# DISABILITY AND EMPLOYER PRACTICES

# DISABILITY AND EMPLOYER PRACTICES

## Research across the Disciplines

SUSANNE M. BRUYÈRE, EDITOR

ILR PRESS

AN IMPRINT OF
CORNELL UNIVERSITY PRESS
ITHACA AND LONDON

The contents of this book were developed under a grant from the
National Institute on Disability, Independent Living, and Rehabilitation
Research (NIDILRR grant number 90RT5010-01-00). NIDILRR is
a Center within the Administration for Community Living (ACL),
Department of Health and Human Services (HHS). The contents of this
book do not necessarily represent the policy of NIDILRR, ACL, HHS,
and you should not assume endorsement by the Federal Government.

Copyright © 2016 by Cornell University

All rights reserved. Except for brief quotations in a review, this book, or
parts thereof, must not be reproduced in any form without permission in
writing from the publisher. For information, address Cornell University
Press, Sage House, 512 East State Street, Ithaca, New York 14850.

First published 2016 by Cornell University Press
Printed in the United States of America

Library of Congress Cataloging-in-Publication Data

Disability and employer practices : research across the
disciplines / Susanne M. Bruyère, editor.
      pages cm
   Includes bibliographical references and index.
   ISBN 978-1-5017-0058-3 (cloth : alk. paper)
   1. People with disabilities—Employment—United States.
2. Personnel management—United States. I. Bruyère, Susanne M., editor.
   HD7256.U5D577   2016
   331.5'90973—dc23        2015030338

Cornell University Press strives to use environmentally responsible
suppliers and materials to the fullest extent possible in the publishing of
its books. Such materials include vegetable-based, low-VOC inks and
acid-free papers that are recycled, totally chlorine-free, or partly composed
of nonwood fibers. For further information, visit our website at
www.cornellpress.cornell.edu.

Cloth printing        10  9  8  7  6  5  4  3  2  1

This book is dedicated to the outstanding team of people who are listed as contributors in both the writing of this book and the research and knowledge translation efforts described herein. It is a distinct privilege to work closely over many months with such talented, hardworking, and dedicated professionals, whose work will make a decided difference in promoting employer practices that can improve employment outcomes for individuals with disabilities. My sincere thanks to each of you for this remarkable experience.

Whatever affects one directly, affects all indirectly. I can never be what I ought to be until you are what you ought to be. This is the interrelated structure of reality.

Martin Luther King Jr.

# Contents

# Preface

The experience of disability touches all of us at some point in our lives, either directly or indirectly. Some of us are born with a disability; many of us incur a short- or longer-term disability in midlife, or care for a child or other family member who has a disability; and most of us will experience disability as a natural consequence of growing old. Disability is endemic in the human experience; it is the great equalizer, in that it is not mindful of socioeconomic, religious, racial/ethnic, and geographic differences or boundaries. So, creating a world where the experience of disability no longer needlessly sets us apart from others should be an imperative for us all.

The ability to contribute our natural talents and fully participate in society is greatly facilitated by the ability to work and to experience economic well-being. Designing workplaces that make possible the full inclusion of individuals with disabilities should be an important national and global goal we all can embrace.

This book has three related purposes:

1. To raise the visibility of the critical issues surrounding equitable employment for people with disabilities, with a focus on workplace policies and practices
2. To provide evidence of the importance of applying the very best science available to address these issues across all facets of the problem
3. To illustrate how combining scientific efforts from different disciplines to work closely on a common purpose, as well as the intimate involvement of key stakeholders, can provide extraordinary results that inform needed changes to policy and practice.

In these pages, we describe the efforts of a transdisciplinary team working toward the common goal of maximum workplace inclusion for individuals with disabilities. What is distinctive about these efforts is how we have drawn from so many disciplines and fields of expertise, data sources, and methodologies to learn where disparities exist in equitable employment opportunities for people with disabilities and to identify workplace policies and practices that can help remedy these inequalities. Our team has included individuals who work and have expertise in the fields of business, economics, education, environmental design and analysis, human resources, management, industrial/organizational psychology, public health, rehabilitation psychology, research methods, survey design, educational measurement, statistics, and vocational rehabilitation counseling.

This description of our efforts includes the data sources and various research methods used and discusses the array of critical stakeholders needed to maximally inform such an effort. It also examines our purposeful focus on working closely with employers and gaining knowledge about their policies and practices through national survey and administrative data, surveys of human resource professionals, and in-depth case studies working in partnership with organizational leaders, gaining their input as well as that of managers and employees.

Such a comprehensive transdisciplinary effort focusing on disability workplace inclusion is, we think, unique. Our desire in writing this book is to share our experience with others. We believe that the data sources and methods identified will serve as an informative research guide for scholars and policy makers engaged in similar research and policy formulation on behalf of individuals with disabilities. We have strived to make this work accessible to a wide audience and hope that our efforts and findings may also be of use to human resource professionals, administrators of disability employment services, disability advocates, persons with disabilities themselves, and their family members.

# ACKNOWLEDGMENTS

The authors would like to extend sincerest appreciation to the many partners and collaborators who have made this work possible. First of all, the research described here was funded by a grant from the U.S. Department of Health and Human Service National Institute on Disability, Independent Living, and Rehabilitation Research (NIDILRR) to Cornell University for a Rehabilitation Research and Training Center on Employer Practices Related to Employment Outcomes among Individuals with Disabilities (Grant No. 90RT5010-01-00). We would like to thank NIDILRR for this funding support and also our NIDILRR project officer, Leslie Caplan, who provided invaluable support and feedback to this project throughout the five-year effort. A special thanks must go also to Frances Benson, ILR Press editorial director, who helped us shape this book and supported it as an important story to tell.

We are most grateful to individuals whose names may not appear on chapters in this book but who have contributed significantly along the way. Among these are Tom Moehrle at the United States Bureau of Labor

Statistics, for his help with the data used in the study described in chapter 3 using restricted-access Bureau of Labor Statistics data, and Xin Jin, assistant professor of economics at the University of South Florida, who was also a collaborator on this research program while a doctoral student at Cornell University. Ron Edwards from the U.S. Equal Employment Opportunity Commission afforded us access to the EEOC Integrated Mission System data discussed in chapter 4, with which our disability discrimination research was conducted. John Hough, from the National Center for Health Statistics and the Agency for Healthcare Research and Quality, both in Bethesda, Maryland, facilitated access for our work with the Medical Expenditure Panel Survey also discussed in chapter 3.

Sincere thanks also go to those federal agency, business, research, disability advocacy, and United Nations organizations whose representatives graciously shared their time and knowledgeable perspective to contribute to our state-of-the-science conference in October 2013, which significantly enriched the contents of this book. These include representatives from the Army and Air Force Exchange Services; U.S. Department of Defense; Department of Labor Office of Disability Employment Policy; Equal Employment Opportunity Commission; National Institute on Disability and Rehabilitation Research; Office of Federal Contract Compliance Programs; Office of Personnel Management; Rehabilitation Services Administration; American Association on Health and Disability; Association of University Centers for Disabilities; International Labor Organization; Merck & Company; National Federation of Independent Business; National Industry Liaison Group; Northrup Grumman; Rutgers University; Society for Human Resource Management; The Conference Board; U.S. Business Leadership Network; WFD Consulting; and World@Work.

Many people in the Employment and Disability Institute and the ILR School at Cornell University more broadly have supported this effort. Our sincere thanks go to Margaret Waelder Graber and Kate MacDowell, project assistants; Camille Lee, Joe Williams, Brett Blanchard, and the EDI web team members; Aurora Clegg, ILR School student; Melissa Bjelland, research associate; Kristie McAlpine, ILR doctoral student; and the ILR School Communications and Marketing Office, including Joe Zappala, Donald Bazley, David Yantorno, and Mary Catt, who collectively provided many months of painstaking effort to develop the websites, online tools, research briefs, publications, webcasts and social media outreach efforts described in this book, as well as organize and implement a successful state-of-the-science conference in Washington, D.C., and this manuscript; and Yasamin Miller and the team from the Survey Research Institute at Cornell University for their assistance in developing and implementing the surveys described in this work.

Finally, we want to express our gratitude to the supportive lead liaisons at our case study organizations who put their belief in strong inclusive workplaces into action and the extensive network of employer association and individual employer representatives that we have had the great privilege to be able to work with and learn from over these many months. Without your willingness to partner with us, and to share your concerns and your triumphs in designing, testing, and implementing the workplace policies and practices that improve employment outcomes for people with disabilities, this work would not have been possible. Special thanks to the following:

The Center for Advanced Human Resource Studies at the Cornell University ILR School—Chris Collins, Steven Miranda, and Jo Hagin

The Conference Board—Peter Linkow, Mary Wright, Ivelys Figueroa, Charles Mitchell, Lorrie Foster, and Timothy Dennison

The Society for Human Resource Management—Mark Schmidt, Evren Esen, and Nancy Hammer

The Disability Management Employers Coalition—Marcia Carruthers and Charlie Fox

The American Association of People with Disabilities—Mark Periello and Frankie Mastrangelo

We are exceedingly grateful to each of you for your willingness to contribute your significant expertise, energy, and enthusiasm in support of this work, but most importantly in the shared vision of improving employment outcomes for individuals with disabilities who deserve an equal position in the U.S. labor force and the opportunity to contribute their talents and enjoy the full socioeconomic and social participation that is their right.

# Abbreviations

| | |
|---|---|
| AAPD | American Association of People with Disabilities |
| ACS | American Community Survey |
| ADA | Americans with Disabilities Act |
| ADEA | Age Discrimination in Employment Act |
| BLS | Bureau of Labor Statistics |
| BRFSS | Behavioral Risk Factor Surveillance System |
| CAHRS | Center for Advanced Human Resource Studies |
| CATI | computer-assisted telephone interviewing |
| CDC | Centers for Disease Control and Prevention |
| CPS | Current Population Survey |
| CRA | Civil Rights Act (of 1964) |
| DCV Catalog | Disability and Compensation Variables Catalog |
| DM | disability management |
| DMEC | Disability Management Employer Coalition |
| ECEC | Employer Costs for Employee Compensation |
| EEO | equal opportunity officer |

| | |
|---|---|
| EEOC | Equal Employment Opportunity Commission |
| EPRRTC | Employment Practices Rehabilitation Research and Training Center |
| FEVS | Federal Employee Viewpoint Survey |
| HR | human resources |
| HRS | Health and Retirement Study |
| ICF | International Classification of Functioning, Disability, and Health |
| IMS | Integrated Mission System |
| I-O | industrial-organizational (psychology) |
| IRB | Institutional Review Board |
| IRS | Internal Revenue Service |
| IT | information technology |
| KT | knowledge translation |
| MEPS | Medical Expenditure Panel Survey |
| NBGH | National Business Group on Health |
| NHIS-D | National Health Interview Survey on Disability |
| NIA | National Institute on Aging |
| NLTS2 | National Longitudinal Transition Study-2 |
| NOD | National Organization on Disability |
| OFCCP | Office of Federal Contract Compliance Programs |
| O*NET | Occupational Information Network |
| OPM | Office of Personnel Management |
| PSID | Panel Study of Income Dynamics |
| PTFEAD | Presidential Task Force on the Employment of Adults with Disabilities |
| PTSD | post-traumatic stress disorder |
| SHRM | Society for Human Resource Management |
| SIPP | Survey of Income and Program Participation |
| SSA | Social Security Administration |
| SSDI | Social Security Disability Insurance |
| TBI | traumatic brain injury |
| TCB | The Conference Board |

1

# Disability and Employment: Framing the Problem, and Our Transdisciplinary Approach

Susanne M. Bruyère, Sara VanLooy, Sarah von Schrader,
and Linda Barrington

This book is about the employment of people with disabilities in the United States and the important role of employer practices. Scenarios like the following play out in American workplaces daily:

- An HR recruitment professional in a large electronics company is asked to design a strategy to identify several hundred qualified individuals with disabilities within six months to fill positions across the organization's job categories in an effort to meet the 7 percent hiring target now required of U.S. federal government subcontractors.
- A Deaf package handler working for a mail delivery company successfully executes his job but cannot participate in company meetings without sign language interpretation services. He is afraid to ask for this assistance in case others would think less of him for needing it, or worse yet, he might lose his job after making this request.
- An HR talent acquisition professional for a large multinational technology company that has successfully employed over one thousand people with disabilities through hiring and effective medical leave and

return-to-work policies finds that there has been 65 percent turnover among these employees in the last year and needs to identify the reasons why.

- A successful longtime high-level executive in an advertising company who disclosed to his company that he has progressive multiple sclerosis, so that he could take intermittent leave when needed, learns that he has not been given the incremental salary increases given to others in comparable positions within the firm.
- An HR diversity and inclusion professional is asked to establish an employee resource group for individuals with disabilities in an effort to create a more inclusive climate for these individuals. She finds that few people are willing to come to the group, because they are uncomfortable identifying themselves as people with disabilities.

These scenarios are drawn from the range of challenges we have encountered in our work to increase access to and equitable inclusion in the workplace for people with disabilities. They accurately demonstrate the dilemmas faced by employers and the human resource professionals within companies who are tasked to create a diverse workforce that includes individuals with disabilities. A significant gap remains between ideal workplace disability policies and current realities. To improve this situation, effective disability-inclusive policies and practices must be pervasive in the workplace and throughout the employment process, including recruitment and hiring, compensation and benefits, workplace accommodations, retention, promotion, and advancement.

Underpinning this discussion is the recognition that there is no consensus on the best approach to address the challenge of incorporating the measurement of disability status within surveys and administrative records. There is no single, universally accepted definition of disability (Livermore and She 2007). Numerous definitions have been used over time—some focusing on medical conditions, some on functional limitations, and some on limitations on the ability to work. Mashaw and Reno (1996) counted over twenty definitions of disability used by public or private benefit programs, government agencies, and statisticians. Two prominent conceptualizations of disability dominate discussions. One defines certain conditions as disabling and counts people with those conditions as disabled. The other conceptualization views disability as an impairment that limits a person's capacity to function at work, in society, or in daily life.

A frequently applied framework of disability is the World Health Organization's (2001) International Classification of Functioning, Disability, and Health (ICF). This model views disability as a decrease in the ability to functionally engage and participate in the activities of life. Such decreases in function are seen as resulting from interactions between various health conditions and the environment in which they are experienced (Jette 2006). Although the sources of data from national and administrative surveys and original research herein described use an array of definitions, this framework is the one upon which this book lies philosophically. The heart of this book is built upon the belief that it is the environment and the nature of how we view and interact with people with disabilities that create disability, and not the nature of a person's impairment itself.

## The Disability Employment Conundrum

People with disabilities make up at least 10 percent of the U.S. working-age population, yet national workforce participation statistics reveal that people with disabilities are not accessing employment at anywhere near the rates of their peers without disabilities. U.S. employers are missing out on a large portion of the available labor force. In 2013, the employment rate of Americans ages twenty-one to sixty-four with disabilities was 34.5 percent, compared to 76.8 percent for people without disabilities (Erickson, Lee, and von Schrader 2014). Unequal employment opportunities for people with disabilities result in a loss for this population, as they may not be able to access the financial security and community integration that come with working at a good job. People with disabilities who are employed earn less than nondisabled workers, and the earnings inequality increases among those with more education (Yin, Shaewitz, and Megra 2014). Top talent may be missed if employers are not prepared to hire and retain candidates who may have disabilities. Even among those with a bachelor's degree or higher, people with disabilities are employed at far lower levels than their nondisabled peers (58 percent vs. 85 percent, respectively) (Erickson et al. 2012, 278). By increasing our understanding of employment disparities and how employer practices are related to these disparate employment outcomes, we may be able to guide practice to bridge this gap.

Highlighting research approaches to build this type of understanding is the goal of this volume.

The intent of Sections 501 and 503 of the Rehabilitation Act of 1973, and later Title I of the Americans with Disabilities Act of 1990 (ADA), was the improvement of employment outcomes and the elimination of employment discrimination against individuals with disabilities. These groundbreaking laws affirmed that equal employment opportunity is a right of people with disabilities and led to important changes in employer practices around disability (Bruyère, Golden, and VanLooy, 2011). Despite the passage of the ADA, the employment gap (as well as gaps on other key economic indicators) between people with and without disabilities has remained significant over time (Bjelland et al. 2011). Recessionary periods have tended to make the situation even worse; for example, the recent "Great Recession" disproportionately affected workers with disabilities, with a 9 percent decrease in the representation of individuals with disabilities among the employed population in the United States (Kaye 2010). While employment for people without disabilities is on the rise again, the situation for workers with disabilities has not been as quick to bounce back (Kessler Foundation 2014).

These statistics not only confirm the existence of employment disparities for people with disabilities in the United States; they also reflect the loss to the American workforce of a significant pool of talent that remains largely untapped. A 2010 survey by the Kessler Foundation and the National Organization on Disability (NOD) reported that more than half of individuals with disabilities who were not employed said that lack of work or not being able to find work was the reason (Kessler/NOD 2010a). This is problematic not only for the individuals with disabilities who are unable to access work, but also for employers and the public welfare more broadly. The percentage of adults ages twenty-five to sixty-four receiving Social Security Disability Insurance (SSDI) benefits doubled between 1989 and 2009, from 2.3 to 4.6 percent. At the same time, "cash payments to SSDI recipients (adjusted for inflation) tripled to $121 billion, and Medicare expenditures for SSDI recipients rose from $18 billion to $69 billion" (Autor 2011, 5–6). In 2008, sixty-three federal programs spent more than $357 billion, and states spent $71 billion, on programs to support working-age people with disabilities (Stapleton and Livermore 2011). Many are individuals with prior employment histories who are seasoned workers, who have been forced to leave the workforce because of a significant health condition, illness, or accident that resulted in a disability. These are often individuals who might be employed if the workplace was receptive to accommodations that would enable them to remain at work and if public policies were designed in a way to support return to work without prematurely removing all SSDI safety nets (Burkhauser, Butler, and Kim 1995; Stapleton and Livermore 2011). Therefore, the importance of addressing the issue of the employment of individuals with disabilities goes beyond furthering the goal of all individuals' having equal employment opportunities, to reducing the escalating costs of social programs that may actually be disincentives to work for people with disabilities. Considerable research has been conducted on barriers to employment for people with disabilities, but significant knowledge gaps remain. In particular, more research is needed to examine the employer's side of the employment relationship to understand what is behind the continuing disparity in employment.

## The Focus of This Book

This is no simple problem; many forces impact employment disparities for individuals with disabilities. In this volume, we describe the approaches and findings of a transdisciplinary team of researchers at Cornell University who are working to better understand employment disparities and how employer practices are related to employment outcomes and workplace experiences of people with disabilities.

Disability employment has traditionally been studied from the point of view of the "supply side," examining the medical, educational, psychological, and vocational inputs that affect a person's functioning and job skills (Chan et al. 2010). This approach, however, ignores the fact that labor market outcomes such as employment are determined when the *supply of* individuals' labor aligns with *demand for* labor on the part of employers. Our research has demonstrated that these resulting labor market outcomes are very different for people with and without disabilities. Regulatory policies are an attempt to level the playing field on which market outcomes are determined, influencing both individuals' opportunities and employer practices. Figure 1.1 represents a simplified version of the many forces influencing employment outcomes. While it is essential to understand the entire context in which employment outcomes exist, we focus this research initiative on employer practices that may impact outcomes. Specifically, we are conducting research on a wide range of aspects of the employment process, including recruitment and hiring, technology and accessibility, total compensation, workplace inclusion, and retention and promotion, with the goal of better understanding what is working and what may serve as a barrier to full access to employment for people with disabilities.

From 2011 through 2015, the U.S. Department of Education's National Institute on Disability and Rehabilitation Research (NIDRR) provided funding for a Rehabilitation Research and Training Center on Employer Practices Related to Employment Outcomes among Individuals with Disabilities (EPRRTC) to the Employment and Disability Institute in the Cornell University ILR School.[1] This project's goals were (1) to create new knowledge about employer practices around disability, (2) to increase knowledge of how these practices relate to successful hiring, retention, and promotion of individuals with disabilities, and (3) to assist employers in incorporating these findings into policy and practice. Before describing

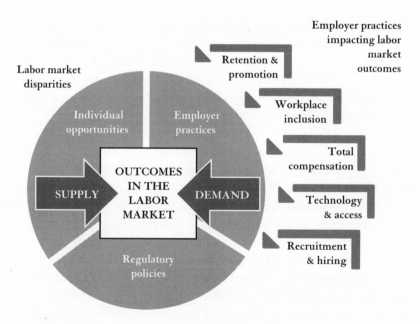

**Figure 1.1**  Labor market outcomes: individual disparities and employer practices

how our team approached research on employment practices that may ameliorate employment disparities, we must take a step back to describe the current context of and barriers to disability employment and why this research is so desperately needed.

## Current Labor Market Context

While disability employment disparities have been present for years, there is an increasing urgency to addresses these issues as demographics shift. With an aging workforce and increasing numbers of veterans who became disabled in overseas conflicts, American workplaces must be better equipped to deal proactively with the attendant needs for accommodations and a disability-inclusive culture.

### Aging Workforce, Returning Veterans, Students with Disabilities

By 2020, it is anticipated that nearly one in four Americans in the civilian labor force will be over the age of fifty-five (Toosi 2012). With the age of workers increasing, the incidence, severity, and duration of disability among workers is also likely to increase. To deal with these demographic changes, employers are being encouraged to align their benefits plans, physical facilities design, administrative procedures, and workplace culture to support and retain older workers (Vargo and Grzanowicz 2002). Although many employers are thinking about such changes, far fewer have actually begun to put needed changes in place. A 2013 study conducted by Cornell University and the Disability Management Employers Coalition revealed that although 86 percent of employers polled were concerned about the impacts of an aging workforce, only 36 percent addressed aging in the design of their disability and absence management programs (von Schrader et al. 2013).

In 2013, there were 21.4 million veterans age eighteen or over. Nearly one-half were veterans of World War II, the Korean War, or the Vietnam War; these veterans were all at least fifty-five years old, and over 70 percent were over sixty-five (U.S. Bureau of Labor Statistics 2014c). Among younger veterans, for the 2.8 million who served during the Iraq War (2003 onward), the unemployment rate in 2013 was 8.8 percent for men and 9.6 percent for women—much higher than the rates for the 3.2 million veterans of the Persian Gulf War (First Gulf War) era (1990–2001), which were 5.7 and 5.3 percent, respectively (U.S. Bureau of Labor Statistics 2014c). In 2013, about 15 percent of all veterans had a service-connected disability. Among veterans of the Iraq War, nearly 30 percent reported a service-connected disability, and 70 percent of that group were in the labor force (U.S. Bureau of Labor Statistics 2014c).

Two specific disabilities have become "signature disabilities" for veterans of Iraq and Afghanistan—traumatic brain injury (TBI) and post-traumatic stress disorder (PTSD). In 2008, RAND reported that the studies it analyzed found that up to 15 percent of service members were affected by PTSD. Research on the prevalence of TBI is lacking, but the numbers may be roughly similar (RAND 2008). A 2009 study used modeling to predict that up to 40 percent of active military and up to 32 percent of reservists may ultimately exhibit PTSD symptoms (Atkinson, Guetz, and Wein 2009).

Findings from a study conducted by Rudstam, Gower, and Cook (2012), which asked employers about their knowledge of returning veterans with disabilities, suggest that many employers believe employing veterans with disabilities would benefit their organizations. Yet most employers are largely not aware of, and therefore do not use, the available resources that would enable them to find, recruit, hire, and accommodate veterans. Also, employers demonstrated significant gaps in knowledge related to hiring and accommodating employees with PTSD and TBI (Rudstam, Gower, and Cook 2012).

Another demographic that is now influencing the nature of the workforce and will necessitate an increased awareness of disability and accommodation in the workplace is the generation of potential workers born after the passage of the ADA. These youth and young adults, or the "ADA generation," as they have been called by Senator Tom Harkin, "have attained unprecedented education levels in inclusive settings and have an expectation to be included as valued members of the American workforce" (U.S. Senate 2013, 2). They have been educated and participate in a society made more accessible and accommodating by the ADA, and they are aware of the rights the ADA affords them. They have had more equitable access than preceding generations not only to educational opportunities, but also to the social and cultural riches of community life such as movie and entertainment venues, public libraries, museums, health facilities, sports facilities, and other recreational, cultural, and athletic opportunities made possible through the provisions of the ADA.

Although physical and programmatic access to educational preparation has improved as a result of regulatory changes like the ADA and also the Individuals with Disabilities Education Act, inequities in opportunities for workforce participation remain for these young workers. Disparities in workforce participation begin in the teenage years; teenagers (between ages sixteen and nineteen) with disabilities had a labor force participation rate 3.5 percentage points lower than their peers without disabilities in 2013. This gap increases with age, rising to a 29-percentage-point difference among those ages twenty to twenty-four, and a 45.5-point difference for people ages twenty-five to thirty-four (U.S. Bureau of Labor Statistics 2014d, table 1). Disparities are even larger for racial and ethnic minorities with disabilities. Young veterans with service-connected disabilities also have lower employment rates than their nondisabled counterparts (U.S. Senate 2013).

Pervasive inequality in employment, income, and poverty calls for our attention to directly address this issue. Employment for individuals with disabilities should be an important area of concern for the American people and policy makers, as people with disabilities are largely an untapped labor force. Changing demographics that include an aging workforce, significant numbers of veterans with disabilities, and increasing numbers of young people with disabilities who expect to be able to use their talents in the workforce make this a compelling item on our national agenda. Identification of the barriers to full employment and the facilitators that can lead to meaningful and lasting change in employment outcomes for individuals with disabilities is critical.

## Employer Barriers to Employing People with Disabilities

In surveys and focus groups, employers frequently identify "pipeline problems" as barriers to employing more people with disabilities; that is, they point to a lack of qualified applicants, or a lack of experience or necessary skills and training in the applicants with disabilities they attract (Broussard 2006; Bruyère 2000; Bruyère, Erickson, and Horne 2002a; Lengnick-Hall, Gaunt, and Kulkarni 2008; Linkow et al. 2013; Rivera 2012). Employers also indicate that their own lack of knowledge about accommodations, the perceived cost of accommodations, and the attitudes and stereotypes about disability held by supervisors and coworkers also create barriers to employment for people with disabilities (Able Trust 2003; Blanck and Schartz 2005; Brannick and Bruyère 1999; Bruyère 2000, 2002; Dixon, Kruse, and Van Horn 2003; Domzal, Houtenville, and Sharma 2008; Gilbride et al. 2003).

Rivera (2012) looked at the hiring of diverse employees in elite firms by interviewing 120 hiring decision-makers at top-tier firms. She found that the majority believed their hiring processes were fair and attributed existing disparities in their workforce to "the pipeline." With this conceptualization, their diversity programs have focused on increasing the number of applicants they have to choose from, rather than on reducing bias in their decision-making processes. Rivera highlights a key issue with diversity practices in the companies she studied—there was a gulf between the recruiting process, which was primarily designed and conducted by the HR staff, and the final hiring decisions, which were made by the "revenue-generating professionals." This is similar to Bruyère's finding (2000) that in private-sector organizations, the immediate supervisor was most often cited as the final decision maker about accommodations, even though the majority of disability nondiscrimination training had been focused on HR personnel.

Much of the experimental research to date focuses on attitudes toward applicants and employees with disabilities and attitudes about disability itself. While employers generally report feeling positively toward people with disabilities, they also express concerns about hiring and accommodating that are at odds with their stated willingness to employ them (Burke et al. 2013). Many researchers report that the attitudes of supervisors and coworkers have a strong effect on the experiences of employees with disabilities (Bruyère, Erickson, and Ferrentino 2003; Colella 1996, 2001; Colella, DeNisi, and Varma 1998; Florey and Harrison 2000; Hernandez, Keys, and Balcazar 2004; Schur et al. 2014). A number of studies focused on employment discrimination claims (Bjelland et al. 2010; McMahon, Shaw, and Jaet 1995; Moss, Ullman, Starrett, et al. 1999) find that while alleged unlawful discharge complaints are most common, employees with disabilities perceive discrimination throughout the employment process—from hiring to on-the-job harassment to unlawful termination.

While employer surveys have generally found that employers express positive attitudes toward the idea of hiring people with disabilities (Colella and Bruyère 2011), these findings do not seem to translate to real-world behaviors, perhaps because respondents to such surveys tend to give socially desirable answers (Colella and Stone 2005; Unger 2002) or because the respondents may not be the people making the decisions (Colella and Stone 2005; Rivera 2012). Ren, Paetzold, and Colella (2008) conducted a meta-analysis of experimental studies of HR judgments of people with disabilities. They found that disability had a clear negative effect on performance expectations and hiring decisions, and that the negative effect was worse for mental disabilities than physical disabilities.

Fewer studies have focused on measuring employer practices and related outcomes (U.S. Department of Education 2010), and very little research has considered the question of how company policies and practices affect the employment of people with disabilities (Disability Case Study Research Consortium 2008). Studies seeking answers to the question of how best to improve employer practices around disability employment have frequently asked employers about their perceptions of effectiveness of practices, rather than whether the practice has actually been implemented in their workplace (Erickson et al. 2013).

## Need for New Research on Disability-Related Employer Practices

The next step to improve employment outcomes for persons with disabilities will require researchers to draw from a multiplicity of informants and use a variety of data sources and analytical models. By analyzing organizational data and eliciting the perspectives of key organizational leaders, human resource professionals, managers, coworkers, and individuals with disabilities themselves, we can reach a deeper understanding of the remaining barriers to full employment and inclusion of individuals with disabilities in the workplace, and we can find ways to successfully address them. Only by gathering insights from each of these contributors to the experience of disability in the workplace can we more accurately plan needed next steps to address employment disability discrimination and exclusionary practices.

Many of the barriers identified by employers regarding the hiring of individuals with disabilities may be reduced or overcome by educating employers on issues of disability, and specifically by providing information on effective workplace policies and practices. Further research on how company policies and practices and the corresponding attitudes of coworkers, supervisors, and hiring managers affect the employment opportunities of people with disabilities is needed to inform the development of evidence-based practices to address these barriers (Disability Case Study Research Consortium 2008; Vornholt, Uitdewilligen, and Nijhuis 2013).

Little measurement has been done to date to determine whether the identified practices in the management of diversity, and especially disability diversity, show real-world promise in improving employment rates for people with disabilities. Yang and Konrad (2011) state that "implementation is an under-researched area in diversity management" (16). They go on to recommend that investigation is needed on organizational practices, such as "the number of practices, the extent to which the practices extend across the entire organization, and the consistency with which people managers use diversity management practices."

A recent scoping review of the research literature around employer responses to disability in the workplace found that the number of studies on the topic has increased significantly since 1991 (Karpur, VanLooy, and Bruyère 2014). More and more employer research is being done, but it is still largely concentrated on studies of attitudes toward disability, it widely employs hypothetical scenarios administered under laboratory conditions rather than real-world data, and it relies heavily on survey methodologies to capture employer behavior. Most studies have analyzed self-reported perceptions of employer practices without placing these reports in the context of evidence from employer secondary data. Employer data could objectively verify perceptions of workplace practices, but this approach has not previously been widely pursued. And, importantly, these studies are being published primarily for an audience of service providers rather than employers, such that their findings are not reaching the audience that is the ultimate decision-maker in employment matters (Karpur, VanLooy, and Bruyère 2014). The existing literature focuses largely on describing employer practices in order to make recommendations for service rehabilitation delivery systems, support promising practices in vocational rehabilitation, and address barriers to implementation within those service-driven environments. Just 27 percent of the examined literature published between 1990 and 2010 was intended for an employer audience (Karpur,

VanLooy, and Bruyère 2014). The scoping review also revealed a paucity of publication outlets for disability research that reach employer audiences. This fact underscores the importance of engaging employers throughout the process of both developing and translating research on employer practices, as the creation of inclusive practices and policies within work environments is critical to the successful career navigation and economic parity of people with disabilities.

## Importance of a Transdisciplinary Perspective

Numerous scholars have pointed to the desirability, if not the necessity, of combining diverse approaches and findings from multiple disciplines to study complex and multifaceted social issues (Kessel and Rosenfield 2008; Nissani 1997; Pitt-Catsouphes, Kossek, and Sweet 2006; Qin, Lancaster, and Allen 1997; Rosenfield 1992). New research is needed that not only focuses on the perspective of the employer and draws from the multiple perspectives within the workplace, but also draws from a wider variety of analytical methodologies and data sources. Disability employment inequity is an issue that is multifaceted and interfaces with many fields and functions in intricate ways on multiple levels, such as employment policy, law, human resource studies, rehabilitation medicine, vocational counseling, and workplace policy and practice, to name a few. Such complex problems necessitate solutions that are informed by perspectives from multiple backgrounds that individual disciplinary perspectives might otherwise be unable to provide.

Research on the employment of people with disabilities has been conducted in numerous individual areas such as legal studies,[2] economic policy,[3] vocational rehabilitation counseling,[4] industrial and organizational psychology,[5] and disability management.[6] More recently, Schur, Kruse, and Blanck (2013) provide an overview of the many ways in which people with disabilities have historically been excluded from full participation in community and economic life, drawing from literature across the social sciences, including economics, political science, psychology, disability studies, law, and sociology.

Significant gaps remain between the empirical evidence of disparities and barriers and the identification of real-life interventions that will improve the hiring, workplace retention, and advancement of individuals with disabilities. Simply describing the issue from the viewpoints of different fields has not been sufficient. To date, few if any studies have sought to bring these multiple perspectives together in the field of employment and disability in a systematic way to shed greater light on the issues, identify key factors to resolve barriers, and positively impact employment outcomes for people with disabilities. Truly transdisciplinary approaches to researching how to improve employment outcomes for people with disabilities are critically needed. The term "transdisciplinary" is being used here purposefully. The approaches detailed in this volume are pointedly attempting to transcend the limitations of singular-disciplinary or even multidisciplinary approaches and perspectives that have been applied to employment inequities for people with disabilities.

Wickson, Carew, and Russell (2006) identify the key characteristics of transdisciplinary research as problem focus, evolving methodology, and collaboration. Pohl (2011) distinguishes transdisciplinary research from other research approaches in that it is not focused as much on the evolution of knowledge in a particular disciplinary field, but rather on the application of effort to a comprehensive and multi-perspective approach in order to achieve a better understanding of real-world problems. Other authors identify the distinguishing features of transdisciplinary research as the inclusion of nonacademics, and a focus on the problem rather than individual disciplines, with no individual discipline being seen as having intellectual precedence, thereby requiring effort on the part of the researchers involved to open up their approaches to creative ways of applying their perspectives to a new way of thinking.

Our Cornell team is purposely transdisciplinary, and there are aspects of the model of transdisciplinary research that particularly guide our approaches and thinking. From the outset, our team focused on a clearly defined real-world problem: disparities in the employment of people with disabilities, and specifically how employer practices impact these pervasive disparities. Our approach stresses the importance of dialogue among disciplinary perspectives, stakeholder involvement throughout the research process, and effective translation of the acquired knowledge.

## Diverse Disciplinary Perspectives

Our team includes individuals who work and have expertise in the fields of business, economics, econometrics, education, environmental design and analysis, human resources, management, industrial/organizational psychology, public health, rehabilitation psychology, research methods, survey design, educational measurement, statistics, and vocational rehabilitation counseling. In addition, we engaged staff with a rich array of demonstrated skills and experience in website design and database development, videography, and social media to assist with our extensive knowledge translation activities. Each of these disciplines and areas of expertise offers a unique perspective that can inform our core areas of research—employer practices as they relate to employment disparities for individuals with disabilities—as well as our extensive efforts to disseminate research results to our target stakeholders.

Each of our team members was purposefully selected to address distinct issues of focus for the research described in this book, as well as to inform across-research efforts more broadly, contributing to a truly transdisciplinary approach in our work. Our economist colleagues assisted us generally by identifying relevant information from many large secondary/national survey and administrative datasets, by conducting analyses across the many identified datasets from which we drew relevant information about the status of people with disabilities in the U.S. workforce, and by documenting the extent of continuing economic and employment disparities. The more specialized labor market and compensation expertise of our economist colleagues also enabled us to examine with better precision the disparities in pay, as well as total compensation considered more broadly, between individuals with disabilities and their nondisabled peers.

Our colleagues with business, human resources, and management expertise greatly informed our research design and data collection efforts with employers during our research working groups and targeted membership surveys with multiple national employer representative associations. These colleagues also greatly facilitated access to employer associations and networks and individual employers for organizational case studies.

Our inclusion of the expertise of industrial-organizational (I-O) psychology was very helpful to our employer focus groups described above, but even more critical to our in-depth case studies of particular companies. I-O psychology is the scientific study of the workplace. In its application, the rigor and methods of psychology are applied to issues of critical relevance to business, including talent management, coaching, assessment, selection, training, organizational development, performance, and work-life balance (Society for Industrial Organizational Psychology 2015). In these efforts, we conducted focus groups and key informant interviews, but in addition we surveyed the company workforce, enabling us to capture a much more nuanced understanding of the combination of policies, practices, and workplace climate factors that are most influential for improving employment outcomes of people with disabilities throughout the employment process.

One of the areas of focus for this research was the impact of health benefits on the employment behavior of individuals with disabilities. Our colleagues in the fields of public health, vocational rehabilitation, and rehabilitation psychology provided both cross-cutting and targeted expertise to these efforts. These proficiency areas also more broadly informed the work across the projects, affording a disability-informed perspective to the research. Colleagues with no disability-focused research experience welcomed seasoned disability expertise to inform their research design, implementation, and interpretation efforts.

Members of the team with econometrics, research methods, statistics, survey design, measurement, evaluation, and related expertise contributed to distinct studies, but also regularly consulted across research projects, affording others the benefit of their rigorous methodological knowledge. Statisticians and measurement experts worked between project groups to discover ways to think about existing data, combine datasets, and analyze survey data. These new insights into mathematical models for real-world observations enriched our findings and supported discoveries of patterns in our data.

The rich array of disciplinary and methodological expertise described here has enabled our team to conduct rigorous and relevant research using many data sources and methodologies. What has made it a truly transdisciplinary experience, however, has been the regular and systematic sharing of expertise and viewpoints throughout all stages of the research process. From issue identification, hypothesis building, and research design formulation, through research execution and analysis, research team members regularly discussed their progress and their challenges in implementation and interpretation of findings with others on the research team, as well as with key stakeholders, to maximally inform the work they were conducting.

These transdisciplinary collaborative efforts have been equally important in the knowledge diffusion phases of this work, where we have enriched our dissemination strategies through an informed transdisciplinary perspective in selecting key results for target audiences, as well as the mediums and networks by which distribution can most effectively occur. This has been the area where researchers, website designers, database developers, social media experts, and a strong administrative support team have not only transcended but truly leveraged disciplinary and expertise differences to create outstanding research that can be maximally accessed by others through online tools; an extensive website offering videos by our scientists, policy makers, and employers who use our research; and many related research briefs and scientific publications. The information about stakeholder involvement that follows here further illustrates how we have worked to maximize the intent of true transdisciplinary research.

## Stakeholder Involvement in the Research Process: From Inception to Translation

The incorporation of participatory research methods is seen as paramount in a transdisciplinary model (Stock and Burton 2011). Participatory research is rooted in the idea that research must be done *with* people, rather than *on*, or *for*, people, and has been seen as a desired approach in the past several decades when working with individuals with disabilities (Whyte 1991; Bruyère 1993; Turnbull, Friesen, and Ramirez 1998). Such an approach is characterized by involving stakeholders in research design and data collection, analysis, and interpretation, as well as in the dissemination of the research findings. This approach emphasizes the construction of "communities of inquiry" that evolve around issues that are significant for the co-researchers (Reason and Bradbury 2008). Similarly, transdisciplinary research is said to be characterized by involvement of nonacademics from the very beginning, affording them the opportunity to "influence boundaries and methods" (Stock and Burton 2011, 1101).

Through building stakeholder networks and conducting research informed by the ultimate knowledge user, the transdisciplinary process has the potential to help bridge the knowledge-to-practice gap. When describing an evaluation of a transdisciplinary process, Walter et al. (2007) note that there is "an influence of a transdisciplinary process on the decision-making of stakeholders, especially through social network building and the generation of knowledge relevant for action" (325). This highlights not only that transdisciplinary research is an effective model to address complex social problems, but also the importance of sharing findings to inform needed change. The involvement of stakeholders in addition to academics in the research process can increase the stakeholders' awareness of, and ultimate adoption of, the research findings.

The chief "voice" being sought at an intimate level in this work has been that of employers from a variety of sectors, sizes, and industries. But, within that inquiry, the perspectives of various workplace actors, such as company leadership, equal opportunity officers, and human resource professionals, as well as supervisors, coworkers, and individuals with disabilities themselves, have been an integral part of the process. Knowledge gained from various ways of soliciting information from these stakeholders has contributed to an iterative process of incrementally informing and refining this research and also pointing more decisively to informational products that will contribute to needed workplace changes. "Knowledge translation" is a term first used by the Canadian Institutes of Health Research in 2000, to conceptualize the issues involved in ensuring that research findings are ultimately implemented by the people who are in a position to do so. Knowledge translation has been described as "an interactive process underpinned by effective exchanges between researchers who create new knowledge and those who use it" (Sudsawad 2007, 2). Like transdisciplinary and participatory action research, it emphasizes the involvement throughout the research process of non-researchers who are stakeholders in the subject of the research. Knowledge translation can be conceptualized as a cycle whereby researchers are informed by stakeholders, then inform their stakeholders about new knowledge, and finally learn from the application of that knowledge. Graham et al. (2006) describe this as a "knowledge to action cycle" and emphasize the collaboration between knowledge producers and knowledge users (see figure 1.2).

In conceptualizing a research project, beyond developing a good understanding of what has already been done and what questions remain, it is important to ask the ultimate users of research, those who we hope will use the research to make changes, what they most need to know. This crucial part of knowledge translation is often overlooked, but can ensure that the audience with whom you plan to share the research has a part in identifying the questions of interest, which can make research more impactful (Rudstam et al. 2013).

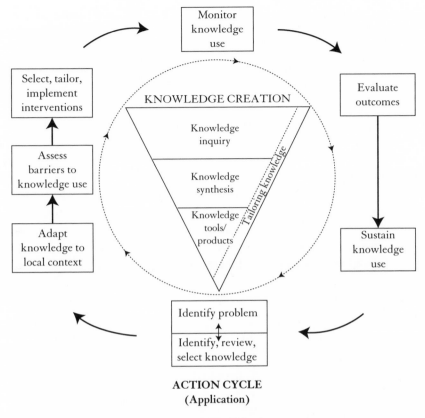

**Figure 1.2** The KT cycle

*Source:* Graham et al. 2006.

## Overview of Our Approach

In the remaining chapters of this volume, we describe the individual and cumulative efforts of a team of Cornell University researchers to address the problem of employment disparities for people with disabilities, using a transdisciplinary approach. Our team has drawn from a wide variety of data sources and employed an array of differing research methodologies to accomplish its intended tasks. Being purposely transdisciplinary in our approach has enabled our researchers to broaden the scope of their investigations and transcend some of the limitations experienced when addressing employment disparities with traditional unidimensional or unidisciplinary approaches. Across all these efforts, we have worked closely with critical stakeholders to bring about desired longer-term success in improving employment outcomes for individuals with disabilities, including key representatives of individual employers and employer associations, disability advocacy organizations, federal policy makers, and rehabilitation and disability employment service providers.

Figure 1.3 graphically presents our initiatives and approaches to building new and relevant knowledge to inform change. Beginning with a scoping review that mapped existing research, and with a series of employer working groups, our initiative framed the challenges and issues of improving labor market outcomes for people with disabilities through the lens of employer practices. Involving stakeholders in this framing (and throughout our initiative), we shaped multiple and transdisciplinary streams of research to understand disparities in labor market outcomes between individuals with and without disabilities and assess workplace practices that impact these outcomes. We continued the transdisciplinary approach and stakeholder involvement through the translation and dissemination of initiative results, striving to most effectively improve employer practices and advance the world of work for people with disabilities.

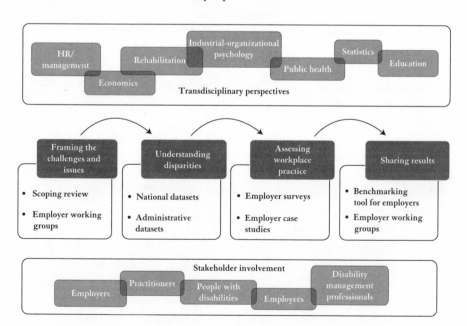

**Figure 1.3** Employer practices and advancing the world of work for people with disabilities

This volume explains the various research methodologies and data sources that we have used to do so, provides relevant examples of related research using these datasets or methodologies that have informed our work, describes key findings that can inform employer policies and practices in minimizing employment disabilities discrimination and maximize employment opportunities for individuals with disabilities, and makes recommendations about additional approaches and data sources that are available for future research, policy analysis, and field-based applications.

These pages represent the expertise and methodologies of a diversity of fields. Some of the approaches described are in-depth reviews of organizational policies and practices literature; analysis of national survey datasets and administrative datasets from federal agencies and business organizations; focus groups of members of business associations; interviews with key informants; surveys of human resource professionals, and of individuals with disabilities; and in-depth organizational case studies. It is not our intent in this volume to provide an in-depth treatise on any of these methodologies. We recognize that in purposefully trying to present the breadth of our efforts, we are depicting a somewhat superficial treatment of each of the methodologies used. To address this potential limitation, we provide references/referrals to related sources for a more comprehensive treatment of many of the methodologies that we discuss here.

In addition, we describe the ways in which we have attempted to approximate the central core value in transdisciplinary research of involving multiple stakeholders across all facets of the research process, as well as resulting knowledge translation to real-world problems. Our intent in doing so is to encourage other researchers to consider some of the various research approaches and datasets that we have found useful in our efforts, to describe findings from our specific research efforts, and to share the transdisciplinary knowledge gained by our approach and proposals for its real-life application in the work environment. A brief description of each of the chapters follows.

## Involving Employers in the Research Process

In chapter 2, "Engaging Employers as Stakeholders," Linda Barrington outlines the premise of this work as a whole, presenting methods for directly involving employers in the research process. This is the critical basis of the work described in this volume, since employers both provide key information in the research process and are the chief audience for dissemination of our findings if they are to effect meaningful workplace change over time. In addition, the research team early on and throughout the research process intimately engaged the employer perspective. Often, those attempting to address employment inequities for people with disabilities view employers solely as the *object* of change rather than as stakeholders in the change process. Barrington discusses the value of intimately involving employers in research that examines workplace barriers for people with disabilities, exploring the belief that if researchers hope to truly understand the issues at hand, and subsequently to effect changes in the workplace based on their findings, employers themselves must be involved more directly.

Chapter 2 reviews the characteristics of employers that should be considered when trying to better understand workplace policies and practices. Barrington also considers challenges in working closely with employers, such as gaining buy-in early in the research process, gaining the trust of the organization, identifying a key organizational contact, and negotiating continued participation in the research process. Research protocols such as assurances for the protection of human subjects can also present unique challenges. Chapter 2 ends with selected "lessons learned" from our own research over the past several years in working across many employer interests.

## Using National Survey Datasets

Researchers studying employer behaviors often need to approach their subject from multiple vantage points, especially when there is no single data source with complete coverage of relevant information. Large national survey and administrative datasets that provide information on employers and employment can provide otherwise absent perspectives (Nazarov, Erickson, and Bruyère 2014).

In chapter 3, "Exploring National Survey Data," William Erickson, Arun Karpur, and Kevin Hallock provide a broad overview of some interesting and important national datasets and how they can help inform research on the employment of individuals with disabilities. They first outline a selected set of available national survey data sources that cover both employer practices and disability status and therefore inform about select factors related to the employment of people with disabilities. They then present a subset of sources, some of which are linkable, that include demographic data on individuals, disability status of individuals, and information on labor market outcomes including employer practices. They discuss the difficulties in using such data sources and describe some novel efforts they have made to take advantage of existing data sources in furthering the study of employment outcomes for individuals with disabilities. Finally, they describe some of the specific findings of empirical work that take advantage of the sources they have previously described and collected.

## Administrative Datasets Informing Employer Practices

Hassan Enayati and Sarah von Schrader consider the applications of administrative datasets in chapter 4, "Using Administrative Data." Administrative data are generally collected by an organization in the course of its regular operations. Their fundamental purpose is to document institutional transactions or practices, and these datasets are maintained by many types of organizations, from government agencies to independent businesses of all sizes.

Administrative data are particularly useful simply because they already exist; no additional effort is needed to generate a dataset. Also, they are generally updated regularly with new information, which makes them ideal for longitudinal studies. Their comprehensive nature and the need for accuracy of organization-relevant variables imposed by business necessity are advantages. However, data of interest to researchers but less relevant to organizations may be less complete or not collected in administrative records. Also, administrative data often do not include counterfactual populations for comparison or socio-demographic control variables, so researchers must locate proxy data for their ideal variables.

Enayati and von Schrader continue their chapter by presenting examples of specific administrative datasets with utility for researchers interested in examining employer practices, and conclude by discussing the value of integrating detailed administrative data with survey data.

Use of Surveys to Inform Employer Practices

William Erickson, Sarah von Schrader, and Sara VanLooy address survey research in chapter 5, "Surveying Employers and Individuals with Disabilities." They examine this frequently used approach with an eye to understanding its strengths and limitations, presenting practical approaches and considerations specifically with regard to gathering information about employer practices and disability employment issues. One of the primary strengths of surveys is the ability to collect data from a large population to address specific research questions and to explore emerging issues that are not addressed in existing national survey data. There are several challenges to using a survey approach, especially with regard to accessing the most appropriate informants and sampling in such a way that allows generalization to a known population. While surveys can be tightly targeted, making them ideal for the collection of quantitative information, they are not as effective for the more in-depth, qualitative information that is best collected through interviews or focus group approaches.

The chapter begins with a discussion of surveys as a primary data collection approach for disability and employment data and discusses several possible types of survey informants for employer practices research, each of whom have access to different types of information and provide different perspectives. The authors then provide an overview of some key considerations that can affect the generalizability of results, including sampling approaches, survey administration mode, and strategies to increase response rate. Of course, as the perspectives of individuals with disabilities may be the focus of a survey, special considerations in surveying individuals with disabilities are discussed.

Use of In-Depth Case Studies in Private and Public Workplaces

In chapter 6, "Conducting Case Studies," Lisa Nishii and Susanne Bruyère review the purpose of case study research as a complement to the cross-organization studies described in the previous chapters, with in-depth data collected from employees *within* organizations. The authors begin with a discussion of how a case study can complement the previously described methodologies. Within-organization research can examine internal factors that are not usually captured in administrative, national, or cross-organization datasets, and can study the interactions between individual experience and organizational context in great detail. There are numerous subjective perceptions, attitudes, and experiences about which researchers can learn only by asking employees themselves. The experience of each employee with managers and coworkers, and the environment created by the synthesis of policy, practice, and attitude within the organization, shape the final employment outcome.

This process can be examined with a case-study approach, using individual and multilevel analyses, combining the results of survey responses from employees from varying levels of the organizations. The authors also consider the value of combining the results of organizational survey efforts with findings from the interviews of key personnel such as senior managers and supervisors, and focus groups of employees with and without disabilities, and managers who perhaps have or have not had an opportunity to supervise an individual with a disability.

## Knowledge Translation, and Implications for Policy, Practice, and Future Research

In chapter 7, Susanne Bruyère, Ellice Switzer, Sarah von Schrader, Sara Van-Looy, and Linda Barrington trace the pathways from knowledge creation to knowledge diffusion that can be used to fully realize the benefits of a transdisciplinary model. They describe the advantages and challenges of traditional dissemination approaches such as conference presentations and the publication of scholarly articles, as well as newer approaches such as webcasts, webinars, blogs, and social media. Bruyère et al. describe their efforts to disseminate the knowledge about employer practices and behaviors that was acquired in the course of this research in order to persuade employers to make real changes and implement best practices, as well as to inform the disability advocacy community and individuals with disabilities themselves which practices to encourage employers to adopt in their respective workplaces.

Chapter 7 also summarizes the ways in which the transdisciplinary team involved in this research worked across their respective expertise, data sources, and methodological approaches to learn from and inform their own work and the cumulative findings across all research activities. The scientific knowledge gained, along with the personal and professional growth that occurs in such a process, is discussed. The chapter ends with a summary of the implications of this work and these findings for employer practices, workplace policy, and future research.

The purpose of Chapter 1 has been to provide an overview of the critical importance of a focus on employment outcomes for individuals with disabilities in the United States and globally, to confirm the importance of the application of theoretical and analytical expertise across many disciplines to address these issues, and to describe how a team of Cornell University researchers have responded to this challenge across their collective expertise and experiences over an intensive five-year effort. The pages that follow track our cumulative efforts throughout these many months: drawing from related prior work to inform the current research; acquiring new knowledge from the use of existing datasets; collecting new information from employer focus groups, interviews, and in-depth case studies; and presenting the preliminary findings, benefits, and limitations of each approach. We illustrate with specific examples how findings from one study have iteratively and additively informed the work for the others in a layered and enriching process. In addition, we describe how we have taken our cumulative knowledge to design informational products and online tools that we hope will contribute to an enhanced understanding of ways to improve employment outcomes for individuals with disabilities and that are accessible to employers, policy makers, people with disabilities and their family members, disability advocacy organizations, rehabilitation and disability services providers, the media, other researchers, and the general public. We hope you will find our work useful.

# 2

# ENGAGING EMPLOYERS
## AS STAKEHOLDERS

Linda Barrington

Aside from self-employment or entrepreneurship, the employment and career advancement of individuals with disabilities must be addressed within a workplace setting. Progressive change in the workplace for individuals with disabilities can be effected by outside forces pushing in (such as regulators, consumers, communities, or advocacy groups) or by inside agents improving their own organizations and work environments (employers and coworkers, and of course employees with disabilities themselves). Whether change comes from within or without, these groups are all stakeholders in advancing employment outcomes for individuals with disabilities. Often, however, external advocates view employers solely as the object of change but not as stakeholders in the change process.

The term "stakeholder," as applied in the business context, identifies the multiple parties internal or external to an organization that can affect or be affected by that organization's behavior or success. R. Edward Freeman produced what became the classic work on stakeholder theory, *Strategic Management: A Stakeholder Approach* (1984), and earned himself the (unsought) title of "the father of stakeholder theory" (Laplume, Sonpar, and Litz 2008, 1152). Freeman argued that decision makers (in a company) must "take into account all of those groups and individuals that can affect, or are affected by, the accomplishment of the business enterprise" (Freeman 1984, 25).

In the broadest use of the term today, a stakeholder is anyone who has an interest or investment in a particular organization or course of action. In this framing, the employing organizations and the managers thereof are themselves stakeholders in any course of action intended to advance individuals with disabilities in the workplace. Consistent with the principles of participatory action research, the more aligned all stakeholders can be in embracing change, the more likely the change process is to succeed; alignment is easier if all parties are "brought along" in the process. Following this logic, the efficacy of research aimed at identifying actions likely to advance employment opportunities for individuals with disabilities can only be strengthened by successfully engaging employers in such studies.

Successful engagement, however, is much easier advised than achieved, and is defined by collaboration that both sustains academic freedom and research integrity, and results in a completed project where all parties feel they have gained insight and no harm has been done. But before a joint research project can be completed successfully, it has to be conceptualized and mutually agreed upon. Mindruta (2013) describes three key features of the "matching" that occurs in the initial forming of a research alliance: mutual gain, credibility, and constraint on "the number of simultaneous alliances firms can pursue" (647). While Mindruta is modeling the research alliance in the context of patentable scientific exploration, his main characterization of it as a "two-sided process" is perfectly applicable to any employer collaboration. Both the practitioner and the academician must feel there is gain from the joint effort. Each must see the other as having the expertise, sophistication, and commitment to carry through as intended. And both must find the project to be more valuable than what could be gained from spending those same resources elsewhere.

One of the most distinguishing features of the research conducted as part of our transdisciplinary initiative has been deep and direct involvement with employers. Engaging employers in this research, while a requirement of the funding agency, was also the desire of our team of researchers, who sought a truly transdisciplinary and participatory approach to employer practice research. Our engagement with employers was facilitated by the long-standing deep relationships that the members of our research team have built with employer associations and networks, as well as individual corporations and federal agencies.

This chapter outlines some considerations in forming and conducting employer-engaged research that will uphold academic integrity and ethical standards—doing no harm through the research—and provide valuable information for the research collaborators, both scholar and employer. We summarize the wealth of learning about collaborative employer research that we have gained in the course of this initiative as well as accumulated from decades of research collaborations with employer representatives across numerous projects. We start with some overarching principles and lessons learned about working effectively with employers on collaborative research, which have been gathered more broadly, and conclude with illustrative specific insights gained from our work with two separate employer associations. We also include preliminary findings from focus groups, which have informed our dissemination efforts, described more fully in chapter 7. In our discussions, we use the terms "partnerships," "alliances," "engagement," and "collaborations" interchangeably to refer to research that requires some sort of approval from or agreement with an employing or employer organization. The knowledge we present in this chapter about engaging employers in the research process is not from empirically tested, peer-reviewed findings. It is rather peer-accrued and vetted wisdom from decades of cumulative experience. We hope that this chapter provides valuable context and framing for researchers considering how best to engage employers successfully in the research process.

## Types of Employers

Employers are not a monolithic mass. Organizations employing individuals can operate in the private sector (either privately held or publicly held for-profit companies), or in the public sector (either governmental or not-for-profit organizations). Within each of these, there are further variants of size, industry, charitable status, status as government contractor, geographic scope, mission, and so on. Figure 2.1 provides a schematic for considering such varying characteristics.

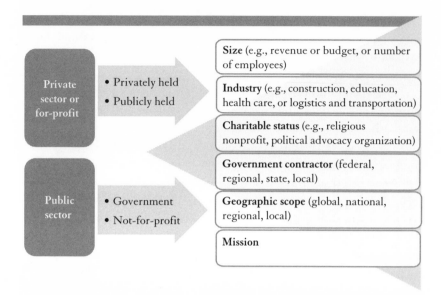

**Figure 2.1** Types of organizations and examples of defining characteristics

Cornell University, for example, has some sixteen hundred full-time and part-time professorial faculty and another eight-thousand-plus non-professorial employees. This workforce is most heavily concentrated in Ithaca, New York, although some are based in offices in New York City or even further afield. Cornell's mission is, in part, to "to discover, preserve, and disseminate knowledge; produce creative work; and promote a culture of broad inquiry throughout and beyond the Cornell community" (Cornell University, 2015). Cornell is a U.S. government contractor and therefore concerned with all Office of Federal Contract Compliance Programs (OFCCP) regulations and guidelines. Contrast Cornell, however, with Wal-Mart Stores Inc., which is also a U.S. government contractor. Walmart's global employee population is over 2.2 million, with 1.3 million of those employed in the United States. Its mission has been stated as "Saving People Money So They Can Live Better" (Scott 2008). While both Cornell University and Walmart are federal contractor employers in the United States, they differ in many ways.

Researchers recognize that these differences need to be considered when attempting to draw generalizable conclusions from any study of one organization or another, but such characterizations also matter for undertaking successful research partnerships with employers. For example, when it comes to navigating an organization's bureaucracy for project approval, smaller organizations may have fewer bureaucratic layers, potentially simplifying the approval process. Larger organizations, on the other hand, may have a human resources analytics function that is already undertaking HR practice research and understands the perspective, tools, and motivation of scholarly researchers. This can ease the effort needed to justify particulars of the study's research methods. Government contractors may have extra incentive to learn more effective ways to meet the OFCCP's new regulations to improve job opportunities for individuals with disabilities. A small, privately held mom-and-pop organization with deep community roots in a limited geographic area might consider it part of its corporate social responsibility to collaborate with the local college or university community through research.

Understanding the perspective of the potential employer-partner and how it views its mission and brand is key to laying the foundation for the two-way trust necessary for a collaborative match and ensuing research. It is also fundamentally important to articulating a "value proposition" that persuades the potential employer-partner to collaborate. The value proposition is further discussed later in this chapter.

## Types of Research Alliances

Single organization case studies may most immediately come to mind when considering employer-engaged research. Case study research focuses on just one employer and can involve gathering and exploring original data collected through focus groups, surveys of employees, or analyzing the employer's existing organizational practices and administrative data (see chapter 4).

Working with a single organization, however, is not the only way to partner with employers directly on workplace practice research. Partnerships, alliances, or collaborations could be formed to conduct research with a consortium of organizations, a business membership group, or using a focus group of business professionals. For example, while case studies of an individual for-profit company and a governmental organization were conducted as part of our overall research efforts (see chapter 6), other related projects also undertook survey collaborations with the Society for Human Resource Management (SHRM) and Disability Management Employer Coalition (DMEC) (see chapter 5). Partnerships with The Conference Board (TCB) and the Center for Advanced Human Resource Studies (CAHRS) in the Cornell University ILR School were established to conduct research "working group" meetings with executives whose job functions include responsibilities for their organizations' practices regarding employees with disabilities. SHRM and DMEC are business associations whose members are individual professionals in the field of human resources or absence and disability management, respectively. CAHRS and TCB are associations whose members are the companies themselves, with employees thereof participating in member activities based on their job function.

## Importance of Employers' Voice in Shaping the Research Agenda

The purpose of research is to discover new knowledge. If the purpose of a given project is to discover new knowledge for the specific aim of effecting progressive change in the workplace for individuals with disabilities, then consideration of the study's potential for workplace impact is important as well. One value of direct engagement of employers in the research process is to gain insight into what are the biggest barriers to workplace advancement for employees with disabilities as seen by those organizational representatives who will ultimately do more or less to promote such advancement. How do workplace decision-makers prioritize the related challenges and concerns within their organizations in terms of both opportunities for improvement and the costs of making progressive change? Building such inside knowledge into the focus and framing of the research project increases the likelihood that the study's results will find an interested audience among organizational change agents.

That said, most practitioners have many demands on their time that limit their ability to keep up with scholarly research and research methods. While they do see merit in academia pushing the envelope of knowledge, they are also cautious in believing that academic work will provide insights relevant to their job responsibilities. Accordingly, they look for clues or clear signals that a new study is worth paying attention to.

One such signal of relevance to employers is that the research involves actual companies, preferably in one's own industry, or whose business success they wish to emulate. A description that makes the characteristics of the employer clear (size, industry, geographies or regions of employee base) can help to validate the research in the eyes of the business community. Being able to make public the name of the employer-collaborator(s) provides even more powerful validation. While it may be ideal, for example, to be able to name the organization that was the case study, it is very difficult to gain permission to do so. Naming names, however, is not the only way to gain legitimacy. Naming companies whose individual representatives were active in an advisory role on the project can also increase a study's credibility to the business audience.

## Scholarly Standards Present Their Own Credibility Barriers

Securing academic credibility with a scholarly audience for employer-partnered research brings challenges as well. While business-friendly terms such as "value proposition" may be necessary to negotiate parameters of the study with the potential employer collaborators, this may not appeal to some academic coauthors. In addition, there may be further and more substantial conflicts to overcome.

Scholarly research standards and practitioner standards for relevance are quite frequently at odds over foundational issues such as the age of the data, sample size, wording of survey questions, confidentiality procedures, and integrity-maintaining independence in conducting the research. For employers concerned with quarterly and annual business results, a study of business practices, the results of which will not be known for a year or more, may seem to be a waste of time and resources. Careful analysis and peer review are rarely completed on "business time." Survey fatigue in the workplace and among business decision-makers in particular means that what is an acceptable response rate on a survey to practitioners may be quite different from what is acceptable to academic researchers. Achieving academic standards in response rates, sampling precision, and survey-writing methods may be expensive, requiring additional project resources to underwrite the cost of multiple follow-up procedures. The effort deemed necessary from an academic perspective to achieve sufficient

data may be considered wasteful through the lens of the employer collaborator, something we experienced among our own employer network
partners. Perhaps the biggest challenge may be in balancing standards for
confidentiality and independence in the project overall (discussed more
fully in the next section).

In academic literature, much has been written about the rigor-relevance
or academic-practice gap. Kieser and Leiner (2009) point to a 1959 Ford
Foundation report as launching the debate. The authors of that seminal
report argued that business education in the United States was not sufficiently underpinned by science—in essence, pointing to *too much* relevance
and not enough rigor. Over the past five and a half decades the expanse of
rigor in management education has turned the tables on the debate. The
cry is now for bringing scholarly research (back) into the realm of relevance. A classic work in this regard is Gibbons et al. (1994). In this book,
the authors call for what they term "Mode 2" research, where application is
ever-present in the construct of knowledge creation, and research evaluation is conducted through a more practice-inclusive quality review process.

Some more recent literature attempts to analyze the rigor-relevance gap
empirically in order to shed light on what possible paths could bridge the
academic-practitioner knowledge creation gap. Nicolai, Schulz, and Gobel
(2011) analyze differences in the referee reports of academic and practitioner reviewers for a long-established "bridging" journal, *ZFO*, whose
target audience is both academia and practice. Flickinger et al. (2014) use
meta-analytical techniques to investigate how rigor and relevance of specific studies are linked to the impact they have within the discipline. Wasti
and Robert (2004) examine the topic and citation patterns of over three
hundred articles appearing in both academic and practitioner journals.

These scholars seem to be rather negative, however, about the feasibility
of bridging practice and scholarly research. Nicolai et al. (2011, 53) describe
academics' and practitioners' perspectives as "hardly compatible" and
"creating a striking incongruence between the two groups' ideas of practical relevance." Flickinger et al. (2014) find that while, on average, a study's
relevance is not negatively associated with the legitimacy it gains in the
discipline, "the academic community attributes legitimacy to studies based
on their rigor rather than their relevance" (120). Wasti and Robert (2004)
conclude that academic research has "failed in producing research that is
relevant for IHRM [international HR management]" (229), and citation

patterns reveal that academics appear "unconcerned with discussing the practical implications of their work" (209). Perhaps more blunt and discouraging is Kieser and Leiner's assessment that the academic-practitioner gap has become "unbridgeable" in management research and that thinking otherwise may be "false hope" (529).

Against the dark tone set by numerous academics, we believe our experience offers some useful complementary, and hopefully contrary, examples. We find employer collaborations are possible and relevance can be translated from otherwise publishable academic work.

## The Institutional Review Board and Do No Harm

The biggest challenge in bridging the relevance-rigor gap and conducting practitioner-academic research may be research integrity processes and standards. From the academic perspective, the Institutional Review Board (IRB) is the most recognized part of the research integrity process. The IRB defines a process that operationalizes the aspiration for research to do no harm to human subjects, and the practical parameters for executing against this ambitious aim. Revelations from the Nuremberg war crimes trials about experimentation on captives by German scientists during World War II, and the 1950s and 1960s Tuskegee experiments that withheld medical treatment from African Americans, "forced the reexamination of ethical standards and the gradual development of a consensus that potential human subjects needed to be protected from being used as 'guinea pigs' in scientific research" (Trochim 2006). It is on this foundation, and following the 1979 Belmont Report (U.S. Department of Health, Education, and Welfare 1979), that academic institutions have established IRB procedures so that "researchers will consider all relevant ethical issues in formulating research plans" (Trochim 2006).

Academic researchers, who consider the IRB process a given, may find it odd that convincing an employer collaborator of the value of academic research standards in general, and of the IRB in particular, may be necessary. Organizations and business membership associations without a mission related to scholarly (peer-reviewed) research will not typically have IRB processes in place. They will, therefore, likely not be sensitive to the need or value of such, or have experience in navigating the process.

In the case of our various research projects, the IRB process was completed successfully by our immediate team, but select partners had not previously undergone it and were not prepared for the time and effort it took to complete Cornell University's IRB procedure. It is important to note that, in the end, the system worked as intended. The employer representatives agreed they had learned much by going through the IRB process and were prompted into important reflection about the parameters and structure of the research project. One even adopted a new consent form within their own setting as a result.

Underpinning the IRB process is a desire to protect human subjects that was prompted by the discovery of medical research abuses. Employer collaboration on workplace practice research may not easily fit into the standard IRB questionnaires and procedure. We found this especially true in the case of employer representatives participating in working groups that functioned in both a quasi-advisory and quasi-focus-group capacity.

While each institution determines its own IRB procedure, the Office for Human Research Protections within the U.S. Department of Health and Human Services is the federal authority.[1] The Office for Human Research Protections also releases the *International Compilation of Human Research Standards* annually to assist researchers in meeting expectations and regulations internationally (U.S. Department of Health and Human Services 2014). Ultimately, academics must check with their own organization's IRB office on how best to navigate the process. Direct conversation with the researcher's IRB office in advance of submitting an IRB application is the recommended route for avoiding miscommunication and unnecessary effort down the road.

## Risk to the Organization

Completion of the IRB process, while clearing an institutional hurdle on the part of the researching organization, will likely not provide the employer and its representatives with the assurance they need regarding how potential harm from the research will be allayed. To demonstrate to the employer partner that processes are in place to do no harm, it may be necessary to articulate how the risk from participating in the research will be sufficiently minimized for the employer organization itself, rather than for the individual employees participating in the study. Concern over risks to the organization, rather than direct risks to the human subjects, is an ethical situation different from that encountered in traditional laboratory research experiments.

In a laboratory, no one worries about the potential suffering of the Petri dish within which an experiment takes place. In the workplace setting, however, the employing organization is a "living" Petri dish that can suffer harm beyond that of the specific human subjects engaged in the workplace research. And any harm to the organization creates a secondary risk for those individuals who hold positions of responsibility or whose work experience may be affected by an adverse organizational event. A "Do No Harm" principle proposed to the American Anthropological Association membership for discussion in 2010 can perhaps offer a useful framing here. It included this wording: "[Researchers] share a primary ethical obligation to avoid doing harm to the lives, communities or *environments* they study or that may be impacted by their work. . . . Such work should reflect deliberate and thoughtful consideration of both potential unintended consequences and long-term impacts on individuals, communities, identities, tangible and intangible heritage and *environments*" (American Anthropological Association 2010; italics added).

In the context of workplace research, the workplace itself is an *environment* that must be considered. If collaborative workplace research creates a negative outcome for the organization, and business suffers as a result, employees' jobs could be at risk. While this may sound overly dramatic, our team is aware of a workplace study where the results, when made public, were reported in the media. Re-reporting of results and poorly written headlines culminated in a highly public scrolling news ticker suggesting that the company had discriminated against some of its employees. The company was, at the time, in very sensitive labor negotiations, and negative press could have affected legal outcomes or even its stock price. In the end, the news organization pulled the inaccurate news feed, but parties both at the company involved in the study and on the research team were threatened with employment repercussions, and careful responses were required to protect the integrity of the research and the employment of those involved.

This concern over organizational risk is important to understand before beginning an outreach process to solicit employer partners. It helps to explain why organizations, or individual decision-makers within, may be reticent to jump at an invitation to collaborate on a workplace-practice study. Understanding this perspective also helps in planning what needs to be done by the researcher in advance to address these concerns.

There are certainly advantages gained from being able to publicly reveal the identity of the organization in which the research took place. While the researcher may rarely, if ever, seek permission from an individual human subject to reveal her or his identity, identifying the organizational partner(s) in a workplace study is almost always desirable. It can add credibility to the study not only in the world of peer-reviewed scholarship, but also for those in the employer audience meant to be influenced by the research.

It must be acknowledged that as difficult as it is to secure agreement from an organization to participate in an employer practices research study, obtaining permission from the organization to make its name public is even less likely. If, however, the research was being conducted on a group or consortium of organizations, then the specific participating organizations might be more willing to publicly acknowledge their participation in the study. Being one among many participants in an employer study might provide an organization with sufficient confidence that specific results would not be linked back to itself to grant permission to release its name. An organization might also be willing to have itself identified as a research partner if the research demonstrated some very favorable result for the company (for example, a very successful workplace practice) that could help it in recruiting new employees or unconditionally advance its public image. It is extremely unlikely, however, that a single employer would agree to be identified prior to seeing the final report of the results.

The timeline for presenting or publishing results is also an important topic for conversation with a potential employer collaborator. Many organizations hold decision makers accountable for quarterly and/or annual results. On the one hand, the pace of academic research and publication may feel far too slow for relevance to an individual's job responsibilities. On the other hand, collaborating on a study that may not be public for some five years (owing to the academic publishing process) may feel less threatening because any potential negative fallout to the organization's competitive advantage or brand from the study could be perceived as being an eternity away. In building a persuasive case for collaboration, consider proposing to not publish or make public in any way the results of the collaboration until some explicit future date with which the company would be comfortable.

Some helpful steps to consider with respect to overcoming the employer's (and its legal department's) confidentiality concerns are summarized in figure 2.2.

**Step**

**Action**

**Purpose**

**1**

Familiarize yourself with any recent workplace controversy or challenges the organization has experienced (mergers and acquisitions, lawsuits, union actions, etc.)

Avoid pitfalls and faux pas from being unaware of organizationally sensitive situations. Demonstrate you've done your homework and understand their issues.

**2**

If possible, connect first through a network contact so the introduction can include reference to a known acquaintance.

Establish legitimacy through personal network connections and increase the likelihood your e-mail or phone call will be answered.

**3**

Offer to sign a confidentiality agreement at the very start of discussing the project. Have your own organization's confidentiality form to offer, but be prepared for signing theirs, if your organization allows.

Signal professionalism in your approach to their confidentiality concerns.

**4**

Assure the employer that the identity of the organization (as well as any individuals participating) will be kept confidential. Only under a separate expressly written agreement would any identity be revealed.

Strengthen employer's confidence that information will not be unwillingly revealed publicly.

**5**

Design a sequencing to your research collaboration that starts with lower (legal) risk activities and progresses to higher-risk activities, as trust grows.

Build trust in the working relationship before undertaking stages of research that create more confidentiality challenges.

**6**

Discuss a realistic timeline for when results are first shared with the organization and then publicly (in any form), through to publication in a scholarly journal or book. Consider how long an "embargo" of the results could be tolerable.

Make explicit the length of time between research and any academic presentation or publication, and involve the employer in this conversation, to ease confidentiality concerns.

**Figure 2.2** Steps toward successful collaboration

## Making It Happen—from Start to Successful Completion

Convincing Business Collaborators of the Value
They Receive: The "Value Proposition"

As mentioned earlier, bringing an employer into a research alliance requires being able to effectively articulate the cumulative value that participation affords the employer representative. This reasoning might be called
the "value proposition" of the research collaboration.

The value proposition, in business parlance, "is a marketing tool that
explains why customers can benefit from a company's products or services. It can also be created for recruitment purposes, to show applicants
the value of becoming an employee of the company" (*Ultimate Business
Dictionary* 2003). To recruit employer collaborators, the researcher is es-
sentially marketing to and engaging the employer representative(s). Researchers may find the notion of marketing a research project as somehow
anti-intellectual—after all, shouldn't the intrinsic value of the research
merit it as worthy enough? The reality is, however, that the intrinsic scholarly or advocacy value of research will need to be communicated in a manner that engages and persuades the sought-after employer, and the value
proposition is a familiar business concept.

Anderson, Narus, and van Rossum (2006) offer a schematic of the cas-
cading effectiveness of the value proposition, reproduced here in table 2.1.
In reference to this exhibit, they advise that, in business, "best-practice suppliers base their value proposition on the few elements that matter most to
target customers, demonstrate the value of this superior performance, and
communicate it in a way that conveys a sophisticated understanding of the
customer's business priorities" (93).

Modifying the exhibit to be applicable to a research collaboration can be
done simply enough by replacing the words "customer" with "employer
representative," "market offering" with "research project," and "pur-
chase" with "participate in." After modifying the terminology, the challenging but valuable exercise remains to actually articulate the value of a
proposed employer-collaboration research project within the guidance of
this framework. What are the benefits for the employer of participating
in the research? Why should the organization devote resources, including employee time, to collaborating on this project over all other efforts to

**TABLE 2.1.**  Conveying the value proposition

| | "Which alternative conveys value to customers?" | | |
| --- | --- | --- | --- |
| Value proposition: | All benefits | Favorable points | Resonating focus |
| Consists of: | All benefits customers receive from a market offering | All favorable points of difference a market offering has relative to the next best alternative | The one or two points of difference (and perhaps a point of parity) whose improvement will deliver the greatest value to the customer for the foreseeable future |
| Answers the customer question: | "Why should our firm purchase your offering?" | "Why should our firm purchase your offering instead of your competitor's?" | "What is most worthwhile to our firm to keep in mind about your offering?" |
| Requires: | Knowledge of own market offering | Knowledge of own market offering and next best alternative | Knowledge of how own market offering delivers superior value to customer compared to the next best alternative |
| Has the potential pitfall: | Benefit assertion | Value presumption | Requires customer value research |

*Source:* Exhibit "Which Alternative Conveys Value to Customers?," from James C. Anderson, James A. Narus, and Wouter van Rossum, "Customer Value Propositions in Business Markets," *Harvard Business Review*, March 2006, http://hbr.org/2006/03/customer-value-propositions-in-business-markets/ ar/1.

which those resources could be devoted? And what are the most important outcomes to the specific employer-partner being targeted that could result from undertaking this research collaboration?

Organizations are concerned with how to fulfill their missions or do their business better. It may be expected that an outcome of the collaboration will be new insights on how to achieve this, described in a report or brief composed for the organization's own internal or external audience. This summary would be separate from, and in addition to, the ensuing scholarly research publications and presentations, as the employer audience will expect business-writing style, rather than academic. Without a customized summary (written or presented), a partnering organization will likely feel it has not received sufficient value from its participation. This summary of results will also need to be completed on a "business schedule," which will likely limit or even prohibit peer-review input at this point. (The timeline for such a summary of results would best be included in the project agreement.)

While it will be most important to articulate how the research will produce new knowledge to improve the employer's business operations or processes, there may also be interest in what the research collaboration can do for the organization's public image. And those individuals who will be the project's liaison or "champion" in the organization may also have a personal stake in being associated with the project and its successful completion.

One additional aspect to consider is specific language or terminology used in describing the project and its value. Terms that are regularly used by researchers may carry different, possibility negative connotations in the business world. Survey researchers, for example, will often refer to types of survey respondents as "informants." This term identifies the person who is actively answering survey questions, possibly on behalf of others, and allows a researcher to differentiate between that person and the "subject," who is the person about whom the information is being collected. This term, however, may be off-putting to business partners who may sense conspiratorial overtones to the discussion, especially if already concerned about risks to the organization from participating. Describing the research in the language of employers, where possible, and translating scholarly or technical jargon, can benefit the employer-recruitment process.

## Value to Organization's Image

*Being a Workplace Practice Leader*     Collaborating with academics can provide organizations (or the individuals within) with the patina of being a leading employer. While the term "best practice" may be overused, many organizations still seek to appear as, if not be, early adopters of innovative workplace practices that provide competitive advantage over their peers. Partnering on cutting-edge research may provide the organization with some bragging rights when trying to attract new employees or get the notice of analysts looking to find companies that are innovative throughout their workplace practices. Suggesting how the organization might be able to use its participation in the study to enhance its reputation as a workplace practice leader may add to the case in favor of research collaboration.

*Being a Good Corporate Citizen*    In the realm of advancing employment outcomes for individuals with disabilities, public opinion surveys do suggest that consumers care about an organization's workplace practices. As stated in one of our employer-partner reports, "Eighty-seven percent of consumers 'agree' or 'strongly agree' that they would prefer to give their business to companies that employ people with disabilities, and 92 percent of consumers are 'more favorable' or 'much more favorable' towards companies that hire people with disabilities" (Linkow et al. 2013, 13, citing Siperstein et al. 2006).

Actively furthering the knowledge frontier through workplace-practice research related to employees with disabilities provides the organization with an opportunity to showcase its corporate social responsibility in this arena. Being a good corporate citizen also means being compliant with all governmental regulations. Those companies who are federal contractors may have additional compliance requirements with respect to employees with disabilities—most recently, the newly implemented regulations from the U.S. Department of Labor's Office of Federal Contract Compliance Programs relating to Section 503 of the Rehabilitation Act. Not surprisingly, federal contractors' attention to improving their workplace practices for employees with disabilities has been heightened. Participating in collaborative research may be seen as more beneficial by federal contractors because of both the direct learning that can result, and the potential "good citizen" signal such research collaboration can send to governmental agencies.

It should be noted that from the staunch business perspective, building a value proposition for research collaboration that argues partnering on the project is a socially responsible thing to do may be considered at odds with stressing how the project can contribute to the organization's "bottom line." While some decision makers may understand that profitability and social responsibility are not necessarily mutually exclusive, many view the former as at the core of their responsibilities and the latter as "charity" that reduces resources available for doing the business of the company. For this reason, the business value of a collaborative research project may be the better persuasion for potential employer collaborators, and the good-citizen argument, an additional (and marginal) inducement.

## Reputational Value to the Individual Collaborator

In considering how to articulate the value proposition for an employer-partner research project, it is helpful to consider what value there might be for the individuals within that organization who would be involved in the project. Being on the research team may be an activity that can meet an individual's professional development or other work objective. Many organizations want partners or higher-level managers/executives to serve on advisory boards. Being the organization's liaison to the research project could be considered providing value or prestige to the individual in that role. In many workplaces, employees have objectives for personal development. Participating in a research group could be considered continuing education for these purposes.

Three examples that members of our team experienced in previous research collaborations illustrate how such professional value can accrue to the individual employee within the partnering employer organization. In one multi-employer research project, it was agreed by the participating companies that all the companies' names should be listed as contributors in the final report. Someone then asked that the names of the project leaders from each company also be listed. As the individual explained it, she needed her own name listed in the back of the report, along with the company's, to document for her manager and the HR department the active role she played in the research collaboration.

In another employer research project, an individual collaborator from the partner organization advocated for extending the research project beyond the original research plan and his own work responsibilities. Two months after the report targeting a business audience was released, this individual moved to a new job with responsibilities in the focus area he had supported expanding the research study to include. In retrospect, for this individual, redirecting his career was part of the value proposition of collaborating on the research project.

After the completion of a statistics-heavy collaborative research project, one team member from the employer organization went on to receive the honor of being appointed to a statistical association. Her post-project application to this position included a letter of support solicited from the academic lead of the study, who through this joint project was able to speak knowledgeably of the individual's statistical acumen and research collaboration skills.

While the ultimate gains to the individuals involved may not be realized for some time after the project concludes, and may not be anticipated at the start, it is worth thinking about the possibilities and asking the organizational liaisons what development value the project could provide to individual employees.

## The Employer Association or Business Network

Just as every academic discipline has its professional association, so too do business functions or job responsibilities. The list of jobs for which a professional association or network exists is seemingly endless: CFOs, supply chain managers, compliance officers, practitioners in training and development, human resources, compensation, and disability management or return-to-work. These organizations are also potential collaborators for engaging employers in the research process. Existing professional associations provide an established aggregation of members that can provide a structure into which a research collaboration could be inserted. An additional benefit of partnering with business associations is that they often produce their own conferences, webcasts, publications, or other communication channels to their membership. These are useful opportunities for disseminating project results more directly to an audience of workplace decision-makers (see chapter 7 for more discussion of content dissemination).

It is also possible to create a new or onetime consortium of employers around a single study or issue. The advantage with this path is being able to negotiate your own agenda. The disadvantage is that you have to convince participants of the value of the association *and* the project, as well as develop or provide any necessary infrastructure.

Reaching out to an existing business or professional association still requires creating a value proposition. What is the mission of the group, and how does this project help serve its interests? Often professional associations exist, at least in some part, to bring new knowledge and better practices to their members. Any research collaboration will be more willingly considered if there is a convincing argument that the study can help improve the effectiveness of the members or the field overall.

**Employer Engagement through Association Partnerships: Approach and Lessons**

As described in chapter 1, the research conducted under the auspices of our transdisciplinary initiative incorporated collaborative employer research across the spectrum of our activities. Employer representatives were engaged in "working groups" to help identify issues and challenges, with survey and case studies to assess workplace practices, and again through working groups that provided feedback on how to disseminate our findings to effect progressive workplace change. With the exception of the case studies, partnerships with four business or professional membership associations facilitated the employer engagement: The Conference Board (TCB), Cornell's Center for Advanced Human Resource Studies (CAHRS), the Disability Management Employer Coalition (DMEC), and the Society for Human Resource Management (SHRM). The research partnerships with DMEC and SHRM were built around an opportunity to conduct a poll and survey of their respective memberships. Discussion of the employer research partnerships with DMEC and SHRM, and those from the individual organization case studies, is presented in chapters 5 and 6, respectively. The collaboration with TCB and CAHRS afforded face-to-face, peer conversations over multiple "working group" meetings (see table 2.2). The CAHRS and TCB projects are each summarized in what follows, with discussion of the juxtaposition of these collaborations against a pure consortium benchmarking approach.

Consortium Benchmarking

In comparing our partnership with TCB to that with CAHRS, the TCB working group was the closer of the two to a consortium benchmarking approach. Schiele and Krummaker (2011) define consortium benchmarking as follows:

> A large research team of practitioners as well as academics visits and benchmarks each best-practices firm. They listen to presentations, conduct topical discussions, talk to managers, visit the firms' installations and review internal documents. After each visit, the consortium jointly analyzes the data, discusses emerging concepts and examines relationships between diverse concepts and/or variables. Consortium benchmarking advances traditional

**TABLE 2.2.**  Collaborative research meetings with corporate membership associations: The Conference Board (TCB) and Cornell Center for Advanced Human Resource Studies (CAHRS)

|  | **First meeting** | **Second meeting** | **Third meeting** | **Fourth meeting** |
|---|---|---|---|---|
| TCB Research Working Group | Research Working Group on Improving Employment Outcomes for People with Disabilities | Research Working Group on Improving Employment Outcomes for People with Disabilities | Research Working Group on Improving Employment Outcomes for People with Disabilities | |
| | Host: Employment and Disability Institute, Cornell—ILR School, New York City | Host: Lockheed Martin, Bethesda, Maryland | Host: Mattel, Los Angeles | |
| | June 2011 | September 2011 | December 2011 | |
| CAHRS Working Group | Working Group on Attraction, Retention and Reward for Employees with Disabilities | Working Group on Organizational Culture and Employer Practices with Respect to Persons with Disabilities | Working Group on Diversity and Inclusion | Working Group on Diversity and Inclusion |
| | Host: Aetna, New York City | Host: Charles Schwab, San Francisco | Host: JPMorgan Chase, New York City | Host: Verizon, New York City |
| | October 14, 2011 | February 15, 2012 | December 10, 2014 | March 20, 2015 |

*Source:* Linkow et al. 2013; CAHRS 2011, 2012.

multi-case approaches by including practitioners, not only as key informants but as co-researchers. Furthermore, since consortium benchmarking is a team-based approach focusing on best-practices cases, relevant discussions between academic and practitioners, or "meta discourses," are likely to emerge and flourish. (1138)

To a large degree, this characterizes the Research Working Group on Improving Employment Outcomes for People with Disabilities. The team included both Cornell University researchers and practitioner researchers from the service-providing/consulting organization, WFD Consulting. In addition, practitioners from participating firms contributed to shaping the final research report and also shared their own organizations' relevant workplace practices. The author of the published report incorporated these presentations and documents into the research process, but also sought to identify "promising practices" external to the group. The three two-day meetings and additional webcasts certainly flourished with "meta discourses," as Schiele and Krummaker term them. Perhaps the most notable deviations from a strict consortium benchmarking is that the full Improving Employment Outcomes for People with Disabilities consortium did not conduct any data analysis jointly, and the planned research publication was not designed to report quantitative benchmarking results, but rather more holistically address in the allotted time what the consortium determined were the key challenges of interest.

## The Conference Board Research Working Group

The Conference Board is a global, independent business membership and research association.[2] Its membership includes mostly corporate organizations, concentrated primarily within the United States, then Europe, and lastly Asia. In addition to convening meetings by corporate functional area and topical issue, TCB produces the U.S. Consumer Confidence Index ® and the Leading Economic Index ®.

Our collaboration with The Conference Board formed the Research Working Group on Improving Employment Outcomes for People with Disabilities, which met three times, each time for two days. The group was formed with sixteen organizational representatives from the business and government sectors, including Alcoa; Bayer; CVS Caremark; the U.S. Department of Veterans Affairs, Vocational Rehabilitation and Employment Service; Discovery Communications; Fidelity Investments; Goldman Sachs; KPMG LLP; Lockheed Martin; Mattel; New York Life Insurance; the U.S. Department of Treasury, Comptroller of Currency; the Pennsylvania Department of Labor and Industry; the U.S. Department of Defense; the U.S. Department of the Army; and Waste Management (Linkow et al. 2013, 6). Some of the job titles held by participants were associate director, analyst, director HR, VP diversity, executive director inclusion, manager workforce inclusion, supervisor rehabilitation special-ist, and integrated marketing/supply chain.

To encourage discussion on sensitive topics, these meetings were run under the agreement that no comments would be attributed in a man-ner that identified individuals or their organizations without their express written permission. It was the group members themselves, through facili-tated discussion, who shaped the scope of the ultimate report, focusing it on four questions (Linkow et al. 2013, 6):

1. The business case: Is it advantageous for organizations to employ peo-ple with disabilities?
2. Organizational readiness: What should organizations do to create a workplace that helps people with disabilities thrive and advance?
3. Measurement: How can success for both people with disabilities and the organization itself be determined?
4. Self-disclosure: How can people with disabilities, especially those whose disabilities are not obvious, be encouraged to identify themselves so that resources can be directed toward them and outcomes can be measured?

In answering these questions, a literature review was conducted and inte-grated with synthesis of the group discussions and selected practices as pre-sented by invited expert speakers and the business members themselves.

*The Business Case*　The business case for hiring and advancing employ-ees with disabilities was summarized through seven lenses identified as critical from a review of the literature and conversation of the group: talent pool; costs (workers' compensation, health care, accommodation, legal and related); benefits (retention, productivity, workers' compensa-tion cost savings, safety, customer engagement, profitability); revenue and market share (market for assistive technologies and support services, con-sumer market); work-group performance; financial incentives (tax cred-its); and fulfillment of executive and legislative mandates. In addition to compelling demographics (such as articulated in the previous chapter), the business case noted consumer market statistics, including the fact that the combined market for support services (excluding medical services and overnight housing) and assistive technologies (including eyeglasses and contact lenses) is larger than the gross domestic product (GDP) of 151 countries (Linkow et al. 2013, 13). The synthesis of the business case on other financial measures, while generally positive, was not as strong, and "more definitive research is needed" (Linkow et al. 2013, 16). Regardless, the fulfillment of executive and legislative mandates and the provision for government subsidies and tax credits were noted as substantial business case considerations.

*Organizational Readiness*     An important conclusion of the working group's deliberations was that organizations cannot successfully implement furthering employment and advancement of people with disabilities without working toward more holistic "organizational readiness" (Linkow et al. 2013, 17–50). This readiness includes (1) a foundation of values and beliefs, (2) top management commitment, (3) communications—both internal and external, (4) integrative infrastructure, (5) an employment process that "flows from the initial job description to efforts for career development and advancement" (Linkow et al. 2013, 22), (6) measurement and self-disclosure, and (7) organizational climate.

*Measurement and Self-Disclosure*     As is evident from the four questions that the working group jointly constructed, measurement and self-disclosure are current high-priority challenges for employers. The tried-and-true business adage "what gets measured gets done" still appears to carry much weight. This working group broke the amorphous category of measurement into five actionable categories, summarized here in table 2.3.

**TABLE 2.3.** Measurement considerations to advance workplace progress

| 1. | Accountability | Quantitative goals for improvement must be set and progress against those goals evaluated. |
|---|---|---|
| 2. | Vendors | As employers are themselves customers in the business-to-business supply chain marketplace, they can also set standards and objectives for their vendors, applying pressure on their suppliers to improve their practices regarding employees with disabilities. |
| 3. | Culture | Disability status can be included on employee surveys, as other demographic characteristics such as gender and race typically are, to determine how workplace culture perceptions differ for employees with and without disabilities. |

| 4. | Representation throughout employment pipeline | Representation statistics for individuals with disabilities "starting with applications, to interviews, to hiring, to advancement and developmental opportunities" (Barrington et al. 2013, 63) provide a fuller picture for assessing progress. |
| 5. | Return on Investment (ROI) on training | It is possible to apply quantitative analysis to measure the impact that training and development around diversity in general and people with disabilities in particular have on outcomes for the inclusion and advancement of employees with disabilities. |

*Source:* Linkow et al. 2013

Employers in the working group additionally pointed out that the challenges of measurement and self-disclosure are inseparable. If employees with disabilities do not disclose those disabilities, there is no measurement that can be used to drive progress. Throughout the process of engagement with this stakeholder group, an attempt was made to galvanize thoughts and perceptions around the many-faceted issue of disability disclosure—to understand the concept within the context of the current regulatory environment, and to reconcile the employer's desire to know with an individual's incentive (or lack thereof) to tell. Table 2.4 presents an original framework created within the research working group for considering who gains what from varying degrees of disclosure. It articulates how self-identification of disability status can happen with varying degrees of anonymity; and while employers may have a good reason for offering an opportunity for self-identification, the reason for the request may not include direct benefit to the employee.

For example, if the employer wishes to improve workforce planning by incorporating representation goals for employees with disabilities, questions on an anonymous employee survey regarding career intentions could be useful and would not require knowing an individual's name and disability status. On the other hand, if the employer wants to develop a high-potential mentoring program for employees with disabilities, individuals with disabilities would need to identify themselves for inclusion in the program. Even this scenario, however, does not require the employees to self-identify to managers who are not directly involved in the program.

The full public report produced from this multi-employer collaboration (written to target a business audience) can be found in Linkow et al.

**TABLE 2.4.** Self-disclosure decision matrix

| Self-disclosure matrix | | PURPOSE SERVED FOR: | |
|---|---|---|---|
| Degree of identification | Collection process | Individual employee | Employer |
| None | • No proactive collection of disclosure data | • Protect individual confidentiality and privacy | • Presumably reduce legal risks* |
| Anonymous | • Employee survey<br>• Employee focus groups and interviews conducted by third party<br>• Data collected/kept separately from all other individual information, such as job applications | • Support organizational improvement<br>• Help drive high-level culture or process change | • Gather top-line metrics on representation as well as recruitment, hiring, and advancement<br>• Create accountability measures<br>• Improve workforce planning |
| Individual identified | • Verbal notification by individual<br>• Form with name identified<br>• Data kept in HR or other company data systems (e.g., emergency preparedness database) | • Receive an accommodation<br>• Take advantage of any company career advancement opportunities for people with disabilities<br>• Safety/emergency preparedness<br>• Affirm identity and individual empowerment | • Improve employee performance<br>• Strengthen accountability measures for representation, recruitment, hiring, retention, and advancement<br>• Improve talent development |

* Avoidance of data collection is no guarantee of protection from legal risk.
*Source:* Linkow et al. 2013, 39.

2013; the executive summary is in Linkow and Figueroa 2013. Information obtained from the working group discussions and research was also applied to other parts of the larger transdisciplinary research agenda.

## The Cornell Center for Advanced Human Resource Studies Working Groups

The Cornell Center for Advanced Human Resource Studies is the leading business-academia partnership devoted to global HR management, with more than seventy corporate members.[3] The CAHRS working groups provided insight into and feedback on the various research activities of the larger project. There were four meetings in all, attracting a range of participants from a dozen to upward of twenty-five, with job titles including director of HR, director of diversity and inclusion, compliance manager, diversity analyst, manager employee engagement, senior director of talent acquisition, and HR generalist. Each meeting lasted two-thirds of a day, was hosted at a partner company, and focused on a predetermined theme. CAHRS research faculty members facilitated the discussions.

To allow for open and frank conversation, the terms of the working group meetings were that no comments would be attributed to individuals or their organizations without their express written permission. The publicly available output from these meetings consisted of high-level, anonymized summaries (CAHRS 2011, 2012). As with TCB collaborations, insights from these discussions were also applied in shaping the surveys and analytics of other research studies within the overall initiative.

Conversations among working group participants helped to prioritize our immediate and future research agendas by pointing to what questions, in the eyes of the employer representatives present, were most in need of answering to reduce barriers and further advancement in the workplace for individuals with disabilities. Some of the issues about which there was consensus were the following (CAHRS 2011, 2012):

- What are the particulars of workplace culture that make employees with disabilities more comfortable with self-disclosure?
- How do return-to-work programs affect perceptions of people with disabilities, and how can negative stereotypes of return-to-work programs be reduced?
- What keeps a person with a targeted disability out of the labor force versus in the labor force but unemployed? Why do some want to work and can't find employment while others are not seeking employment?
- What holds people back from self-reporting a disability? Is it different for employees of different ages or levels in the organization? Do people with differing disabilities have differing reasons for not disclosing?

Another valuable contribution of these in-person conversations with employers was their anecdotes of their experiences. These stories are very helpful in disseminating research conclusions to a practitioner audience. Some academics may downplay such narrative as simply "color commentary" (to borrow a sports-media term), but storytelling has become a promoted skill in business management and strategic communications (Denning 2006; McKee and Fryer 2003; Morgan and Dennehy 1997). In the words of one author, "more and more firms grasp that narrative is central to addressing many of today's key leadership challenges" (Denning 2006, 42). One example of such a story that we gleaned from the working group adds palpable applicability to our research finding that increasing the comfort of self-disclosure of a disability is important at every part of the employment pipeline.

> A phone interview turned into the successful hire of a top engineering candidate because one recruiter let her curiosity lead her. The job candidate looked great on paper, but something was amiss on the phone interview. In the post-interview debrief, the company's representatives wondered openly if the person on the phone was even the actual applicant who applied for the job. Instead of crossing the candidate off the list, one of the recruiters decided to probe further. Curious at the disconnect between what the company's recruiters had expected and what they heard on the phone interview, the recruiter dug deeper. She learned the strong engineering candidate was deaf [and] . . . had made his own accommodations for the interview. . . . [The] recruiter worked with the candidate to provide accommodation for the rest of the interviewing process. The candidate was ultimately selected and successfully hired. The new employee has not only brought top talent and diversity to his team, but also a more collaborative energy that's improved the team's overall functioning. [The] take away: Better training of recruiters and strengthening candidates' willingness to ask for accommodation can secure top talent that might otherwise be regrettably overlooked. (CAHRS 2011, 2)

Another example of a research-supporting anecdote—this one quantitative—reinforces studies that show third-party anonymous surveys increase self-disclosure rates (see discussion of anonymity and self-identification in chapter 6). One participant representing a multinational and federal contracting corporation shared that when employees were given an opportunity to disclose their disability status on our employee culture survey along with other demographic information, the measured workforce representation of employees with disabilities was more than three times greater than the measurement according to the company's internal HR disclosure records.

Another valuable conversation took place in our first CAHRS working group around the preferred metrics for tracking long-term progress among these employers (CAHRS 2011). Participants identified the representation statistic for people with disabilities in these four categories as one important measure of whether progress will have been made a decade from now:

- Interns
- Recruits from "pedigree" colleges and universities
- Total employee base
- Senior management

Other metrics identified as top progress measures were

- More university offices of student services for students with disabilities involved in the recruiting process
- Increased ease of hiring and on-boarding employees with disabilities, specifically shortened time from application to hire for candidates with disabilities
- Greater presence of and employee participation in an employee resource group related to disability, including employees with and without a disability
- Whether or not metrics for tracking progress on inclusion of employees with disabilities have become as common as those for tracking progress by gender or other dimensions of diversity

The final two CAHRS meetings focused on the discussion of the results of the case study research conducted as part of our initiative (see chapter 6) and improving dissemination of our transdisciplinary research results to employers through the BenchmarkABILITY online tool described in chapter 7. An early prototype of BenchmarkABILITY was shared with the participants of the third CAHRS working group. Modifications were then made in response to the feedback, and an enhanced prototype was shared at the fourth working-group meeting.

## Further Workplace Practice Research

In the remainder of the book, lessons learned from several other workplace-practice research projects are summarized. Each project with direct involvement from employer representatives had its own unique challenges and benefits. In each case, we feel that the benefits from employer collaboration certainly exceeded the challenges encountered. As with all research endeavors, we have unearthed new questions and potential for future research. We believe our engagement with organizational decision-makers has been instrumental in embedding into our future research the priorities and perspectives of those making the workplace-practice decisions that will directly affect employment opportunities and career advancement for individuals with disabilities.

# 3

# EXPLORING NATIONAL SURVEY DATA

William A. Erickson, Arun Karpur, and Kevin F. Hallock

Much of our knowledge of the existing employment situation of people with disabilities comes from analyses of national survey data. These surveys, conducted to provide federal and state governments with the information they need to manage and evaluate their programs and policies, among other reasons, also provide the primary source of statistics on the entire population. They contain a wealth of information regarding a wide variety of topics, and most of the data are readily available for researchers to access and analyze. National survey data offer a number of significant advantages to researchers. In most cases the data can be easily downloaded from the Internet, and the files are usually well documented. Analysis of existing national datasets can provide the groundwork needed to inform further research. Results can independently confirm (or deny) findings from analysis of other data sources and further strengthen researchers' conclusions or call them into question.

What follows is not meant to be an exhaustive discussion of these sources but rather an attempt to describe the datasets and innovative ways to combine them, and to highlight some of the important findings that can result. We begin with a high-level overview of some of the different national surveys available, describing some of the strengths and limitations of working with these data, and the way they have historically been used to explore disability and employer practices. We then describe ten key national surveys that include information on the disability status of individuals as well as on labor market outcomes and employer practices. We also address considerations in identifying potential national survey data sources for research, and discuss some of the challenges in working with these data.

To illustrate the strength of these national survey datasets, we present two empirical examples from our transdisciplinary initiative. These include applications to the level and form of employment compensation and to wellness, including novel ways of combining existing data to address some of the shortcomings of national surveys.

Finally, we describe the Disability and Compensation Variables Catalog (DCV Catalog), which is an online tool created as part of the team's work, specifically designed to provide an easy way to browse and identify variables regarding disability as well as employer practices, including a variety of measures of compensation across ten national surveys. We describe several ways that the DCV Catalog can be used, including both identifying potential data sources and variables for analysis, as well as for identifying questions to use in other research efforts.

## Working with National Survey Data

Generally, little monetary investment is required beyond the time required to become familiar with the data. These data sources can provide a large sample with which to work, permitting the identification of subtle differences among populations and offering the potential for subgroup analyses. Some have large enough samples to permit the development of state-level estimates and enable between-state comparisons. Statistical weights are often available in order to develop national and in some cases state-level estimates.

Most of the larger national surveys are *cross-sectional*, collecting data on a unique sample at a specific point in time. This provides information that can be used to make inferences about a population of interest, including key indicators, such as prevalence or employment rates. Other national surveys are *longitudinal*, allowing for the examination of the same sample of individuals over time. Longitudinal, or panel, surveys may permit the study of an acquired disability with respect to a person's employment and other labor market outcomes. National surveys can be used to identify issues and serve as a foundation for further research studies, especially if they are conducted annually, making it feasible to examine trends over time. Identification of trends in national data can assist researchers in drafting their own surveys and planning case studies.

A major limitation of these datasets is that they may not identify the specific population of interest or contain the precise information needed to ideally address a research question. The fact that these data are preexisting saves time and resources, but removes any opportunity for customized language or sample selection. Sorting through the numerous existing national survey data sources to identify which ones contain the most appropriate variables for a specific research question or topic of interest can be challenging. As the most useful variables for a given research project may be contained in multiple national surveys, it is sometimes possible to creatively combine different data sources to fill in gaps or supplement the available data. We discuss this and provide an example of our work in this regard further along in this chapter.

Because the questions on national surveys are predetermined, and their wording is out of secondary users' control, questions and response categories can change over time. This can potentially preclude the examination of trends over time or combination of data from multiple years. It is essential to carefully examine the actual survey questions and coding of every variable, especially when comparing data that are collected with regular frequency (for example, multiple panels or years of data).

Most national data sources are quite efficient in ensuring complete surveys, but there are always instances where a respondent refuses or otherwise does not provide an answer to a question. While this missing information can result in some problems, many national survey data sources utilize methods to "impute" missing responses. Imputation is a procedure for substituting a value for a missing or unusable response, often based on other available information about the respondent. Some survey data provide additional variables that identify, or flag, cases where this has been done. This allows researchers to examine differences in respondents and nonrespondents, exclude those imputed cases, or apply alternative imputation approaches. Missing data is a potentially greater issue in the case of longitudinal or panel surveys that require significant efforts to retain respondents and follow them over time.

## Research Using National Survey Data

National survey data have been used extensively to examine disability and employer practices and policies. The following are just a few examples of the numerous papers using national survey data.[1] The Current Population Survey (CPS) data have been used to understand the main reasons for nonstandard work arrangements (Schur 2002, 2003; Schur and Kruse 2002), while Hotchkiss (2004) used these data to explore the part-time employment experience of workers with disabilities over time. The Behavioral Risk Factor Surveillance System (BRFSS) has been used to explore how the level of disability is related to income and the likelihood of employment (Randolph 2004) as well as the relationship between exercise and employment for persons with disabilities (Ipsen 2006). Kaye (2009) combined information from the Department of Labor's Occupational Information Network (O*NET) database and the American Community Survey (ACS) data to examine the occupational characteristics of workers with disabilities. Within our transdisciplinary initiative, Hallock, Jin, and Barrington (2014) used three different surveys, the ACS, the CPS, and the Health and Retirement Survey (HRS), to examine pay and total compensation gaps between persons with and without disabilities.

The ACS has been used to develop estimates by disability status for various issues including employment, full-time/full-year employment, earnings, household income, poverty, Supplemental Security Income (SSI) receipt, and health insurance for working-age persons with and without disabilities (Erickson, Lee, and von Schrader 2014). O'Hara (2000) used the Survey of Income and Program Participation (SIPP) and the National Health Interview Survey on Disability (NHIS-D) to examine discrimination against persons with disabilities in employment transitions as measured by wage penalties and different types of disabilities that were more or less likely to elicit prejudicial responses. Meyer and Mok (2006) used the Panel Study of Income Dynamics (PSID) to examine disability status and its association with employment, hours worked, earnings, income, and consumption. DeLeire (2000) used the SIPP to explore wage and employment effects of the Americans with Disabilities Act (ADA).

Workplace accommodations were examined through analysis of the NHIS-D (Zwerling et al. 2003) as well as the HRS (Charles 2004; Burkhauser et al. 1999; Burkhauser, Butler, Yang-Woo 1995). Daly and Bound (1996) used the HRS to examine worker adaptation and employer accommodation after the onset of a health impairment, while von Schrader, Xu, and Bruyère (2014) used the CPS Disability supplement to examine accommodation requests and receipt.

These studies are just the tip of the iceberg in terms of research that has been done. Later in this chapter we provide additional information on the data sources mentioned above and describe where additional detail on the actual content of these major national surveys can be accessed.


## National Survey Data Sources

One of the difficulties in working with national survey data is identifying which of the many available surveys can inform a research question. Given the focus of our research program on employer practices and persons with disabilities in the United States, we focused on identifying existing publicly available national survey data sources that contain information on both employer practices and disability status. We began by building a set of data sources that contain person-level information and were collected relatively recently—in the year 2000 or later. Each data source had to contain information regarding demographic characteristics, individual measures of disability, and characteristics related to employment such as occupation, industry, region, and certain human resource practices, such as level of wages and other forms of compensation (such as health insurance).

The following ten national surveys were identified based on these criteria: the American Community Survey; the Behavioral Risk Factor Surveillance System; the Decennial Census of Population (Census 2000); the Current Population Survey; the Health and Retirement Study; the Medical Expenditure Panel Survey; the National Health Interview Survey; the National Longitudinal Transition Study-2; the Panel Study of Income

**TABLE 3.1.** Ten major datasets with disability variables

| Abbreviation | Full name | URL | Design | Years | Frequency | Sample size |
|---|---|---|---|---|---|---|
| ACS | American Community Survey | http://www.census.gov/acs/www/ | Cross-sectional | 2000– | Annual | Approx. 3 million individuals |
| BRFSS | Behavioral Risk Factor Surveillance System | http://www.cdc.gov/brfss/ | Cross-sectional | 1994– | Annual | 432,607 individuals (2009) |
| Census | Decennial Census | http://www.census.gov/main/www/cen2000.html | Cross-sectional | 1790– | Decennial | |
| CPS | Current Population Survey | http://www.census.gov/cps/ | Cross-sectional | 1940– | Annual | 60,000 households (monthly) |
| HRS | Health and Retirement Study | http://hrsonline.isr.umich.edu | Longitudinal | 1992– | Biennial | 12,652 individuals in 1st cohort |
| MEPS | Medical Expenditure Panel Survey | http://meps.ahrq.gov/mepsweb/ | Longitudinal | 1996– | Annual | 32,320 individuals (2005) |
| NHIS | National Health Interview Survey | http://www.cdc.gov/nchs/nhis/about_nhis.htm | Cross-sectional | 1957– | Annual | 88,446 individuals (2009) |
| NLTS2 | National Longitudinal Transition Study-2 | http://www.nlts2.org/ | Longitudinal | 2000–2010 | Biannual | 11,270 individuals |
| PSID | Panel Study of Income Dynamics | http://psidonline.isr.umich.edu/ | Longitudinal | 1968– | Annually 1968–1996, biannual 1997– | Approximately 22,000 individuals |
| SIPP | Survey of Income and Program Participation | http://www.census.gov/sipp/ | Longitudinal | Panels at intervals, 1984–2008 | Quarterly panel | 46,500 households (2004) |

Dynamics; and the Survey of Income and Program Participation. To help to illustrate the wide variety of sources available, brief descriptions of these ten data sources follow. A summary with a link to each survey's home page can be found in table 3.1.

1. *The American Community Survey* (ACS) is an annual cross-sectional survey first fielded in 2000. It is conducted by the U.S. Census Bureau and is designed to collect information on a sample of the institutionalized and noninstitutionalized population. It is the largest annual survey fielded in the United States and is distributed to over 3 million households. The survey covers a broad range of topics including age, gender, race, family and relationships, income and benefits, health insurance, education, veteran status, and disabilities, as well as housing characteristics. The objective of the ACS is to provide federal, state, and local governments with up-to-date information to help plan investments and services. Information from the survey aids in the determination of how more than $400 billion in federal and state funds are distributed each year. Note that the disability questions were changed several times but have remained consistent from 2008 to 2015. Since 2008, the six-question set of disability items from the ACS has been included in a number of other national-level surveys, including the CPS, the SIPP, the BRFSS, the National Crime Victimization Survey (NCVS), and the American Housing Survey (AHS).

2. *The Behavioral Risk Factor Surveillance System* (BRFSS) is an annual cross-sectional survey first conducted in 1984. Designed by the Centers for Disease Control and Prevention (CDC), it collects uniform, state-specific data on preventive health practices and risk behaviors linked to chronic diseases, injuries, and preventable infectious diseases that affect the adult population. Although it is a CDC-supported survey, it is unique in that it is actually conducted by individual state health departments. The BRFSS also includes a number of optional modules focusing on specific health issues that states can choose to include.

3. *The Decennial Census of Population* is a cross-sectional survey that occurs every ten years to enumerate every resident in the United States and is mandated by Article I, Section 2 of the U.S. Constitution. The U.S. Census Bureau uses the data to determine the number of seats each state has in the U.S. House of Representatives, and the information is also used to distribute billions in federal funds to local communities. The census questionnaire has expanded, contracted, and evolved throughout history, especially its questions pertaining to per-

sons with disabilities (Barrington and Bruyère 2012). The most recent iteration, the 2010 Decennial Census, utilized only a "short form" survey. It limited data collected to just basic information such as age, gender, race and ethnicity and contains no disability data. The annual ACS took over the collection of the more detailed information traditionally collected in the Decennial Census "long form."

4. *The Current Population Survey* (CPS) is a U.S. Bureau of Labor Statistics (BLS) cross-sectional survey, conducted by the United States Census Bureau to gather estimates of employment, unemployment, earnings, hours of work, and other indicators. It collects a variety of demographic characteristics, including age, gender, race, marital status, and educational attainment, as well as employment-related information such as occupation, industry, and class of worker. The "work limitation" disability question was first included in 1981 in the March Supplement, and the six disability questions based on the ACS were added into the monthly survey in 2008. Supplemental questionnaires are occasionally funded to produce estimates on various topics, including school enrollment, income, previous work experience, health, employee benefits, and work schedules. Of particular interest is the CPS disability supplement fielded in May 2012. It focused on a variety of issues of interest, including labor force participation, work history, types of workplace accommodations, and barriers to employment for persons with disabilities.

5. *The Health and Retirement Study* (HRS), first fielded in 1992, is a longitudinal study run by the University of Michigan and supported by the National Institute on Aging (NIA) and the Social Security Administration. It is a large-scale project that follows a representative sample of about twenty-six thousand Americans over the age of fifty every two years. It studies the labor force participation and health transitions that individuals undergo toward the end of their work lives and the following years. It collects a wide variety of information including disability, physical health and functioning, cognitive functioning, health insurance and health care expenditures, as well as work, accommodations provided, income, assets, and pension plans.

6. *The Medical Expenditure Panel Survey* (MEPS) is a longitudinal panel survey first fielded in 1996 and conducted annually by the Agency for Health Care Quality. It provides nationally representative estimates of health care utilization and expenditures, sources of payments, and health insurance for the noninstitutionalized U.S. civilian population. The Household Component (MEPS-HC) of the MEPS is widely used, whereas the Medical Provider Component, Insurance Component, and Nursing

Home Component are restricted-access datasets and require special approvals for researchers. Each year, the MEPS-HC sample is established to form a panel, and everyone within the panel is interviewed five times over a period of thirty months. The MEPS-HC collects information on key socio-demographic factors, medical conditions/events, functional limitations, cost or expenditure for medical services including physician services, drugs, procedures, hospitalization and ambulatory care, as well as information on employment, hourly wages, access to health insurance, and workplace characteristics in every interview round.

7. *The National Health Interview Survey* (NHIS) is an annual cross-sectional survey that is one of the major data collection efforts of the National Center for Health Statistics (NCHS). First conducted in 1957, it is designed to monitor the health of the civilian noninstitutionalized population of the United States through the collection and analysis of data on a broad range of health topics. A major strength of this survey lies in the ability to display these health characteristics by a wide variety of demographic and socioeconomic characteristics.

8. *The National Longitudinal Transition Study-2* (NLTS2) was an annual longitudinal study funded by the U.S. Department of Education to document the experiences of a national sample of students receiving special education who were thirteen to sixteen years of age in 2000, as they moved from secondary school into adult roles. The study collected information regarding a wide range of topics, including high school coursework, extracurricular activities, academic performance, postsecondary education and training, employment, independent living, and community participation. The original NLTS was a six-year study beginning in 1985. The NLTS2 began in 2000, and final data collection occurred in 2010. A third study, the NLTS 2012, began in 2012.

9. *The Panel Study of Income Dynamics* (PSID) is a biennial longitudinal household survey that since 1968 has followed a nationally representative sample of over eighteen thousand individuals living in five thousand families in the United States. Information on these individuals and their descendants has been collected continuously for over forty years. The PSID collects data regarding employment, income, wealth, expenditures, health, marriage, childbearing, child development, philanthropy, education, and numerous other topics.

10. *The Survey of Income and Program Participation* (SIPP) is a longitudinal survey conducted by the United States Census Bureau. The first panel was fielded in 1984. It collects a wide variety of information, including source and amount of income, labor force information,

program participation and eligibility data, and general demographic characteristics. It measures the effectiveness of existing federal, state, and local programs, estimates future costs and coverage for government programs such as food stamps, and provides statistics on the distribution of income and measures of economic well-being in the United States. Note that a number of changes have occurred in the disability questions over time.

## Data Source Considerations

Although each of the ten surveys described above provides data regarding disability as well as compensation information, not all surveys are equal, and the actual content varies greatly. How should researchers, policy makers, and interested others go about deciding the survey with which they should work? There are a number of considerations that will help determine which is best suited to respond to a specific research question. Some of the major considerations include the population of interest (that is, working-age, transition-age youth, and older population), topical coverage, and the specific variables and questions available for analysis.

Surveys are based on different samples and populations; some focus on a specific segment of a population. Depending on the population of interest, this may help narrow down which data sources are most appropriate to use. For example, the ACS collects information on the institutionalized and noninstitutionalized population of all ages, while the CPS surveys only the civilian noninstitutional population sixteen years of age and older. For a researcher specifically interested in those currently serving in the military, the ACS would clearly be a better source of data. Other surveys use different criteria: the SIPP is limited to household members ages fifteen and older, and the BRFSS surveys only household members ages eighteen and older. The NLTS2 and the HRS examine two specific populations at the opposite ends of the age spectrum: youth and persons age fifty and older. This information is often referred to as the "sampling frame" and is typically available in the survey documentation.

As can be seen in the basic descriptions, the surveys are supported by several different government agencies, each of which has special interests that are in turn reflected in the content of the surveys. The Census Bureau's ACS and the Decennial Census of Population are both quite broad in nature, while the CPS (BLS) is primarily focused on labor and employment information. The surveys supported by the CDC and related entities tend to be oriented toward medical and health issues: BRFSS, MEPS, and NHIS are more likely to include detailed health measures than are the other surveys.

Another significant challenge is presented by the great diversity in the definition of (and the questions used to identify) the concept of disability. Most surveys use a set of questions to identify the population with disabilities, but those questions may vary significantly across surveys. Determining what combinations of disability variables will be used to define the population called "disabled" is essential and should be carefully considered. Specific disability types may be better identified in certain surveys, and may not be identified at all in others. Specific health conditions are more likely to be collected in the health-oriented surveys; some surveys collect detailed functional and activity limitation information, while others such as the ACS and CPS use a more limited six-question disability set, which may or may not identify the researcher's population of interest.

Even when identifying similar disability types, the questions used across surveys may be different. A researcher interested in disabilities with respect to "grasping" will discover that there are four data sources (MEPS, NHIS, NLTS2, and SIPP) with individual-level information regarding "difficulty grasping." However, there are differences in the specific questions used to obtain this information. The HRS asks, "Because of a health problem do you have any difficulty with picking up a dime from a table?" In the MEPS, the grasping question is phrased as, "How much difficulty does the person have using fingers to grasp or handle something such as picking up a glass from a table or using a pencil to write?" The NHIS asks, "By yourself, and without using any special equipment, how difficult is it for you to . . . use your fingers to grasp or handle small objects?" In the SIPP, the question is, "[Does the respondent] have any difficulty using hands and fingers to do things such as picking up a glass or grasping a pencil?" This foreshadows the empirical results presented later in this chapter that involve estimating the compensation gap between those with disabilities and those without and how that gap differs by data source. Some of these differences could be due to the nature and form of the questions being asked.

## Using Multiple National Surveys in Compensation Research

Using national data sources can be challenging for a variety of reasons, including the diversity of disability definitions and differences in the population sampled as described above. Sometimes existing data sources seem an easy avenue for empirical work, since the data have already been collected. On the other hand, as noted previously, *because* the data sources already exist, they are fixed, the questions cannot be changed or the variables altered, and thus they may not have precisely the data that are necessary to answer a particular question. In order to make significant research progress in this situation, it is sometimes necessary to combine various data sources.

As an illustration, for one project, members of our team sought detailed information about an individual's compensation (we describe how this related to individuals with disabilities later in this chapter). This is difficult information to locate; while many surveys include data on the wage and salary income of individuals, only about 70 percent of the cost of an employee is given directly to the employee as wage or salary income (Hallock 2012). The remainder is made up of a host of other forms of compensation, including vacation time, holiday pay, sick pay, insurance, retirement contributions, and so on. These additional types of compensation are essential in gaining an understanding of the total compensation that individuals receive from their employment.

Few data sources contain this type of rich information on the nonwage and salary parts of individuals' pay, except, perhaps, for senior executives of publicly traded companies. One data source that does have rich information on the costs of compensation to employers is the Employer Costs for Employee Compensation (ECEC) survey. Unfortunately, this data source asks employers about *occupations* in their organizations, making it impossible to immediately link compensation information with data on measures of disability for individuals. However, the ECEC occupational-level data can be linked to records in national surveys that include the individual's occupation as well as age, race, gender, disability measures, and other variables.

An additional issue is that the publicly available ECEC data are available only for very large aggregated occupations. In order to get a finer level of detail, we applied for and were granted access to restricted ECEC data that included hundreds of specific occupations. These data allowed us to make comparisons between persons with and without disabilities for both the basic wage gap and the total compensation gap. We hypothesized that the latter gap would be smaller in percentage terms, because those with disabilities may differentially enter into occupations that had relatively more-generous (health) insurance benefits than those without disabilities. As we show in the next section, that is precisely what we found.

## Empirical Findings with National Data

Our research examined many areas related to the relationship between "employer practices" and persons with disabilities. We highlight just three of them here, all of which build from a more holistic view of employer practices regarding employer-provided employee compensation. According to the U.S. Bureau of Labor Statistics (2014b) on average, wage or salary income accounts for only 70 percent of the total cost that employers pay for employee compensation in the United States. In making workplace hiring and other business decisions, employers consider the entire cost of employees—including health, vacation, training, and accommodation, etc.—not simply wages or salaries paid. Individual employees, of course, consider these factors as well.

The first two examples of our research discussed in the following section use the MEPS to examine health-care expenses of individuals with disabilities and how employer-paid health insurance is related to the probability of job change for persons with disabilities. This is followed by an examination of the compensation gap between persons with disabilities and persons without disabilities, estimating total compensation, beyond just wages and salaries, as best we could.

### Employer-Paid Health Insurance and Job Retention

For employers, employee health-care benefits are both a cost concern and are acknowledged as a valuable recruitment and retention tool. One survey found that 79 percent of employers who provided coverage were very concerned about cost control (Society for Human Resource Management 2014), while in another survey, a similar proportion (83 percent) considered health benefits an important part of their offerings, and intended to continue to subsidize them (Towers Watson 2014).

One of our research projects focused on understanding the potential reduction in excess health-care expenditures that might be realized by increasing access to workplace wellness programs for employees with disabilities. The MEPS-HC data offer a rich resource to study various aspects of employment, including access to employer-provided workplace benefits, type of employment, hours worked, and industry. On average, employees with disabilities had health-care expenditures that were three times higher than those of employees without disabilities. It was evident, using attributable risk fractions, that preventing the occurrence of secondary health conditions had the potential to reduce annual average health-care expenditures by 16 to 25 percent for working individuals with disabilities. This research pointed out the need for employers, who in most instances provide workplace wellness programs, to consider the accessibility of such initiatives for employees with disabilities (Karpur and Bruyère 2012).

As indicated by Rimmer (2005), workplace wellness programs have yet to be made inclusive for people with disabilities. Our research, by estimating the potential reduction in average annual health-care expenditures, provides an argument for employers to consider disability accommodations in the design and delivery of workplace wellness programs to stem the increasing costs of health-care premiums for their workers with disabilities.

In assessing employer practices and their impact on worker retention, another study utilized MEPS-HC data to assess the impact of having access to employer-paid health insurance on job-change probabilities for employees with disabilities (Karpur, Bjelland, and Nazarov 2013). The aging of the American workforce means more workers will be individuals with disabilities or will experience chronic health conditions, making this question especially important to employers. Within the MEPS-HC, participants are asked at each round if they were still in the job they previously reported or if they had switched jobs or retired from work. If there was a change, the reasons are documented, which allows the study of the dynamics of employment patterns. Using this information, it was determined that employees with disabilities who have employer-paid health insurance change jobs far less frequently than employees with disabilities who do not have employer-paid health insurance. Though a similar trend was observed for workers without disability, the magnitude of the relationship between not having employer-paid health insurance and job-change probability was higher among workers with disabilities. Of course, the implementation of the Affordable Care Act may influence these observed patterns; an employer mandate could potentially increase access to health insurance in conjunction with the availability of subsidized health-care plans through statewide health insurance exchanges.

## Compensation Gap for Persons with Disabilities

Although there was previous work on estimating the wage gap between people with and without disabilities, these studies did not present a clear investigation of the total compensation gap between those with disabilities and those without disabilities. Investigating the gap in total compensation is important because of the magnitude of noncash compensation in the United States—employees as well as employers may be making employment choices based in part on this noncash pay. As a corollary to our finding that access to employer-paid health insurance is related to the probability of job change for employees with disabilities, we hypothesized that the total pay gap between the two groups would be smaller in percentage terms than the wage and salary gap.[2]

On the surface this appears to be a simple and straightforward question; however, it becomes complicated very quickly, since the data are not easily accessible. Once we merge in detailed information on nonwage and salary forms of compensation, there are a host of options for demographic datasets of individuals with which to merge and analyze.

But suppose we choose only one of those datasets (for example, the Current Population Survey). Even with that simple decision, we are then faced with the diversity of measures of disability. For example, figure 3.1 shows seven measures of disability (for full-time female workers): disabled in any form, hearing difficulty, vision difficulty, cognitive difficulty, ambulatory difficulty, self-care difficulty, and independent living difficulty. The figure also shows an interesting diversity in the fraction of that sample with a disability by occupation type.

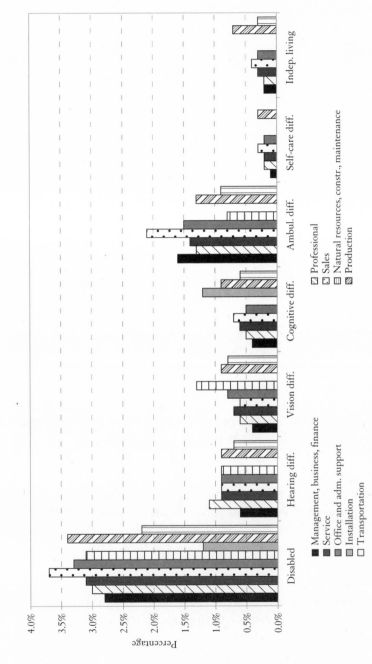

**Figure 3.1** Percentage of full-time female workers with a disability, by disability status and occupation (CPS, March 2010)

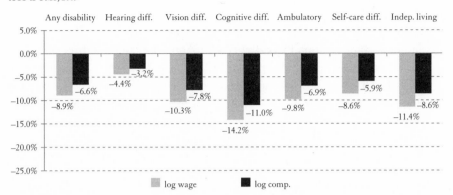

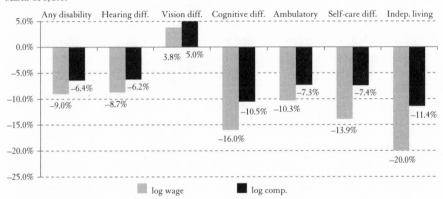

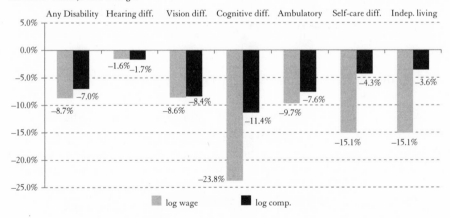

**Figure 3.2** Ordinary Least Squares (OLS) estimates for intermediate occupation controls (full-time female workers; wage and compensation truncated at top 5 percent)

Figure 3.2 gets to the main point of the compensation studies (wage and total compensation by disability status) and does this for three different datasets (each merged with the ECEC): the ACS, the CPS, and the SIPP. In all but only a few cases, the results are just as we hypothesized. For example, consider the CPS in figure 3.2. The first column shows that, controlling for a set of covariates as described in Barrington, Hallock, and Jin (2014), individuals with any disability earn approximately 9 percent less than those without any disability. On the other hand, those with any disability are compensated 6.4 percent less (in total pay) than those without any disability. This is consistent with our idea that people with disabilities may be more likely to be matched in a job with relatively better nonwage benefits. It is clear that this main point holds up (the percentage wage gap is larger than the percentage total compensation gap) almost universally, irrespective of the measure of disability (read across the figure from left to right) or across data source (read across the figure top to bottom).

These results demonstrate some of the empirical differences across data sources, even though the general main point seems to hold. For researchers and policy makers, we feel this highlights that empirical studies should include multiple sources of data whenever possible, to increase credibility and identify data source–specific weaknesses in results. For employers looking to increase recruitment and retention of employees with disabilities, the overall consistency across datasets strengthens the implication that compensation beyond wage and salary pay should be looked to in designing attractive compensation packages.

## Locating Specific National Survey Data

Without the wealth of data available in national survey sources, the studies described above would not have been feasible. Unfortunately, identifying which sources contain the specific information that can address a research question can be a huge undertaking. It requires working through the survey documentation, including both the actual survey instrument and the survey's data dictionary (the document that lists the variables available), to determine if the survey includes information that can answer the research question. For example, if a researcher had an interest in health insurance coverage for an individual, there are seven surveys described here (ACS, CPS, HRS, MEPS, NLTS2, PSID, and SIPP) that collect some information regarding that topic. However, for a researcher interested in studying the employer contribution to health insurance, only three of those datasets (CPS, HRS, and SIPP) will be of use.

To assist researchers and others in overcoming the significant difficulties and barriers to understanding, identifying, and working with national survey data, we developed the Disability and Compensation Variables Catalog (DCV Catalog). The catalog allows us to share the results of our own efforts to identify national survey data with content relevant to the study of disability and employer practices, and was designed to help promote the use of these valuable resources by other researchers.

## The Disability and Compensation Variables Catalog

The DCV Catalog[3] (described in Hallock 2013a) is an online guide that provides an easy way for researchers and others to explore hundreds of variables related to disability and health conditions, work, compensation (that is, pay and benefits), and employer characteristics available in the ten national survey datasets described in this chapter, along with one administrative dataset. Its development was spurred by our own transdisciplinary research. Members of our team began cataloging what relevant variables exist in national survey data for our respective projects. As we shared our early progress, we realized that coordinating and formalizing our individual data inventories could create a valuable tool, useful for researchers beyond our immediate team. Consistent with a transdisciplinary approach and the principles of participatory action research, and to ensure a user-friendly and functional interface, the team conducted extensive usability testing with internal and external researchers, graduate students and scholars (both academic and government sector) in the fields of economics and rehabilitation.

Researchers and others can use the DCV Catalog as a means to identify which datasets and associated variables are of greatest use to explore with regard to a number of topics, including disability, employer, and employee characteristics. The catalog provides information not readily available elsewhere, allowing researchers to quickly and easily identify,

# Cross-Dataset Catalog of Disability and Compensation Variables

Browse or search across 11 major datasets for variables related to: disability and health conditions, work and employer characteristics including compensation such as pay and benefits. The catalog provides: variable names, survey questions, response categories and related variables that can be exported into an excel spreadsheet for your use.

Note: This tool is designed to provide an overview across multiple datasets - always use the dataset's codebook/dictionary to guide actual analysis. To view dataset descriptions and caveats click on dataset acronym.

Screen Reader Friendly Version

**Search by Topic, Data Set, or Keyword**  Keyword Search: [        ]  [Search]

| Select Topic | Select Data Set | | | | | | | | | RESET ALL SELECTIONS |

| | ACS | BRFSS | Census | CPS | HRS | MEPS | NHIS | NLTS2 | PSID | RSA-911 | SIPP |
|---|---|---|---|---|---|---|---|---|---|---|---|
| [Open All] [Close All] | ☐ | ☐ | ☐ | ☐ | ☐ | ☐ | ☐ | ☐ | ☐ | ☐ | ☐ |
| ⊟ **Employee Disability & Health** | ☐ | ☐ | ☐ | ☐ | ☐ | ☐ | ☐ | ☐ | ☐ | ☐ | ☐ |
| ⊞ ☐ Activity/Functional Limitation | ☐ | ☐ | ☐ | ☐ | ☐ | ☐ | ☐ | ☐ | ☐ | ☐ | |
| ⊞ ☐ Childhood Specific | | | | | ☐ | | | ☐ | | | |
| ⊞ ☐ General | ☐ | | ☐ | ☐ | | | | ☐ | | | |
| ⊞ ☐ Health Condition | | | ☐ | | ☐ | ☐ | ☐ | | ☐ | ☐ | ☐ |
| ⊞ ☐ Impairment | ☐ | | | ☐ | | | | | | ☐ | ☐ |
| ⊢ ☐ Onset/Timing | | | | | ☐ | | | | | | |
| ⊞ ☐ Participation Restriction | ☐ | | | ☐ | ☐ | ☐ | ☐ | | ☐ | | ☐ |
| ⊢ ☐ Work Injury | | | | | ☐ | | | | | | |
| ⊟ **Employer Characteristics** | ☐ | | ☐ | ☐ | ☐ | ☐ | ☐ | | ☐ | | ☐ |
| ⊢ ☐ Industry | ☐ | | ☐ | ☐ | ☐ | ☐ | ☐ | | ☐ | | ☐ |
| ⊢ ☐ Location | ☐ | | ☐ | | | | | | | | |
| ⊢ ☐ Number of Employees | | | | ☐ | ☐ | ☐ | ☐ | | ☐ | | ☐ |
| ⊢ ☐ Ownership | ☐ | | | ☐ | ☐ | ☐ | | | ☐ | | ☐ |
| ⊢ ☐ Unionized | | | | ☐ | ☐ | ☐ | | | ☐ | | ☐ |
| ⊟ ☐ **Employer Compensation** | ☐ | ☐ | ☐ | ☐ | ☐ | ☐ | ☐ | ☐ | ☐ | ☐ | ☐ |

**Figure 3.3** Screen shot of front page of the DCV Catalog

| Select Topic | Select Data Set | | | | | | | | | RESET ALL SELECTIONS |

| | ACS | BRFSS | Census | CPS | HRS | MEPS | NHIS | NLTS2 | PSID | RSA-911 | SIPP |
|---|---|---|---|---|---|---|---|---|---|---|---|
| [Open All] [Close All] | ☐ | ☐ | ☐ | ☐ | ☐ | ☐ | ☐ | ☐ | ☐ | ☐ | ☐ |
| ⊟ **Employee Disability & Health** | ☐ | ☐ | ☐ | ☐ | ☐ | ☐ | ☐ | ☐ | ☐ | ☐ | ☐ |
| ⊞ ☐ Activity/Functional Limitation | ☐ | ☐ | ☐ | ☐ | ☐ | ☐ | ☐ | ☐ | ☐ | ☐ | |
| ⊞ ☐ Childhood Specific | | | | | ☐ | | | ☐ | ☐ | | |
| ⊞ ☐ General | ☐ | | ☐ | ☐ | | | | ☐ | | | |
| ⊞ ☐ Health Condition | | | ☐ | | ☐ | ☐ | ☐ | | ☐ | ☐ | ☐ |
| ⊞ ☐ Impairment | ☐ | | ☐ | | ☐ | ☐ | | | ☐ | ☐ | ☐ |
| ⊢ ☐ Onset/Timing | | | | | ☐ | | | | | | |
| ⊞ ☐ Participation Restriction | ☐ | | ☐ | ☐ | ☐ | ☐ | ☐ | | ☐ | | ☐ |
| ⊢ ☐ Work Injury | | | | | ☐ | | | | | | |
| ⊟ **Employer Characteristics** | ☐ | | ☐ | ☐ | ☐ | ☐ | ☐ | | ☐ | | ☐ |
| ⊢ ☐ Industry | ☐ | | ☐ | ☐ | ☐ | ☐ | ☐ | | ☐ | | ☐ |
| ⊢ ☐ Location | ☐ | | ☐ | | | | | | | | |
| ⊢ ☐ Number of Employees | | | | ☐ | ☐ | ☐ | ☐ | | ☐ | | ☐ |
| ⊢ ☐ Ownership | ☐ | | | ☐ | ☐ | ☐ | | | ☐ | | ☐ |
| ⊢ ☐ Unionized | | | | ☐ | ☐ | ☐ | | | ☐ | | ☐ |
| ⊟ ■ **Employer Compensation** | ☐ | | ☐ | ☐ | ☐ | ☐ | ☐ | | ☐ | ☐ | ☐ |
| ⊟ ■ Benefits | ☐ | | ☐ | ☐ | ☐ | ☐ | ☐ | | ☐ | | ☐ |
| ⊞ ☐ Education/Training | | | | | | | | | | | ☐ |
| ⊟ ■ Health Insurance | ☐ | | ☐ | ☐ | ☐ | ☐ | ☐ | | ☐ | | ☐ |
| ⊢ ☑ Coverage | ☑ | | ☐ | ☑ | ☑ | ☑ | | ☑ | | | ☑ |
| ⊢ ☐ Employee Contribution | | | | | | | | | | | ☐ |
| ⊢ ☐ Employer Contribution | | | | ☐ | ☐ | | | | | | ☐ |
| ⊢ ☐ Plan Type | | | | | ☐ | | | ☐ | ☐ | | ☐ |
| ⊢ ☐ Provider | | | | ☐ | | ☐ | | | ☐ | | ☐ |
| ⊢ ☐ Leave (Time off) | | | | ☐ | ☐ | ☐ | ☐ | | | | ☐ |

**Figure 3.4** Screen shot of variable availability for health insurance coverage

compare, and contrast variables and survey questions across the various data sources. As is visible in figure 3.3, it provides access to a consistently organized display broken down by topic and subtopics across the various data sources.

Variables with more refined categories can be expanded through a drop-down list. For example, "Employer Compensation" has subcategories of "Benefits" and "Pay." Benefits as a category, in turn, has subcategories of Education/Training, Health Insurance, Leave, Retirement Incentives and Pension, and Other. Health Insurance can be refined to reveal Coverage, Employer and Employee Contributions, Plan Type, and Provider. Figure 3.4 is a screen shot that shows the display for Health Insurance Coverage, and that within the datasets covered by the DCV Catalog, variables for health insurance coverage of respondents are contained in the ACS, CPS, HRS, MEPS, NLTS2, and the SIPP.

More detailed information is accessible, beyond the variable name and label. The actual survey question text, the range of responses, and other related items and notes can also be revealed. Variables similar or related to the primary item that may be of potential interest to researchers are also documented, along with such items as follow-up questions. The content of the catalog was based on the most recent data that was available at the time of development.

The DCV Catalog can be especially helpful for researchers in the early stages of exploring data sources, as it quickly reveals whether a topic is covered in a given dataset and the specific variables available regarding that topic. Individuals who are developing their own survey can also make use of the catalog to see how different surveys have captured information and identify questions to potentially include. If an identical question or set of questions is used in a survey, comparisons can be made between the new survey population and that of the existing data source. We have found that this catalog has helped us in our own research plans and goals, and it has proven a valuable resource for others interested in the field in providing a better understanding of the different national surveys, the contents of the datasets, and identifying potential variables of interest.

National survey data provide a wealth of opportunities for better understanding the employment of individuals with disabilities. The relative ease of access, large sample size, and national representativeness offer tremendous value and allow for the examination of a variety of topics related to disability, employment, and employer practices. Our desire to encourage others to explore the viability and use of these data sources to conduct their research led to the development of the DCV Catalog.

In chapter 7, we discuss other ways that we have promoted the use of national survey data, as well as other datasets and research methodologies covered in other chapters. In the context of the other methods described in this volume, existing data should ideally be carefully examined before researchers commit to a new data collection effort to see how much can be answered through the analysis of existing national survey and administrative data. Strategies such as combining different data sources to address information gaps, as illustrated in the examples provided, should be explored. Analysis of existing data can potentially serve as a foundation and provide some direction on which to base other data collection efforts. Specific questions used in national surveys can be utilized in other surveys to provide a bridge between the existing survey and the new research findings. These are just a few of the myriad of ways in which national survey data can provide great value to researchers in addressing many of the important questions regarding employment and disability issues.

4

# Using Administrative Data

Hassan Enayati and Sarah von Schrader

As the term suggests, administrative data are collected as part of an entity's operations and are often gathered as a means of record keeping (for example, the employment records maintained by a firm for payroll). The increased use of computers in routine operations means that these data are typically recorded electronically and updated regularly. Given the fundamental purpose of documenting registration, transactions, or enrollment, the entities that collect administrative data range from government agencies to independent businesses, and the records contain everything from medical information to employment information to demographics. School districts across the country maintain records of enrollment and academic performance. The Internal Revenue Service (IRS) collects information on income for individuals and businesses. Disability, retirement, and survivors' benefits are compiled by the Social Security Administration (SSA). The National Vital Statistics System of the Centers for Disease Control and Prevention (CDC) assembles data from various sources on birth, marriage, divorce, and death. Thus, information documenting a wide range of circumstances that may influence labor market outcomes is captured by administrative data.

## Using Administrative Data for Research

Chapter 3 outlined available national survey data sets and described ways many researchers are using them as a source for information on disability employment. Compared with national survey data, administrative data are an underused source of information. Our team believes that the wide range of data collected for administrative purposes by federal and state agencies, businesses, and other organizations offers innovative opportunities to explore the manner in which worker characteristics and employer practices affect the employment outcomes for individuals with disabilities. The research advantages of using these data are driven by their relatively low cost, longitudinal nature, universal coverage of the population (for instance, all company employees or program participants), as well as by their ability in some cases to be linked to other data sources. Our project team has used administrative data to examine questions around disability discrimination, specifically examining characteristics of both disability discrimination charges and the employers who receive them, and team members see many promising new research opportunities available to government agencies and individual firms for developing a richer understanding of the employment outcomes for people with disabilities.

The possibilities for new research using administrative data have sparked the interest of the academic community. In a response to the National Science Foundation's call for white papers on "Future Research in the Social, Behavioral, and Economic Sciences," Card et al. (2010) argue that the expansion of access to administrative data is paramount for the United States to be at the frontier of research, and more crucially, to accurately inform policy makers. In a 2012 presentation to the National Bureau of Economic Research, Raj Chetty highlighted the rising popularity of the use of administrative data in micro-data-focused papers published in the leading economics journals (for example, the share of such articles published in the *Quarterly Journal of Economics* jumped from less than 20 percent in 1980 to over 60 percent in 2010). More recently, Nazarov and coauthors advocate for linking administrative records with national surveys to more deeply analyze how workplace factors impact the employment outcomes for individuals with disabilities. They argue that integrated files contain more robust information that is better suited for more in-depth studies (Nazarov, Erickson, and Bruyère 2014).

## Advantages of Using Administrative Data in Research

One of the primary advantages of administrative data is that the data have already been collected. Businesses and government agencies gather and organize their records for their own purposes, whereas with survey data, hundreds to thousands of responses must be collected specifically to generate a dataset for research purposes. From a research perspective, it is much less expensive to use administrative data than to construct and field a new survey. As an example, consider the Current Population Survey, a national survey dataset discussed in chapter 3. The CPS is produced by the Bureau of Labor Statistics and provides detailed information on the labor force by surveying sixty thousand households each month. In its 2014 Congressional Budget Justification, the BLS requested $1,577,000 to add an annual supplement to the existing CPS (U.S. Bureau of Labor Statistics 2014a). Another example comes from the twenty-seven-item Hospital Consumer Assessment of Healthcare Providers and Systems survey developed by the Centers for Medicare and Medicaid Services to examine inpatient care. The estimated costs of the survey ranged from $3 to $20 per completed survey, depending on the delivery method (Abt Associates 2005). Meanwhile, the cost *to a researcher* for collecting administrative data is zero.[1] Thus, administrative data are normally less expensive than survey data, which has been a primary attraction of these data.

The nature of the collection of administrative data can also be considered a benefit. First, it is relatively easy to update the data with a new wave of information. Because the data exist as a form of record keeping, new events are entered into the data, often as they occur. Not only are newer observations available with administrative data, but historical information is also often available. This means that administrative data are often longitudinal in nature, which allows for a more complete analysis of the impact of policies and practices, another important benefit of these data. Suppose we wanted to know the impact of a change in employer practices on the employment outcomes for individuals with disabilities.

Longitudinal data allow for statistical methods that control for both observed employment patterns and certain unobserved individual characteristics.[2] Consistent collection techniques can also be a benefit resulting from the manner in which the administrative data are collected, particularly in either a large business's or national agency's record-keeping systems—for example, the IRS's wage information (McNabb et al. 2009). Unfortunately, as we will describe below, collection consistency is not always the case with administrative data.

Several advantages of administrative data revolve around who is represented in the data. First and foremost, while surveys can be designed to target a particular population, administrative data have universal, within-program coverage.[3] National agencies collecting information on participation in welfare programs, for example, keep track of every individual receiving those benefits. As a result of comprehensive inclusion of program participants, administrative data tend to be more reliable than survey data for analyses focused on low prevalence subpopulations (for instance, specific racial or ethnic subgroups, disability categories, or local geographic areas). Because administrative records are maintained for all individuals related to the record-keeping entity's operations, the selection of individuals described in administrative data is broader than in a survey.

The final set of advantages we discuss here relate to the quality of administrative data. Because the data exist as a way for an entity to maintain its records, the entity has an incentive to guarantee that the variables of interest are accurate and detailed. School districts, for example, accurately track the school a student attends; however, they may less reliably record peripheral information such as a parent's level of education. As opposed to survey data, which are often self-reported, administrative data benefit the researcher with their lower levels of attrition, nonresponse, and measurement error. Slud and Bailey (2006) show that the Census Bureau's Survey of Income and Program Participation (SIPP) panels lose 14 percent of participants one-third of the way through the panel and 30 percent by the end of the panel. Beyond the issues of attrition, the SIPP also exhibits evidence of measurement error. Examining the 2004 American Community Survey and 2005 Annual Social and Economic Supplement of the Current Population Survey, Nelson (2006) finds that between 15 to 29 percent of income from Supplemental Security Income (SSI) must be imputed due to nonresponse. Huynh, Rupp, and Sears (2002) find that only 75 to 81 percent of individuals receiving income from both the Old Age, Survivors and Disability Insurance Program and SSI report receipt of both on the SIPP.

## Limitations of Using Administrative Data in Research

While administrative data do not suffer from attrition, nonresponse, and measurement error in the same way that survey data do, they too have quality concerns (Card et al. 2010). Primarily, variables of less interest to the recording entity are less reliable. For example, socio-demographic data of interest to a researcher may not be available (Grosse et al. 2010). Because of their bookkeeping nature, administrative data may have poorer-quality documentation and context, as the data were not created for use outside the interest of the entity. For example, the definition of a variable may change over time but maintain the same name in the dataset and even in the documentation, which in turn creates problems for the researcher when comparing the variable over time (Virnig and Maderia 2012).

Quality concerns notwithstanding, the most significant limitation to the use of administrative data for research purposes is its applicability. Survey questions are designed and validated by researchers with the direct objective of answering specific types of research questions. On the other hand, administrative data are collected for record-keeping purposes, so the subset of research questions that an administrative dataset can answer is limited by the variables collected by the recording entity. Many variables that would be highly useful to the research community are not collected, as they are not relevant to the entity collecting data; for example, information on disability status or type may not be collected if it is not relevant to the agency. Even if the data include relevant variables, it is common that proxies for the ideal variable must be used. For example, an administrative dataset might have information on an individual's wages but lack information about household income, which may be the preferred variable. Depending on the dataset, background variables that could be used as control variables in a variety of analyses may not exist (Handel and Kolstad 2015). Clearly, there can be limitations in terms of applicability and coverage of administrative data when addressing certain research questions. However, some of these issues may be overcome by linking the primary administrative dataset with a secondary survey or administrative dataset. Linking different sources of data can be quite challenging, in terms of both getting permission to do the linking and also the practical issues of combining the files.

Another limitation associated with administrative data is access. Whether the administrative data are maintained by a government agency or a private business, researchers are reliant on that provider for access to the data. Card et al. (2010) argue for a fundamental change in the way government agencies share their records with researchers and explain how the restriction of access to these high-quality data has impeded progress of science and sound policy-making in the United States. Accessing administrative data can be quite challenging, as datasets are guarded by data custodians to ensure the privacy and confidentiality of employees, program participants, applicants, and claimants.

For more commonly accessed administrative data, there may be a protocol established for accessing data. Typically, when requesting administrative data, a researcher is required to present a research proposal and describe how the data will be kept confidential. For example, many researchers use the Rehabilitation Services Administration 911 data, de-identified administrative data on cases closed by state vocational rehabilitation agencies. There is a straightforward process for requesting the data and an existing data agreement contract that a researcher can complete in order to gain access to these data.

The level of risk in terms of data confidentiality is often related to the difficulty in accessing data; therefore limiting requests for fields that would potentially identify an individual is a good practice. Often an administrative dataset has not previously been used for research purposes, so there is no prior experience with sharing data or developing data agreements (for example, a business's human resources data). In these cases, a relationship must be developed with the agency or business to build trust and understanding around the research, before the typical steps of requesting administrative data would begin. Chapter 2 provides excellent suggestions for collaborating with employer organizations. Such collaborations could potentially include gaining access to their data, as is further discussed in chapter 6. In particular, table 2.2 in chapter 2 offers some concrete actions and recommendations for building research relationships with organizations based on our team's experience, and later in this chapter we highlight the importance of demonstrating to potential partners that allowing a researcher to access data can be mutually beneficial.

While the universal, within-program coverage and longitudinal nature of administrative data are advantages, these data are not always representative of the full population of interest; for example, they cover only program participants. Using the example of records from a welfare program agency, the administrative records would accurately track the benefits of each recipient; however, the records would not contain information on nonrecipients (McNabb et al. 2009). Another example from our own team's research with administrative data is our work with the Equal Employment Opportunity Commission's (EEOC) administrative data on employers who receive charges of employment discrimination filed under the Americans with Disabilities Act (ADA); these data contain no information on employers who do not receive charges. If specific characteristics affected the likelihood of charge receipt, the administrative data alone would not be able to identify these impactful variables, as no control group exists within the data (von Schrader and Nazarov 2014). Additionally, researchers may be interested in understanding the differential roles of a policy or practice by subgroup, such as disability status. As opposed to a survey's well-documented sampling process, administrative data users are restricted to the individuals who are part of the entity's program or product. Consequently, the statistical theory and methods that guide research using survey data may be inappropriate within an administrative data context. Wallgren and Wallgren (2007) call for the development of new methods for analyzing administrative data.

The final limitation discussed here centers on the ethical use of administrative data and is related to the confidentiality issues discussed above. The Belmont Report (U.S. Department of Health, Education, and Welfare 1979) outlines the guiding ethical principles in human subjects research. Because survey data are collected specifically for research purposes, the Belmont Report directly informs researchers on how and what can be gathered from participants and also what can be done with the survey data after they have been collected. When administrative data are used to answer research questions, the initial requirements of the Belmont Report guiding the collection procedures have been bypassed, which leads to potential deficiencies in the safeguarding of individual rights. For example, protecting the principle of autonomy (that is, the right to informed consent) is an actively discussed concern. The Belmont Report more directly guides research in terms of how the data can be used post-collection. As with survey data, a primary concern is the breach of confidentiality. The research community is still determining how to best apply the standards of the Belmont Report to the use of administrative data (Stiles and Boothroyd 2012).

## Select Administrative Datasets Related to Employer Practices

Now that we have outlined the advantages and limitations of administrative data, we begin our discussion of select administrative datasets related to disability-focused employer practices. Given the existence of administrative data from every organization that maintains its employment records, the following data sources represent a subset of the available datasets that could inform employers and researchers of practices related to the employment of individuals with disabilities. We focus our discussion on datasets already used or well situated for use by researchers to address issues of discrimination and compensation.

### Datasets Addressing Employment Discrimination

A set of administrative data that has been used to better understand characteristics of perceived disability discrimination in the workplace is data from the EEOC's Integrated Mission System (IMS). The IMS is a database documenting the universe of discrimination charges filed under civil right statues enforced by the EEOC, the ADA, the Age Discrimination in Employment Act, Title VII of the Civil Rights Act (CRA) of 1964, and other less commonly cited statutes. The EEOC tracks every charge of employment discrimination that is filed at EEOC offices and contracting state and local Fair Employment Practice Agencies. These data contain detailed information about every charge, including charging party characteristics (age, gender, race, and ethnicity), alleged discriminatory act (termination or hiring), basis of the charge (disability type, age, and/or race), employer characteristics (size and industry), and the outcome of the charge.

The charge data are not a perfect measure of actual or perceived discrimination in the workplace—that is, they do not capture every event of discrimination, owing to the potential for settlements prior to filing a charge or instances of individuals never reporting the perceived discriminatory act. Despite this limitation, the charge data represent a comprehensive list of the universe of charges filed with these outside agencies. When a construct, like discrimination, is difficult to measure using other methods, administrative data can provide leads that can be further pursued using other sources of data. Tracking patterns in the charge data can inform employers by highlighting where in the employment process employers are struggling (getting more charges), and where employers may need to examine their practices. For example, Bjelland et al. (2010) highlight that discharge is the most commonly cited issue on ADA charges (cited on 55 percent of charges), and failure to provide a reasonable accommodation is the second most common issue (cited on 25 percent of charges).

There has been a wide range of research using the ADA charge data that can inform employer practices. The national EEOC ADA research project has led to the publication of over fifty articles that examine characteristics and outcomes of allegations filed citing specific disability types and various discriminatory issues (McMahon et al. 2005). For example, Hurley (2010) examined characteristics and merit resolution rates for allegations citing discharge, and Conyers, Boomer, and McMahon (2005) examined characteristics of ADA allegations citing HIV/AIDs. Another set of studies has examined administrative enforcement of the ADA by the EEOC, particularly focused on disparities in outcomes for individuals with psychiatric disabilities (Moss et al. 1999; Moss et al. 2002; Ullman et al. 2001). Members of our team have also looked at charge rates—that is, the number of charges per ten thousand individuals in the labor force over time, comparing rates across other antidiscrimination statutes and bases enforced by the EEOC. Bjelland et al. (2010) further examined characteristics of charges that cite the ADA alone, as compared to those that cite the ADA in addition to the Age Discrimination in Employment Act (ADEA). This collection of studies formed an important basis for the research that our team conducted as described later in the chapter.

The IMS collects data on charges against most employers; however, there is a slightly different complaint process for federal employers. The federal data on discrimination complaints are collected within agencies and reported to the EEOC in aggregate as well as posted on agency websites under the No Fear Act.

The EEOC's employer reports are another very useful aggregation of administrative data that can help in understanding segregation and relative representation at the establishment or organizational level. To encourage employers to track equal employment data, Title VII of the CRA allows the federal government to collect and publish data from private employers on equal employment opportunity. Private employers with over one hundred employees or federal contractors with fifty or more employees must track data on the diversity of their workforce and report in the annual EEO-1 employer report (Cartwright, Edwards, and Wang 2011). On this form, employers tabulate the composition of their workforce in terms of race/ethnicity and gender across ten occupational categories. Similar reporting requirements are in place for state and local governments (EEO-4), primary and secondary schools (EEO-5), and referral unions (EEO-3). Using these data, organizations and the federal bodies who collect these data can understand whether the makeup of the organization reflects the local workforce and whether members of certain groups are clustered in lower-level positions, rather than management or professional positions. While these data do not have information on disability, the EEO-1 report has been used extensively to understand the changes over time in the representation of women and racial minority groups in the workforce, allowing researchers to understand variations by sector and industry and how various initiatives, policies, administrations, and shifting employer practices are related to changes (Stainback and Tomaskovic-Devey 2012).

While data collection around disability is just beginning for most companies in the private sector, the federal government (the nation's largest employer) has for years been collecting and reporting its progress toward being a model employer of people with disabilities. In 2010, President Obama signed Executive Order 13548—"Increasing Federal Employment of Individuals with Disabilities," which requires that federal agencies increase efforts to recruit, hire, and retain individuals with disabilities. A descriptive report is produced annually by the Office of Personnel Management (OPM) for the president that documents agency-level progress toward the goals of EO-13548, using their internal human resources data (Enterprise Human Resources Integration—Statistical Data Mart) (U.S. Office of Personnel Management 2012). The EEOC also collects EEO data from a slightly different and broader set of federal agencies using the Management Directive-715 (MD-715) form to track progress related to these EEO initiatives (U.S. Equal Employment Opportunity Commission 2003).

The MD-715 form collects aggregated data from agencies and subagencies across the employment process, breaking down the data by disability status and type, as well as by other demographic characteristics. These data are reported annually in a report by the EEOC (U.S. Equal Employment Opportunity Commission 2011).

The ability to examine outcomes across very diverse federal agencies is an interesting feature of these data for researchers. For larger agencies, the MD-715 collects data on agency practices around being a model EEO employer, including demonstrated commitment by agency leadership; integration of EEO into the agencies' mission; management and program accountability; proactive prevention of discrimination; and an efficient grievance procedure. The opportunity to link agency-level changes in employer policy or practices over time with outcomes in terms of workforce diversity from these MD-715 data could produce very important research on the effectiveness of different employer practices.

With the new Office of Federal Contractor Compliance Programs (OFCCP) regulations around Section 503 of the Rehabilitation Act published in September 2013, federal contractors with contracts of at least $10,000 now are required to collect data on disability through regular surveys, again linking these data with administrative HR data on recruitment, hiring, and retention (U.S. Department of Labor 2014b). While these data are not yet formally reported to the OFCCP, except when an organization is audited, the data collection requirement is an important step toward understanding success in meeting affirmative action goals around disability. If an audit does occur, federal contractors must present data as outlined in the scheduling letter form by documenting the percentage of workers with a disability by job category, as well as the contractor's policies and practices.[4] If these data become available to researchers, there would be the possibility of tracking changes in disability employment at the establishment level, as has been done for race and gender using the EEO-1 employer report. Recently, public-use administrative data on audits conducted by the OFCCP were created for the years 2003 to 2013. These data are de-identified but include information on characteristics of the contractor and parent company, as well as characteristics of the violation, remedies, region, and local unemployment rate of the parent company (Francis and Maxwell 2013).

The Role of Linked Data in Identifying Potential Discrimination

Individual-level data remain challenging to access, as confidentiality issues can be difficult to overcome. However, the government and its contractors have created linked data that can be useful to researchers. Linked data refer to a single dataset created from multiple separate datasets. For example, the U.S. Social Security Administration has linked its own administrative data with both commissioned and ongoing national surveys (like those discussed in chapter 3) for over four decades. SSA records were matched to the SIPP to analyze how features of SSI impact the decision to retire (Powers and Neumark 2005). The key advantage of government agencies, like the SSA, integrating multiple data sources is that it allows for more complete modeling of program effects (McNabb et al. 2009). A new and promising dataset to analyze the employment of individuals with disabilities is the SIPP Synthetic Beta, which integrates interagency individual-level data from the SIPP, SSA, and IRS records and therefore includes detailed disability and earnings measures.

Beyond the linked datasets created by governmental agencies, there are ample opportunities for individual researchers and organizations to ask more nuanced questions by linking administrative data with other data sources themselves. Most administrative or archival data reports, like those from the EEO-1 employer reports, do not contain specific information on employer practices—for example, recruitment and screening practices. While we can observe patterns that suggest workplace discrimination, such as occupational segregation, it is not possible to fully understand the causes using administrative data alone (Kmec 2003). However, administrative data can be linked to individual-level or organizational-level survey data to gain a better understanding of characteristics that may be associated with inequalities in the workplace.

In the federal government there are several sources that if linked could tell an important story about employing people with disabilities. As an example, the federal government has a long history of collecting disability data, which can be linked with other data sources to develop a better picture of the experiences and perceptions of individuals with disabilities. As described in chapter 5, the Federal Employee Viewpoint Survey (FEVS) is a survey administered annually by the OPM and completed by employees across the federal workforce. Analysis of the FEVS finds significant differences in a variety of areas between people with and without disabilities (for example, people with disabilities are less satisfied with their advancement opportunities) (U.S. Office of Personnel Management 2014a, b). By linking these survey data with individual-level HR data, we can better understand individuals' workplace experiences through administrative records rather than self-reports; for example, we can potentially observe an individual's tenure with the organization, pay level, compensation, training, and advancement over time. Further, aggregations of agency data collected through the MD-715 or OPM aggregations can provide additional information about disability prevalence in the organization and across job categories. For larger agencies, the MD-715 also collects data on agency practices around being a model employer. Linking these various sources of data can paint a much more complete picture of possible inequalities and what practices or actions may exacerbate or limit them.

In the private sector, Kalev, Dobbin, and Kelly (2006) conducted an interesting study at the establishment level to better understand the effectiveness of certain practices in increasing the prevalence of minority and female managers. They linked two sources of data from 1971 to 2002, the annual EEO-1 report and survey data on employer practices related to diversity for a sample of private establishments, to better understand the effectiveness of multiple diversity initiatives in the private sector. One of their key findings using these unique linked data was the importance of establishing organization responsibility for increasing diversity—for example, affirmative action plans, diversity committees, or diversity managers. The impact of other diversity initiatives, such as mentoring, networking, and training, was greater when in tandem with these organizational responsibility structures.

## Extending ADA Charge Data Research through Linked Data

As noted earlier, there are many papers that examine the characteristics of charges filed since the implementation of the ADA. While the EEOC charge data alone allow us to address questions about the patterns in charge receipt and outcomes, they cannot help us uncover whether one employer is more likely to receive a charge than another. This limitation is because the charge data do not provide an obvious comparison group; employers not receiving charges are not observed. Also, as noted above, administrative data may be less accurate when the field is not required or regularly used by the organization collecting the data. For example, in the charge data, information about the employer is typically reported by the charging party or investigator, therefore the information may be missing or inaccurate. As noted by Bjelland et al. (2010), more than 20 percent of employer variables are missing in the charge data. However, the EEO-1 data have employer-reported size and industry at least for mid- to large-size private employers. By linking the EEO-1 report with the charge data, we can conduct analyses that compare employers receiving charges to those who do not, and also have more accurate data on employer characteristics. Researchers have linked the EEOC charge data to the EEO-1 employer report to better understand the characteristics of employers receiving sex and race charges (Hirsh and Kornrich 2008); however, this type of research had not yet examined employers receiving disability charges.

Members of our research team found that smaller establishments tend to have higher ADA charge rates, as do establishments that are part of larger parent organizations, federal contractors, and members of the transportation and services industries (von Schrader and Nazarov 2014). In a follow-up study, Nazarov and von Schrader (2014) found that charge receipt under the ADA is positively associated with charge receipt under other statutes, like the ADEA and Title VII of the CRA. Further, there appear to be common characteristics of employers who are receiving charges under each of the three statutes. This type of research can be informative to employers as they assess their risk related to receiving a charge and develop policies and practices intended to limit workplace discrimination. These findings also help agencies and organizations, like the EEOC, who support employers' implementation of nondiscriminatory practices, to target their outreach to employers who need the most support.

While integrated data offer the research community an opportunity to more thoroughly analyze the role of employer practices on the employment of individuals with disabilities, the linking process itself can present obstacles. For example, one challenge faced by researchers in the studies just mentioned is the absence of a unique field allowing the charge data to be linked to an employer in the EEO-1 report. Because administrative data are collected not for research but rather for administrative purposes, they often lack the fields or links that would make the data more useful. While integrating datasets is not always easy, some organizations like the EEOC are working to create links between files.

## The Role of Company-Specific Datasets in Addressing Compensation and Other Employer Practice Issues

Nearly every business or organization collects data electronically about its employees—for example, compensation, tenure, positions, pay grades, absence, performance reviews, accommodations, advancement, training, and turnover. These data can then be used by the organization to develop a set of metrics to better understand how the organization is functioning. While these data are important for internal evaluation and in understanding the return on investment for various initiatives, combining these data with demographic indicators can be particularly helpful in documenting the relative success in providing equal employment opportunities for diverse groups by tracking recruiting, hiring, retention, and equity in practices such as compensation.

While these internal proprietary data are not usually available to researchers, by developing relationships with employers it may be possible to access these data through a data-sharing agreement. As discussed in chapter 2, any academic-employer research collaboration must provide some direct value to the employer whose workplace data are being sought. A researcher may offer data analysis that provides a service to the data-sourcing employer, while also pursuing a research interest (Barrington and Hallock 2013). Barrington and Hallock review a variety of studies that use organizational personnel data; they point out that use of these data is growing and has significant benefits in testing assumptions and addressing targeted questions about workplace practices.

A well-documented example of a mutually beneficial research effort between a private organization and the research community comes from the personnel economics literature. Lazear (2000) worked with Safelite Glass Corporation to analyze the impact of Safelite changing its compensation scheme from hourly wages to a piece-rate system. Using organizational administrative data from 1994 to 1995, Lazear demonstrated that switching to the piece-rate system increased average productivity by 44 percent, increased the realized wages of incumbent workers by 10 percent, and also increased the firm's profits. While this example is not directly related to the employment of individuals with disabilities, this case serves as a classic example of the positive outcomes for both researchers and individual firms that collaborative efforts can produce.

Looking more recently at a total compensation topic, Handel and Kolstad (2015) worked with an anonymous, large self-insured firm to understand what factors influence an employee's choice of health-care plan. The researchers linked firm-level administrative data with survey data that was collected as part of their study to examine the role of employee information asymmetry on health insurance choices, that is, the impact of different levels of understanding regarding insurance choices among employees. They found that information frictions and perceived hassle costs influence consumer health insurance choices, and the authors "argue that integrating survey data with administrative data can produce valuable insights, especially when it is highly unlikely one can obtain rich enough administrative data to answer certain questions" (Handel and Kolstad 2015, 49). This recommendation highlights both the value of linked administrative data and also the depth of understanding achievable when firms implement surveys as outlined in chapters 5 and 6.

While these studies focus on compensation, a wide range of questions could be addressed. With the new regulations around Section 503, more employers will be collecting data around disability and analyzing them to demonstrate success and/or challenges in hiring and retaining employees with disabilities. Additionally, in 2014 the OFCCP proposed new data collection requirements related to employee compensation. Federal contractors and subcontractors with more than one hundred employees would have to begin submitting aggregated W-2 wages for workers within a specific EEO-1 job category by race, ethnicity, and sex (U.S. Department of Labor 2014a). While this proposed requirement from the OFCCP will not directly increase the collection of data by disability status, it might set the stage for these data to be collected in the coming years. The Section 503 changes, as well as the potential of the OFCCP proposed compensation data requirements, represent an incredible opportunity to work with employers to better understand the effectiveness of practices related to employing people with disabilities. Data across the employment process from recruitment, hiring, accommodations, compensation, productivity, performance management, and disability management programs can be used to test theories about what works in disability employment, an area that has not been explored well through administrative data.

The greatest limitation in many of the administrative datasets described, particularly those that are personnel records or aggregations of personnel records, is the lack of a disability measure. The federal government has been collecting data for years using the SF-256 as authorized by the Rehabilitation Act, as amended (29 U.S.C. 701 et seq.); however, up until now the private sector has generally not collected disability information or tracked disability-related metrics (Erickson et al. 2014). Even with the new 503 regulations mandating regular surveys of applicants and employees, disability data are still not likely to be completely accurate, as employees may choose not to self-identify. Many factors influence whether individuals disclose their disability in a work situation, and many choose not to disclose because of concern that they may face discriminatory treatment (von Schrader, Malzer, and Bruyère 2013).

Notwithstanding this significant concern, administrative data have proven useful for understanding charges of disability discrimination and for highlighting differential outcomes for individuals with disabilities, for instance through examining aggregations from personnel records by disability type and status in the federal government. When these administrative data are used in combination with other sources, researchers can address more sophisticated questions. This integration of data moves the research community beyond questions that highlight when and where differences exist and toward explanations describing why those differences may exist and how employer practices may influence observed differences. The linking of massive administrative data sources, such as IRS and SSA data, with national survey data, like the SIPP, provides access to data that have previously not been available to researchers and also holds promise for richer understanding of the employment outcomes for individuals with disabilities and older workers.

Important research can be conducted with company administrative data, research that can inform the company about what is working, as well as answer targeted research questions that may move policy and practice in a direction that leads to better outcomes for individuals with disabilities. Many employers are interested in the business case for employing people with disabilities. This can be addressed in part by examining productivity, absences, turnover, and other metrics by disability status within organizations. If disability data are collected, these topics and more refined analyses can shed light on what employer practices lead to better outcomes. Collaboration between researchers and the holders of administrative data can be mutually beneficial, providing needed information for employers and allowing for important research that can inform a wide range of parties about good practice.

# Surveying Employers and Individuals with Disabilities

William A. Erickson, Sarah von Schrader, and Sara VanLooy

Preexisting data sources such as national surveys and administrative files are convenient to work with, and when based on an entire population or a representative sample they can be weighted to develop broadly generalizable, often nationally representative, estimates. With these sources, however, the researcher has no control over the content coverage or questions used. The data also may not contain the specific information needed to address research questions. In this situation, developing and fielding a survey may be the best way to collect the necessary, targeted information. Survey research can be appropriate when (1) adequate secondary information is not available, (2) generalizing findings to a larger population is desired, (3) the appropriate respondents are accessible, and (4) the data of interest can be obtained via self-report (Rea and Parker 2005). But the costs involved in the fielding of a survey make it worthwhile to explore secondary data options first.

One strand of our transdisciplinary research sought to better understand which disability-inclusive practices are actually in place in organizations and how these practices are (or are perceived to be) related to disability employment outcomes, as well as to begin to understand how individuals with disabilities view these practices. We determined that the national survey datasets discussed in chapter 3, while collecting data on individuals and their employment situations (for example, employment status, occupation, industry, wages, and benefits), did not provide any information regarding the specific disability-inclusive practices employers actually had in place. The administrative datasets we accessed (chapter 4) were similarly limited. It was clear that to explore these topics, we needed to implement surveys specifically designed to collect these types of data from employers across multiple organizations.

## Why Use Cross-Organization Surveys?

This chapter is designed to provide a foundation on the use of surveys to gather information across multiple organizations. We do not intend this as a comprehensive guide to survey development; that topic is far too broad. Entire books and myriad papers address the many nuances of survey work (for examples see Dillman 2000; Fink 2009; Fowler 2009; Scheuren 2004; Sue and Ritter 2014; Zikmund 2003). In order to collect high-quality data from researcher-developed surveys, investigators must (1) identify the purpose of the survey and the target group; (2) draft survey questions, pilot test them, and revise accordingly; (3) select respondents and the data collection approach, including incentives or other appropriate methods to promote high response rates; (4) field the survey; and (5) analyze the results (OECD 2012). Our discussion will focus on select parts of this process—specifically, identifying the target group based on the purpose of the survey, accessing respondents, choosing a survey mode, and maximizing the response rate. We will highlight some important issues and considerations in survey research across organizations and offer recommendations based on existing literature and our own experience using surveys to address research questions on employer practices and disability issues.

We focus on two types of cross-organizational surveys: surveys that collect data from representatives across a large sample of organizations, and surveys that capture the personal experience and perspective of individual employees or individuals with disabilities. This latter case is another way to look across organizations, when the individuals sampled do not work for a particular employer and their responses represent experiences across a variety of organizations. We leave discussion of single-organization "deep-dive" case study surveys to chapter 6.

A survey is a flexible and effective method of obtaining data to describe the incidence of specific phenomena and explore the interrelationships between variables (Rumrill, Bellini, and Webb 1999). Surveys are used to collect information that provides the basis for scientific knowledge across many fields, including economics, psychology, health, political science, and sociology. By gathering information from samples of individuals, surveys offer government, business, and institutions critical information about needs, preferences, and behaviors (Scheuren 2004). Surveys are also the most common methodology used in research regarding employer practices around disability. In a scoping review of the available literature in the area, Karpur, VanLooy, and Bruyère (2014) found that more than half of the research articles employed some form of survey methodology.

Surveys have a number of advantages over other data-gathering approaches. As noted above, one of the greatest is the potential for broad distribution. Surveys enable researchers to collect consistent information from a much larger sample of organizations/respondents than is typically feasible using approaches such as interviews or focus groups. A researcher can use a variety of question and response types in their survey, including multiple-choice and open-ended questions, allowing for the collection of data that is quantitative and qualitative in nature. With e-mail and electronic survey software, researcher-developed surveys can be relatively inexpensive to field. However, obtaining appropriate distribution lists and achieving satisfactory response rates can be expensive, with costs varying significantly depending on sample acquisition technique, mode of survey, and incentives offered.

Surveys also have certain limitations. They are inherently less flexible than more open-ended data-gathering procedures can be. Often, detailed responses to questions and follow-up on interesting responses are less feasible in a survey than when conducting focus groups or personal interviews. And, as with any respondent-based data collection, social desirability bias may affect results, as individuals may tend to respond with a more socially acceptable answer to present themselves in a more positive light (Bowling 2005).

## Identifying the Appropriate Target Group

Some employment research focuses on formal practices and policies. Other studies are more interested in awareness of these practices or their interpretation and implementation in the workplace. Still others attempt to evaluate the actual impact of those practices "on the ground," based on the experiences of rank-and file-employees. Each of these perspectives is important to understand, but cannot be fully addressed by one set of survey respondents. Determining whom to target with a survey about employer practices requires careful consideration of the purpose of the survey, as well as knowledge of "who knows what" in an organization.

Different individuals have experiences and organizational perspectives that can offer unique insights into employer practices and policies. In figure 5.1 we highlight how different groups might map to specific employer-practices research topics. It illustrates the three target populations we

**Figure 5.1** Potential survey respondents by research area

review in this chapter and their relevance to cross-organizational surveys: (1) organizations (where the respondent is an organizational representative); (2) employees, including managers and supervisors; and (3) people with disabilities (who, of course, are also likely included as a part of each group of survey participants). The individual with the relevant experience and institutional knowledge, or who has access to the data needed to respond most accurately, should be selected for the appropriate survey objective.

The approach to accessing a sample of one of these target populations varies, depending on the group of interest; some may be easier to access than others. The approach chosen may also impact the ultimate generalizability of results. A researcher who identifies HR professionals in the United States as the target group of interest would ideally have a complete list of all HR professionals from which to randomly select a sample that would be representative of all HR professionals. A random sample from a known population may be ideal, but is often not feasible (for example, a list of all HR professionals may not be available). When this is the case, alternative approaches may be needed, such as sampling from the membership list of a professional or personal-interest organization. Note that membership in those organizations may not be representative of the entire population of the group, meaning that this approach has implications for the generalizability of findings.

## Organizational Representatives

When a study aims to learn about official practices and policies of organizations, the target population is typically organizations, not individuals. However, for a survey it is necessary to identify a representative who can answer on behalf of each organization in the sample. People who either make or promote these practices and policies, such as executives or human resource managers, are the ideal subjects to provide a perspective on an organization's official positions. These organizational leaders are well positioned to share how their respective organizations are responding to policy changes external to the organization (for example, the Americans with Disabilities Act Amendments Act, or revisions to the regulations from the U.S. Department of Labor Office of Federal Contractor Compliance

Programs). They also have a high-level insight regarding the effectiveness of these policies and practices and can describe barriers that might exist to their implementation.

In addition to executives and HR managers, other candidates within an organization may be appropriate respondents to surveys about disability-related practices. It is vital to consider who within a company would have access to the information the survey is designed to collect. Other knowledgeable organizational executives include equal opportunity officers (EEOs), disability management professionals, compensation and benefits managers, training and development specialists, recruitment and placement specialists, and employee assistance program managers. In many cases, particularly in larger organizations, consultation with more than one individual may be needed both to accurately define an organization's official policies and practices and to understand the "on the ground" implementation throughout the organization. Some surveys take the approach of contacting a representative within an organization and asking to speak with the person most knowledgeable in a specific topical area.

The level within an organization is another consideration in identifying the appropriate representative. For example, an organization such as Walgreens has many individual stores, but also a headquarters; policies and practices may differ between stores and headquarters. A researcher might request that larger businesses with multiple branches nominate a representative from headquarters as the main contact. While this assures that the survey will receive only a single response per company, it also assumes that the chosen respondent is familiar with policies and practices across all the locations, which may not be the case. Another approach is to instruct respondents to consider only their own locations, with which they are presumably more familiar, rather than attempt to answer for the broader organization.

Executive-level representatives are often the easiest to identify within organizations. These individuals are often included in publicly available company directories, listed on websites, or included in membership lists of professional organizations. They can sometimes be located via purchased mailing lists, such as Dun's Market Identifiers (Domzal, Houtenville, and

Sharma 2008). This relative ease of identifying executives is offset by the difficulty in making contact; they often have staff who act as gatekeepers, protecting the executives they assist from being accessible for the purposes of a survey.

HR professionals are frequently tapped as the key respondent for employer studies (Bruyère, Erickson, and VanLooy 2000), but identifying appropriate HR respondents can be challenging. As discussed in chapter 2, one approach is to work with associations of HR professionals that can provide connections with these individuals through a familiar and trusted organization, which can also potentially improve survey response rates. From the perspective of research rigor, a limitation of collaborating with a business membership organization for survey sampling purposes is that the researcher typically cannot know if the membership of such organizations (in this case HR representatives) is representative of all employers, or if it is biased in some systematic manner. There are a few other potential issues that may have implications in working with such organizations. People join some organizations as individuals rather than as representatives of their employer, creating the possibility of receiving multiple survey responses for a single company. Associations may contribute significant positive value to the survey by supporting its development and data collection, but may require the researcher to pay to access their membership.

## Middle Management, Supervisors, and Employees

Although upper-level executives can provide an overview of a company's official practices, actual practices may differ as they filter down and are implemented throughout the organization. As will be discussed in chapter 6, line managers and supervisors are the implementers of policies and can provide an excellent window into the actual practices within the organization. Nishii and Bruyère (2009) found that 70 percent or more of managers were unaware of their organization's disability practices. This apparent knowledge disconnect underlines the importance of determining what line managers and supervisors actually know and what they are actually doing in their day-to-day work. A survey of managers and the rank-and-file employees they supervise can contribute to a better understanding of how employer practices and policies are implemented and how their results are experienced by individuals in the workplace.

Identifying and accessing supervisors across organizations can be very difficult. Unlike with executive-level individuals or HR professionals, there is no common database or professional organization that offers access to a pool of middle-management representatives. However, there are organizations that bring individuals of a particular occupation or industry together, and surveying the membership of such an organization may be helpful, depending on the focus of the research.

As we will describe later, members of our team conducted prior research in the federal sector and were able to access supervisors and managers. Although the federal government is a single employer, it comprises around one hundred individual agencies, and this project allowed the examination of workplace policy implementation across the different agencies. Another federal government data source is the Office of Personnel Management (OPM), which conducts a survey of its employees, the Federal Employee Viewpoint Survey. This survey measures federal employees' perceptions about how effectively agencies manage their workforce (U.S. Office of Personnel Management 2014b, 27), and the results are available to researchers. In 2013, the government-wide response rate was 48.2 percent, and for the first time the survey collected information on disability status, finding that employees with disabilities consistently rate their organizations lower than do their nondisabled peers (U.S. Office of Personnel Management 2014b).

Another approach to getting the perspectives of managers and employees is collaboration with individual employers or organizations via case study research, which has its own unique challenges. Despite this, a few case studies have managed to combine data across employers from surveys of employees and managers about employer practices (Disability Case Study Research Consortium 2008; Schur et al. 2014).

Finding employers willing to collaborate or share existing staff surveys is another approach to access manager and employee respondents. Many organizations conduct regular internal surveys to gauge the level of employee engagement and overall workplace climate. Surveys of this type can help an organization by identifying groups of workers or units that have lower employee engagement compared with their peers. Comparing the responses of individuals with and without disabilities can shed light on differences in their workplace experience. Further, when these data are collected over time within organizations, surveys can help identify how changes in employer practices can affect employee engagement. Rutigliano and O'Connell (2013) demonstrated this, tracking a company that introduced a dedicated diversity manager with a focus on disability and implemented a set of disability employment initiatives including setting hiring goals, measuring progress, and training managers, recruiters, and staff on disability considerations. These changes led to a decrease in the gap on measures of engagement between workers with and without disabilities.

There are significant challenges in developing and maintaining these employer relationships, as chapter 2 described. Furthermore, as discussed in chapter 3, when existing employer surveys are used for secondary research, it is rare to be able to include new questions that specifically address the research question, especially in cross-organization studies. Nonetheless, cross-organization research has been produced that has integrated employee surveys across multiple organizations to great effect.

## People with Disabilities

Offering the opportunity for the disability community to have a voice is critical to developing better policies and practices. When research questions are specific to the experience of people with disabilities, it may be more effective to focus the survey recruitment efforts directly on people with disabilities rather than on the companies that may employ them. Some people may be reluctant to self-identify on a workplace survey as a person with a disability, but willing to participate as an individual. Accessing a wider range of respondents may also allow researchers to focus on a specific disability type or drill down into other relevant demographic characteristics. Only through refinements in collecting and including the voice of people with disabilities and other marginalized groups can improvements in workplace practices grow out of the resulting survey research.

Several strategies exist for finding people with disabilities to participate in survey research. Because people with disabilities are a part of the population as a whole, they will be included within any sample of the general population. Surveys of the general population frequently use random-digit dialing and a set of screener questions across a pool of respondents to identify this group (Mitchell et al. 2006). However, given the disability prevalence rate, this is not a particularly efficient approach and can be prohibitively expensive. It also limits the potential population to individuals with phones, and may inadvertently exclude those with specific disabilities, such as those with significant hearing impairments.

Just as one way to access employer representatives is through business membership organizations, another approach to accessing people with disabilities is through membership or advocacy organizations related to disability, or organizations that provide information or services to individuals with disabilities or their family members. These might include the American Association of People with Disabilities (AAPD), United Cerebral Palsy, or other similar organizations. Electronic surveys can be disseminated via these organizations' social media sites and e-mail lists, with surveys potentially being forwarded or shared with other relevant groups. The primary issue with this approach is the difficulty in making generalizations to the broader population of people with disabilities, since this is not a representative sample. However, the data gathered can still be useful in understanding issues and gathering the voices of people with disabilities.

The barriers to completing a survey vary by disability type and the survey content covered, wording, and method or mode. Mitchell et al. (2006) suggest considering the following three challenges when surveying persons with disabilities: (1) communication, (2) stamina, and (3) cognitive barriers. Communication challenges are potential issues regarding hearing and speech impairments; those with visual impairments may have difficulty reading and responding to online or paper surveys, for example (Wilson et al. 2013). Stamina refers to both physical and mental fatigue that can be an issue when responding to surveys. Cognitive barriers arise when people with intellectual or cognitive impairments have difficulty with abstract or temporal constructs or have lower levels of literacy that can make responding without support challenging.

There is no single recommended mode best suited to surveying people with disabilities, but being mindful of those who will be taking the survey can lead to better survey design and implementation. For example, online surveys present unique challenges. The survey instrument itself may not be accessible to persons with visual impairments, and it may not be compatible with the screen-reader technologies that many individuals with such impairments use on their electronic devices. Several online survey companies, including SurveyMonkey and Qualtrics, either provide automated accessibility checks to alert survey developers of good practices for developing an accessible online survey or provide information on how researchers can do this themselves.[1] A thorough discussion of practices for removing barriers to people with disabilities is offered by several sources, including Mitchell et al. (2006).

## Survey Modes

Once you have identified the target group for the survey, the next step is to consider how to actually perform the survey. Surveys can be administered and data can be collected in a number of "modes." The most common approaches include paper-based mail surveys, online and website-based surveys, and telephone surveys, specifically computer-assisted telephone interviewing (CATI).

Each approach has advantages and disadvantages in successfully reaching our target populations; some are discussed further below. In general, mail-based surveys are relatively inexpensive and have a wide reach (Sue and Ritter 2014). However, they typically have low response rates, a long delay between solicitation and response, and do not work well when asking complex or branching questions. Online surveys are low cost, efficient, permit contingency questions, have a wide geographical reach, and provide direct data entry. However, they also have a number of significant disadvantages, including sample bias due to lack of Internet access for certain populations, reliance on software, and possible loss of control over distribution, creating uncertainty about the makeup of the ultimate respondent pool. Telephone surveys have a wide reach, fast response, and are effective in asking complex questions, but are also expensive, often intrusive, can be confused with sales calls, may have issues with call screening, lack visual supports for respondents, and are susceptible to interviewer error and bias.

### Practicalities in Telephone Surveys

CATI interviewers use software that has survey questions programmed into a data entry interface that provides a script and a form to directly enter responses. Many employer surveys use CATI because this method has a number of advantages. Interviewers can screen respondents and ask the initial respondent to forward the interviewer to the person within the company who can provide the information. Interviewers can assist respondents by providing additional instructions or definitions if needed (Fowler 2009). CATI can be one of the faster data collection modes, and like online surveys it allows complex question branching based on respondent answers (Fowler 2009). CATI response rates also tend to be higher than mail surveys in part because it is a more active approach and makes personal contact with respondents (Fowler 2009). The CATI software can be used to reach a sample from the general population through random-digit dialing, which includes unlisted phone numbers and cell phones.

The CATI approach to data collection also has limitations. It omits those without telephones and is a poor choice to access populations with hearing impairments or language difficulties. The use of call screening, number blocking, and caller ID will affect response rates, and being mistaken for sales calls can result in hang-ups (Sue and Ritter 2014). It can be particularly difficult to reach executive-level respondents in a telephone survey, as they often have staff who screen their calls or voice-mail systems that can severely limit direct contact.

The proliferation of cell phones and decline of landlines means that for a large number of households (28 percent as of 2011) the area code is no longer linked to a geographical location, which potentially creates sampling complications (Siebens 2013). A CDC study found that cell phone owners are more likely to refuse to participate in surveys than persons contacted through landlines, making acceptable response rates more difficult and expensive to achieve (Link et al. 2008). Additionally, the presence of any interviewer may result in greater social desirability bias than is found in self-administered surveys, and if multiple interviewers are used, reactions to their different approaches can result in variability in responses. Careful training and monitoring is required to minimize this effect (Bowling 2005). As with all survey modes, respondents are sensitive to the length of the survey; according to Zikmund (2003), one major study on survey research found that interviews of five minutes or less had a refusal rate of 21 percent compared to 41 percent for interviews of six to twelve minutes, and 47 percent for interviews of thirteen minutes or more.

## Online Surveys

It is sometimes easier to access individuals in the workplace via e-mail invitations to online surveys. Online surveys can be taken at a time that is convenient to the individual rather than interrupting the workday. The dissemination of online surveys to professional or employer organizations can be relatively easy, as organizations can often provide e-mail addresses of their membership and would rather provide this than phone numbers. Online survey development tools such as SurveyMonkey and Qualtrics facilitate the creation and distribution of these surveys. These tools typically allow the researcher to screen respondents for eligibility and present them with different branching question sets depending on their responses to specific questions.

One of the greatest drawbacks of online surveys is their potential for systematic bias. Samples are limited to those with Internet access, and valid e-mail addresses are required (Fowler 2009). E-mails inviting participation in online surveys are easily filtered, ignored, or deleted by those who may have less time, motivation, or interest in participating, while persons interested in the survey topic are much more likely to respond. Online survey respondents are more likely to be male, younger, and more technologically sophisticated than mail survey respondents (Kwak and Radler 2002).

The loss of potential respondents due to bad e-mail addresses or to e-mail spam filters makes it particularly difficult to accurately calculate response rates for online surveys, as the number of potential respondents who actually saw the survey invitation is unknown (Sue and Ritter 2014). When respondents forward survey invitations outside the initial contact list, it further complicates the feasibility of accurately determining the number of potential respondents who were contacted (though this can be an advantage for researchers seeking greater diversity of respondents).

In some situations, mixed-mode survey approaches that combine different data collection methods can have advantages (Fink 2009; Vannieuwenhuyze 2014). An example of this strategy is combining online surveys with CATI. This takes advantage of the low implementation costs of online surveys and their easy distribution to a large sample, while using CATI to reach nonrespondents and offset online surveys' greater nonresponse bias, and keeps costs low by limiting and focusing the use of CATI. This combination can help offset each mode's weaknesses, address respondent preferences, and result in overall better coverage, more respondents, and potentially less-biased responses.

## Response Rates

Response rates and nonresponse bias are two of the largest concerns associated with survey results. Response rates can vary greatly depending on a wide variety of factors, including the respondent pool, respondent interest in the topic, survey length, administration mode, and incentives offered. The lower the response rate to a survey, the greater the likelihood that the respondents differ from nonrespondents in their characteristics. This results in sample bias and reduces the generalizability of the population estimates (Bowling 2005). Respondents and nonrespondents may have very different views on the survey topic. If this is the case, the results will be systematically biased and will not reflect the overall population's perspective or experience. Generally, the higher the survey response rate, the more likely that the results are representative of the population targeted by the survey.

A study of 152 organizational surveys published in top peer-reviewed journals found that the average response rate of individuals in organizations asking about personal attitudes and behaviors in 2005 was 52.7 percent (Baruch and Holtom 2008). The response rate for surveys of executives / organizational representatives focused on organizational-level information was substantially lower, at 35 percent. This result is similar to the 32 percent executive survey response rates found by Cycyota and Harrison (2006) in their examination of 231 nonoverlapping papers that used mail surveys to elicit organizational information from executives between 1992 and 2003. There are indications that survey response rates have been falling over the last few decades (Baruch 1999), and this has been attributed, in part, to the increased number of surveys of all types being fielded, or "survey fatigue" (Porter, Whitcomb, and Weitzer 2004).

Employer surveys frequently have low response rates, and nonacademic employer-focused reports often do not report survey response rates at all. A poor response rate doesn't necessarily invalidate survey results, but it does call into question the generalizability of the findings and who did, and, perhaps more important, who did not participate. There are two strategies for potentially getting a sense of participation. One method is to compare the known characteristics (such as membership information) of the nonrespondents to those of respondents; this can provide a sense of representativeness of respondents. Alternatively, if there is a nationally representative secondary data source of the total population of potential respondents available, it may be possible to compare respondent characteristics to the overall population to determine whether respondents differ significantly from the population of interest.

One of the most important ways to get more survey responses is to ensure the survey's salience to the respondents. Surveys that are designed to address topics of interest to the respondents typically get higher response rates. This was one of the few strategies that was found by Cycyota and Harrison (2006) to improve response rates of executives. They found that surveys that approached executives about a topic of importance to the industry, of current interest, and with potential implications for the organization received higher response rates. Carefully crafting the survey questions and invitation to participate to emphasize the survey's relevance to potential respondents is vital to improving response rates. Engaging employers early on in the research process can help ensure survey relevance and effective recruitment communications.

Survey length is also a key factor to consider. Shorter surveys typically result in higher response rates (Roy and Berger 2005; Deutskens et al. 2004). This may be particularly true for respondents in business studies (Jobber and Saunders 1993). One alternative may be to use short, focused topical surveys or polls, instead of a broader, more extensive survey. Such an approach may result in higher response rates and perhaps greater willingness of organizations to collaborate. A potential downside to this approach is that it may not be possible for a short single survey to assess the broader organizational context that may be important in understanding the responses.

Offering incentives is a common strategy for increasing the number of responses. An incentive may be as simple as a promise to send respondents the report of survey results, especially in advance of public release of the study. Other possible incentives are gift cards, or chances to win larger "prizes" in drawings; however, such incentives must be appropriate for the respondent audience. It is also important to be aware that incentives do not always work. Groves, Presser, and Dipko (2004) found that incentives tended to reduce the willingness to participate of respondents who had an interest in the topic. Cycyota and Harrison (2006) found that the use of incentives appeared to have little or no impact on executive response rates in the studies they examined and suggested that other tactics might be more productive. These included sending preannouncements to respondents via mail or e-mail to alert them to the upcoming survey and providing

follow-up reminders to nonrespondents. For surveys of high-level executives, identifying executive assistants and engaging them with information
about the importance of the study can be valuable. Help from the executive
assistants can range from simply flagging the e-mail for the attention of the
executive to printing a paper copy for the executive to complete and then
transcribing those responses into the online survey form.

## Prior Employer Surveys

Our current transdisciplinary initiative has benefited from having a team
with an extensive history in conducting cross-organizational employer
surveys. Below, we describe some of these studies, as well as those of other
researchers whose approaches and findings influenced us. In our overview,
we highlight the purpose of the survey, target group, and how they were
accessed, information about survey mode and response rate, and some key
findings.

### Cornell/SHRM Private Sector Surveys

As noted previously, HR professionals in their organization are frequently
tapped as the key informant for employer studies (Bruyère, Erickson, and
VanLooy 2000), and in 1998 and 2001 Cornell collaborated with the Society for Human Resource Management (SHRM) to conduct studies on
employer practices around disability. SHRM is the largest organization
dedicated to human resource management in the United States and had
over a quarter of a million members worldwide in 2010. This collaboration was important, as SHRM provided a sample from its membership
to survey, and because endorsement by an existing network like SHRM
can improve response rates compared with survey invitations that come
directly from a researcher (Cycyota and Harrison 2006). Further, researchers at SHRM offered topical knowledge and collaborated on survey development.

The 1998 study was a collaboration between Cornell University,
SHRM, and the National Business Group on Health (NBGH) (Brannick
and Bruyère 1999; Bruyère, Erickson, and Ferrentino 2003; Bruyère, Erickson, and VanLooy 2006). The survey focused on employer workplace

practices in support of the employment provisions of the Americans with Disabilities Act (ADA). Specific topics addressed the accessibility of facilities, the modification of workplace policies, and experiences regarding a variety of disability accommodations and organizational barriers. A stratified sample by employer size was drawn from the total population of the SHRM membership of approximately one hundred thousand professional (nonstudent) members. Based on the distribution of members by organization size, a random sample was drawn proportional to the population within each size strata. The collection mode was CATI for the SHRM sample, and the response rate was 73 percent (n = 813). A mailed paper survey was the primary response mode for NBGH, as the organization wanted to keep its survey process in-house. Nonrespondents received a telephone follow-up offering alternative response modes, resulting in a response rate of 32 percent (n = 52).

This survey was one of the first to examine how employers were responding to the ADA. We found that, the vast majority of the time, organizations had made accommodations to meet the need of employees and had made most existing facilities accessible. The most commonly reported organizational barriers to the employment or advancement of a person with a disability were perceptions regarding the job candidate's lack of related experience, requisite skills, and training, and the supervisor's lack of knowledge about which accommodations to make. The survey also revealed significant differences in employers' abilities to accommodate specific disabilities, including visual and psychiatric disabilities.

In 2003, a follow-up CATI-based survey of the participants in the initial SHRM survey explored issues related to organizational practices regarding accessibility of information technology (IT) used in HR processes for applicants and employees with disabilities (Bruyère, Erickson, and Van-Looy 2005). Those contacted for the 2003 survey had agreed to participate in follow-ups in the previous Cornell/SHRM study, and an 88 percent response rate was achieved (433 respondents). This survey determined that although 90 percent of surveyed organizations used online job applications, very few (13 percent) were familiar with guidelines for accessible website design, and only one in ten said that they were aware of their HR websites having been evaluated for accessibility. The majority of respondents were not aware of key IT accessibility resources, suggesting that a large proportion of employers were unprepared to address issues related to website accessibility for persons with disabilities.

## Cornell Federal Sector HR/EEO Survey

Large organizations can provide excellent opportunities to assess practices across their suborganizations. Cornell worked with the Presidential Task Force on the Employment of Adults with Disabilities (PTFEAD), which was a federal task force established in 1998 by Executive Order 13078, to survey the HR and EEO professionals in the federal government (Bruyère 2000; Bruyère and Horne 1999). The survey captured information on the human resources and equal employment opportunity policies and practices of federal agencies in response to the employment nondiscrimination requirements of federal civil rights legislation. A list of 415 names, including all upper-level HR/EEO personnel across ninety-six federal agencies, was obtained from the OPM Human Resources Management Group. A letter was sent to each potential interviewee approximately two weeks prior to the initiation of the survey. The survey was CATI-based and had a 97 percent response rate; this level of response highlights the importance of high-level organizational support for participating in surveys.

The survey found that the vast majority of federal agencies were making accommodations for their employees with disabilities. Seven out of ten had a formal process in place to do so, but one-fifth had received no accommodation requests in the last fiscal year. Only about one-quarter reported frequently using special provisions for hiring persons with disabilities, and the same proportion reported using the special hiring programs for hiring disabled veterans. As in the private sector HR survey, the respondents reported unfamiliarity with accommodations for visual and hearing disabilities, and the majority indicated needing more information on psychiatric disabilities. The survey also identified some issues; the most common disability discrimination claims reported were those related to failure to provide a reasonable accommodation and failure to promote.

## Cornell Federal Sector Supervisor Survey

In 2001, Cornell conducted a survey of supervisor experiences in the federal government in collaboration with PTFEAD and OPM (Bruyère, Erickson, and Horne 2002b). The project was an extension of the federal sector survey described above (Bruyère and Horne 1999) and used a parallel instrument that allowed for some comparisons of results. The CATI-based survey asked supervisors about the accommodation of people with disabilities as applicants and employees in the federal workforce, as well as their experience and perceptions of the effectiveness of existing and proposed resources to facilitate the hiring, retention, and accommodation of people with disabilities.

A sample composed of three thousand white- and blue-collar supervisors was randomly drawn by OPM from the pool of all supervisors in the seventeen agencies that were members of PTFEAD. From these, a target group of one thousand supervisors was chosen, to represent at least fifty supervisors per agency, with proportionally more drawn from larger agencies. All potential participants received a letter from PTFEAD prior to the survey, stressing the survey's importance and encouraging them to participate. The overall response rate was 93 percent, demonstrating the effect of having upper-level support on survey participation.

The CATI-based survey asked supervisors about the accommodation of people with disabilities as applicants and employees in the federal workforce, as well as their experience and perceptions of the effectiveness of existing and proposed resources to facilitate the hiring, retention, and accommodation of people with disabilities. The study found that nearly two-thirds of federal supervisors had at least one employee with a disability or had made at least one accommodation in the previous five years. Many were not well-informed regarding accommodations, with nearly half not aware of major accommodation resources and most unfamiliar with making accommodations for persons with communication disabilities. This was a notable issue because over half the supervisors also reported they were responsible for making final decisions about the provision of accommodations either alone or in consultation with their immediate supervisor.

The Cornell Federal Sector Supervisor and HR/EEO Surveys demonstrated a benefit of conducting surveys with multiple levels of respondents—the ability to compare viewpoints across respondents and organizations. This further allowed the researchers to compare and contrast perspectives, highlighting where ideal EEO practices differed from the real-world experiences of supervisors in the workplace (Bruyère, Erickson, and Horne 2002a). Further comparative work also examined the differences in private sector and public sector practices (Bruyère 2000), as well as international differences in workplace practices and policies in response to disability nondiscrimination legislation based on findings from a parallel survey in the UK and Ireland (Bruyère, Erickson, and VanLooy 2004).

## U.S. Department of Labor Employer Perspectives Survey

In 2008, the U.S. Department of Labor, Office of Disability Employment Policy, conducted the Survey of Employer Perspectives on the Employment of People with Disabilities (Domzal, Houtenville, and Sharma 2008). The survey focused on assessing the attitudes and practices of employers in twelve industry sectors, including several industries projected to have high growth by the Bureau of Labor Statistics. This CATI-based survey was fielded by WESTAT and used the Dun's Market Identifiers register as the business sampling frame.[2] The sample was stratified by industry and company size, allowing the calculation of nationally representative weighted results of the twelve sectors. In order to find the representative best able to answer the survey questions, WESTAT interviewers asked to speak with the person in the organization "who makes decisions on hiring at the overall company level such as your company president or human resources manager." The response rate was 51.4 percent and included 3,797 respondents. Specific topics included the recruitment, hiring, employment, retention, and advancement of persons with disabilities, familiarity with specific disability resources, and what would encourage organizations to hire persons with disabilities.

This survey provided national estimates of recruitment practices, highlighting that active recruitment is much more common among larger employers: 33.8 percent compared to only 7.0 percent of smaller companies. The findings also revealed what employers perceived to be the challenges and best strategies for hiring, retaining, and advancing individuals with disabilities. Relatively few employers were aware of or used federally supported resources to increase the employment of people with disabilities, including One-Stop Career centers, the Job Accommodation Network, and the Employer Assistance and Resource Network.

## Kessler/NOD Employer Survey

The Kessler Foundation and the National Organization on Disability (NOD) fielded an employer survey in 2010 (Kessler/NOD 2010b). Survey topics included general diversity practices, disability practices, experiences with recruiting, hiring, and evaluation and costs of employees with disabilities, as well as persons with disabilities in leadership positions within the corporation and perceptions of the ADA. The employer sample used Dun and Bradstreet listings and the LinkedIn website to identify a national cross-section of companies with fifty or more employees (Kessler/NOD 2010a). The sampling frame was stratified by company size: small (50–999 employees), medium (1,000–9,999), and large (10,000 or more). The employer representatives were deliberately chosen so that senior executives and human resource managers were equally represented. Harris Interactive performed the data collection effort, which was CATI-based for the Dun and Bradstreet sample, and online for the LinkedIn sample. A minimum of six attempts were made to complete every phone interview, and every respondent was offered a $75 honorarium as an incentive. The LinkedIn sample received an initial invitation from LinkedIn to participate in the survey and received a reminder e-mail approximately two days later. A breakdown by sample source and response rates by mode was not provided, but the overall response rate was rather low at 16 percent (n = 411). Organizations were weighted by number of employees and annual revenue for analysis in order to get nationally representative estimates. However, the low response rate makes the generalization back to the population of employers more tenuous.

This survey highlighted specific ways that employers recruit people with disabilities and discussed their challenge finding qualified candidates. One key finding was that many companies were not using service-provider agencies; those that did use these agencies did not generally find them effective.

## Kessler Foundation / NOD Survey of Americans with Disabilities 2010

Kessler and NOD also collaborated in 2010 on a survey of people with disabilities that included a number of questions relevant to employer practices (Kessler/NOD 2010b). Harris Interactive performed the CATI-based survey, which included 1,001 noninstitutionalized persons with disabilities and 766 noninstitutionalized persons without disabilities ages eighteen and older. The survey used a combination of random-digit dialing and recontacting people who were identified in previous surveys as having a disability, and had a 21 percent overall response rate. This survey also included a supplemental sample of persons with disabilities who were in the labor force. This supplemental sample had previously volunteered to periodically participate in Harris online surveys and completed an online survey focused on employment issues. Note that it is unknown how representative this subsample may have been of the general employed population of persons with disabilities; however, it was an efficient way for Harris to identify this population. Employed persons with disabilities were asked a set of questions regarding their experience with their employers regarding job-related discrimination, workplace disclosure and environment, mentoring, affinity groups, diversity and disability hiring, and flexible workplace arrangements.

This survey found that the majority (79 percent) did not report experiencing any of the negative experiences in the workplace asked about. Approximately one in five respondents were matched with a mentor in their job, and three-quarters of them said that the mentor was important to their success in their organization, with half rating them as very or extremely important. Two-thirds reported that their company was doing a good, very good, or excellent job with regard to hiring, retaining, and promoting persons with disabilities.

## Initiatives from the Current Project

As we considered how to add to existing knowledge through new surveys, we carefully examined the previous research, including the examples above. As noted earlier, our purpose in our survey work was to better understand what disability-related employer practices are in place in organizations, how these practices are (or are perceived to be) related to disability employment outcomes, and to begin to understand how individuals with disabilities perceive these practices. We collaborated with three organizations to access target populations of interest through their membership in SHRM (HR professionals), DMEC (disability management professionals), and AAPD (a national advocacy organization of people with disabilities). We describe below our approaches and what we learned about employer practices through these cross-organizational surveys.

## 2011 Cornell/SHRM Survey

We worked with SHRM to follow up our previous surveys in order to identify changes that had taken place and address some of the gaps identified in the literature, specifically the lack of knowledge of the specific disability-inclusive practices and policies that employers had actually implemented. In 2011, we disseminated a survey to a random stratified (by organization size) sample of SHRM membership designed to identify disability practices that organizations currently had in place (Erickson et al. 2013). The sample identified was completely independent of that used in the earlier Cornell/SHRM survey. The survey used multiple data collection modes to increase response rate and reduce potential nonresponse bias. Initial contact was made via e-mails from SHRM containing a personalized link to a website-based instrument. To promote responses, regular reminders were sent to nonrespondents, and small incentives were offered to early respondents. After approximately one month, nonrespondents were contacted by phone and offered the opportunity to complete the survey by telephone interview. The telephone follow-up was deliberately designed to ensure that the respondents were proportional by organization size to the original sample, and resulted in an overall response rate of 23 percent (n = 690). Despite offering incentives, the response rate was lower than in the 1999 survey, which may reflect survey fatigue that lowered motivation to participate (Gofton 1999).

Combining data has the potential to help answer a wider variety of questions than a single survey can. By asking the same question over time, it is possible to see if changes have occurred over the period. For example, a set of identical questions was asked in the 1999 and 2011 Cornell/SHRM survey (Erickson et al. 2013). This allowed the examination of changes over time in the perception of barriers to the hiring and promotion of persons with disabilities. Figure 5.2 shows that for most items, a significantly smaller proportion of employers saw them as barriers in their organization in the more recent 2011 survey.

The analysis of the survey data allowed the authors to highlight the prevalence of various employer practices in organizations of varying sizes and types and to study which practices were associated with the increasing hiring of individuals with disabilities (Erickson et al. 2014). The proportion of organizations surveyed that implemented specific hiring practices

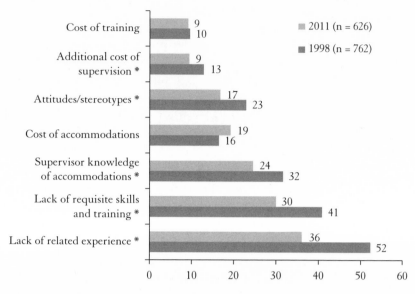

**Figure 5.2** Major barriers to hiring and promotion, 1998 vs. 2011

\* Significant at the p < 0.05 level
*Note:* Percentage of employers who perceived various barriers to the employment and advancement of
people with disabilities.
*Source:* Data from Erickson et al. 2013, figure 6.

can be seen in figure 5.3 below. Nine of the ten practices were found to be
significant at the p < .05 level regarding hiring, after controlling for organizational characteristics. The practices that had the greatest impact were having
internships for persons with disabilities (approximately 5.7 times more likely
to hire a person with a disability) and strong senior management commitment
(approximately 4.8 times more likely to hire a person with a disability).

## Cornell DMEC Poll

While HR professionals provide a useful perspective on many of their organization's practices and policies, often there are silos in organizations. Individuals who focus on disability management (DM) programming, such
as short- and long-term disability, worker compensation, and return-to-
work programs, may not interact regularly with HR. Because these DM
professionals focus on retention of workers, they can be a very knowledgeable source of information regarding practices that promote retention of

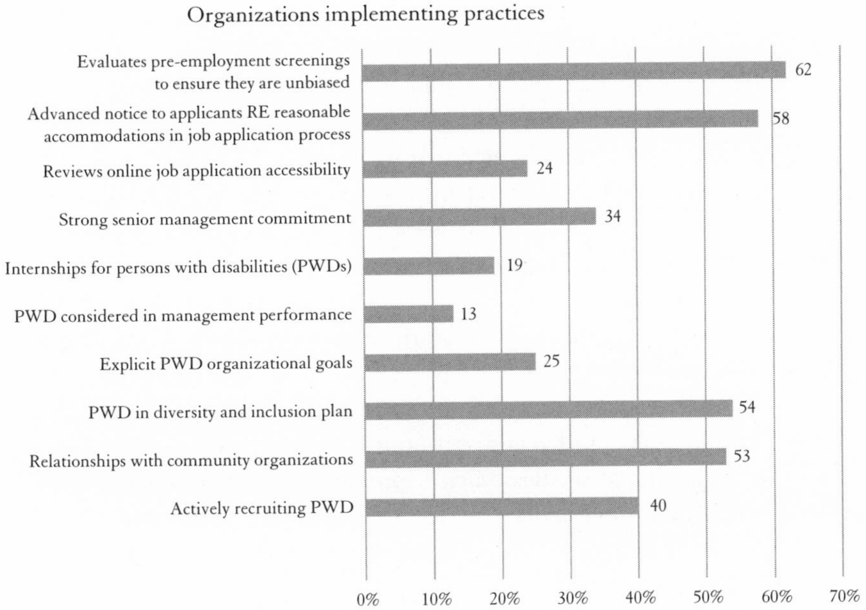

Organizations implementing practices

**Figure 5.3** Percentage of organizations implementing specific recruitment and hiring practices

*Source:* Data from Erickson et al. 2014, table 2.

employees with disabilities within an organization, and potentially offer a perspective different from that of HR representatives. In 2012, Cornell collaborated with the Disability Management Employer Coalition (DMEC) on a study to better understand how disability management programs were responding to an aging workforce. DMEC membership is composed of both "employers" (DM professionals in a company) and "suppliers" (suppliers of DM services to another company). The poll included open-ended items as well as rating-scale items, and focused on the perspective of DM professionals regarding three questions: (1) whether the aging workforce is a concern for their organization, (2) what they perceive as leading practices for retaining an aging workforce, and (3) how they are incorporating aging workforce concerns (von Schrader et al. 2013).

In an effort to increase response rate and encourage open-ended response, the survey was a short poll, designed to take five minutes or less to complete. The poll was distributed to the entire membership of DMEC and recent conference attendees (over forty-five hundred employers and suppliers) and resulted in a 19 percent response rate. While not a particularly high response rate, this was higher than other, longer, surveys conducted with DMEC membership.

The survey results highlighted that while the vast majority of employers (over 85 percent) were concerned about the impact of an aging workforce, relatively few (36 percent) were integrating considerations of an aging workforce into their disability management programming. Many examples of effective practices for retaining an older workforce were elicited using an open-ended item at the end of the survey. There is concern that open-ended items will not be completed; however, in this case over half the respondents replied to this question. The effective practices were wide-ranging, and many were quite creative. These practices fell into the following areas: flexibility, maintaining and enhancing benefits, wellness programming, safety checks, accommodation, stay-at-work and return-to-work programs, and communication with and recognition for older workers.

## Cornell/AAPD Emerging-Issues Survey

In 2011, Cornell University collaborated with AAPD, a disability policy and advocacy organization, to field a website-based survey of people with disabilities on three emerging issues in disability employment: (1) disability disclosure, (2) leave as a reasonable accommodation, and (3) the use of job applicant screeners. The purpose of this survey was to elicit the voices of individuals with disabilities on important policy issues. The topics of the survey were determined jointly with AAPD. Disability disclosure was a particularly important issue in light of new regulations for federal contractors to measure disability recruitment, hiring, and retention. Our conversations with employers (for instance, employer working groups as discussed in chapter 2) had also elicited concerns about whether and how organizations should encourage disclosure.

The survey was disseminated through the networks of AAPD and a federal partner, the Substance Abuse and Mental Health Services Administration. While the electronic survey and the methods for finding people with disabilities limited respondents to those who had access to a computer, this approach elicited responses from approximately six hundred individuals with disabilities. The most successful approach to recruitment was found to be network Listservs, with relatively few people accessing the survey though social media postings (von Schrader, Malzer, and Bruyère 2013). As this approach used a sample of convenience, the results could not be generalized back to the population of individuals with disabilities more broadly. However, the study provided a wealth of information regarding the barriers and facilitators to the disability disclosure decision, as well as offering individuals' stories about their experience with disclosure in the workplace. While accommodation was a main factor for most in the decision to disclose, the survey results highlighted the important roles that the supervisor relationship and the workplace practices and culture play. Again some of the most valuable and interesting data were the open-ended responses that individuals provided about whether they would disclose in the future and why.

Surveys have been widely used and have a number of advantages in soliciting information from organizations and others about employer disability practices, as well as assessing the workplace experiences of employees with disabilities. Several groups exist that researchers may want to consider surveying, each of which has distinct advantages and the selection of which depends upon the topic of interest. A wide array of choices are available when a researcher is planning a study, including whom to survey, how to access the groups of interest, how to distribute the survey, and ways to encourage people to respond. Although we have focused on surveys covering practice and policies related to the employment of persons with disabilities, it is important to be aware that there are a plethora of resources regarding the broader topics of survey design and other studies outside this topical area that could help inform survey approaches.

Organizational representatives are the ideal source for information regarding official policies and practices, especially those that are within HR or at an executive level. Middle-level managers and supervisors can provide information on their knowledge of policies and actual implementation of the practices. Employee surveys and more general population surveys provide a window into the actual experience of the employees with regard to their organization's disability practices or employment experiences. Each of these groups presents unique value to inform the research agenda focused on the relationship between employer practices and employment outcomes for individuals with disabilities, but each also has unique challenges with regard to access as well.

The ideal situation for studying employer practices broadly would be to survey persons across multiple companies and at different levels within companies. Each employee type has a natural advantage for providing insights about relevant policies and their implementations. Executives are best suited for surveys about official organizational policies, while managers/supervisors can provide thorough details about the implementation of these policies, and lower-level employees can supplement this with information about the effects of the policy implementation. Unfortunately, opportunities to access all these tiers across organizations are extremely limited, as they require cooperation and close collaboration with multiple organizations. Chapter 6 will present some examples of this type of approach within a single organization.

Ultimately, researchers must carefully consider the nature of the question they seek to answer and what resources are at their disposal to determine the ideal approach for a given study. Through our transdisciplinary initiative, we have found that the combination of a variety of research methods provided the richest and most informative data.

# 6

# Conducting Case Studies

Lisa H. Nishii and Susanne M. Bruyère

As described in the preceding chapters, there are many benefits to conducting research using national datasets, administrative data, and data from employer surveys. The primary advantage of these approaches is that they allow researchers to identify patterns of findings that are generalizable across organizational contexts—for example, research about the prevalence of disability practices, or about the relationship between the adoption of certain practices and objective firm-level outcomes such as hiring or turnover rates for individuals with disabilities.[1]

## Case Study Research as a Complement to Other Approaches

The purpose of case study research is to complement these cross-organization studies with in-depth data collected from employees *within* organizations (in the case of our own work, two organizations—one each from the federal and private sectors). The two primary advantages of within-organization research are that it allows for an examination of (a) the intrapsychic perceptions, attributions, and attitudes of employees with disabilities that are not (usually) captured in administrative, national, or cross-organization datasets; and (b) the interplay between these individual-level experiences and the particular organizational context within which employees are working. There have been a number of cross-organization surveys conducted to examine the attitudes and experiences of people with disabilities (for example, Schur et al. 2014; von Schrader, Malzer, and Bruyère 2013). Within-organization case studies offer the unique opportunity to examine how the experiences of individuals with disabilities are influenced by surrounding leadership, informational, task, and social attributes (Johns 2001). In this chapter, we will discuss the opportunities afforded by case study research in general and will also describe some of the specific approaches that we adopted in our own case studies, as well as associated research findings.

## The Focus of the Other Approaches

In chapter 5 we described research that was based on data collected from human resource representatives about the disability practices and policies that have been adopted by their organizations. While these data have allowed us to understand organizational-level trends and relationships, organizational-level studies implicitly assume that the disability policies and practices that are reported by organizational representatives as being in place within their organizations are actually implemented as intended (Nishii, Lepak, and Schneider 2008). Yet prior research has revealed that over two-thirds of all managers are unaware of their organization's disability practices (Nishii and Bruyère 2009). This suggests that espoused practices as reported by HR managers may not align with those actually implemented by line managers.

Indeed, we know from HR research that an organization's intended practices are filtered through the line managers who serve as implementers of those practices (Bowen and Ostroff 2004; Wright and Nishii 2013). Depending on the consistency with which managers implement disability practices (both across managers and across time), employees are likely to develop different perceptions of, and reactions to, these practices.

Employees' experiences with these practices shape their perceptions of the organization's disability climate, perceptions that in turn influence the everyday work experiences of individuals with disabilities. By complementing cross-organization research with within-organization research focused on the managerial differences that might explain some of the variation in the way in which practices are executed (e.g., Bowen and Ostroff 2004; Nishii and Wright 2008; Pfeffer 1981), we are able to develop a richer understanding of how specific disability initiatives relate to the employment outcomes and experiences of individuals with disabilities.

Similarly, while administrative datasets such as the Equal Employment Opportunity Commission data described in chapter 4 contribute to an understanding of where claimants are perceiving that disability discrimination is occurring in the employment process, and which types of disabilities these individuals have, these data do not tell us about the workplace factors that might make it more or less likely for individuals with disabilities to experience disability-related discrimination or harassment. By drawing on what is known from diversity research about the within-organization factors associated with reports of discrimination and assessing them in case-study research designs, we are able to understand the organizational climate and managerial and coworker factors that influence the likelihood that individuals with disabilities will experience discrimination.

## Value of Case Studies

In case study research, it is possible to broaden the focus to include an analysis of non-disability-specific workplace factors—factors that have been shown in the HR literature to enhance the advancement and retention of employees in general—as a means of developing a more nuanced and comprehensive understanding of the combination of practices and issues that are most influential for the employment outcomes of people with disabilities. In this research, we build upon prior work that has shown that unit managers exert substantial influence over the experiences of employees with disabilities (Disability Case Studies Research Consortium 2009; Nishii and Bruyère 2009). The quality of the relationships that managers develop with subordinates with disabilities has important implications for the access that those subordinates have to valuable job opportunities, resources for performance success, career and psychological support, and their status relative to other subordinates (Gerstner and Day 1997). In addition, managers have a significant impact on the inclusiveness of work-group climates, the perceived meaningfulness of and fit with one's job, satisfaction with accommodation processes, experiences of disability-related harassment, and overall engagement (Nishii and Bruyère 2009). Therefore, in the case study approach described here, we focused on specifying the characteristics of managers that enhance outcomes for people with disabilities.

In what follows, we first describe the primary sources of data in case study research and review some of the important decisions one should consider related to research design, including issues about which researchers need to be cautious. Next, we discuss the main types of research questions that can be addressed using a case study approach, and include in this discussion some of the specific research questions we examined in the case studies that were part of this transdisciplinary research endeavor and share select findings. We end with a few ideas for future research using a case study approach.

## Designing Case Study Research

### Identifying an Appropriate Employer Case Study Partner

A number of factors should be considered when identifying an organizational partner for case study research. Considerations involved in successfully *recruiting* the organizational partner in collaborative research are discussed in chapter 2. Organizations vary in the extent to which they employ people with disabilities across not only work units but also job function and hierarchical levels. Organizations also vary in their progress in adopting "best practices" to enhance the hiring, engagement, and retention of individuals with disabilities. Although it may be easier to attain needed research sample sizes in organizations that have hired a disproportionately large number of employees with disabilities (Walgreen's distribution centers, for instance) compared with peer organizations, the inherent tradeoff is that findings derived from research with such organizations will be less generalizable to the broader labor market. Such organizations are likely to be characterized by better-tuned disability practices, managers and coworkers who are more knowledgeable about disabilities and associated accommodations, less pronounced stigmas, and fewer barriers to success for employees with disabilities. Partnering with such progressive organizations may help to identify "best practices" that can serve as a source of learning for other, less advanced, organizations, but may be less useful for examining the psychological and practice-based barriers to employment and advancement that continue to exist in the vast majority of organizations.

Regardless of the goals of the research—and therefore the choice of research partners—a critical step in case study research is investing the time and effort required to develop a trust-based relationship with the potential organizational partner. More is written on this in chapter 2, but it is important to reemphasize this point here, as case study research requires a significant time commitment on the part of the organizational partner, and, more important, it requires the willingness to provide access to sensitive data. It is not uncommon for organizations to find it intimidating or intrusive for researchers to survey employees about their experiences and perceptions regarding inclusion, discrimination, and fairness related to a stigmatized identity such as disability. Although the process of nurturing a trusting relationship can take months or even years, it is imperative that the research partnership be viewed as mutually beneficial, because only then is it possible to collect candid employee perceptions and develop a more nuanced understanding of disability issues within organizations.

## Multisource Case Study Data Collection

In case study research, data can be gathered from multiple sources, creating the opportunity for a richness in analysis not possible in many other research methods. Figure 6.1 presents a visual overview of these possibilities, incorporating both administrative and individual sources.

## Organizational Metrics and Documentation

A useful place to begin is with gathering and assessing the organization's official statements of policies, practices and procedures, and existing metrics or measurements that management uses for its own assessments and accountability. What do the organization's documents describe about its

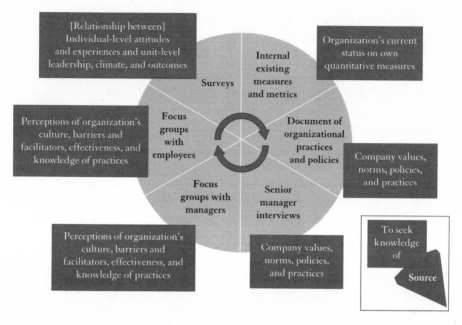

**Figure 6.1** Contributions from multisource case study data collection

workplace practices and culture for employees with disabilities? How does the organization communicate this both internally and externally? What measures are collected, and what do these reveal?

A "wish list" of such data might include: the organization's value statements; EEO-1 reports; affirmative action plans; recruiting, accommodation, and representation statistics (ideally by level and business unit and/ or department); results of past employee surveys; employee handbook descriptions of disability and inclusion-related practices; documentation of recruiting, performance review, and promotion procedures; and descriptions of manager training programs on disabilities, accommodations, and inclusion. Related to disability training, it would be valuable to understand what is covered in training, who is required to take the training and how often, and whether there are follow-up activities to the training. Disability-focused training might include a regulatory compliance focus (for example, the requirements of the employment provisions of the Americans with Disabilities Act); information on the internal accommodation process and resources to determine an appropriate accommodation; disability etiquette; or a more nuanced understanding of the micro-messages that convey bias and stereotypes regarding individuals with disabilities. The content of the training, who receives it, and the organizational messaging around the rationale for training all provide valuable information about the organization's approach to disability issues.

Finally, understanding which linkage and gap analyses are currently being performed by the organization is useful, since these analyses can help inform the design of subsequent surveys. Examples of useful analyses might be: How is the organization analyzing the links between employee data (for example, employment of individuals with disabilities, accommodation rates, or inclusion experiences) and not only internal metrics such as employee engagement data, but also organizational performance metrics such as financial performance, turnover, and customer satisfaction? Are pay or performance gap analyses (for underrepresented groups) regularly performed? While it is highly unlikely to get access to or be able to distill all the existing internal sources of data, each additional source adds to the potential robustness of the case study.

## Interviews and Focus Groups

Interviews with senior managers (in the HR department in particular) can help to identify company values, norms, and practices. Complementary interviews with a sample of managers and supervisors can also be beneficial, as a means of exploring the barriers that they perceive for the successful implementation of disability practices.

Following these interviews, conducting focus groups involving employees with disabilities is a valuable next step. In such focus groups it is useful to inquire about perceptions of how receptive the organization's culture is to employees with disabilities; what types of barriers employees with disabilities face within the organization; and perceptions about how well the organization is doing in recruiting, developing, engaging, and retaining employees with disabilities. It is also helpful to inquire about whether the focus group participants have ever asked for an accommodation, and if so, if they experienced any issues during the process, and whether their coworkers were aware and supportive of their accommodation request. Employees without disabilities who have worked with a colleague with a known disability are also a good source of information. Asking similar questions about the receptivity of the organization's culture, possible barriers facing employees with disabilities, the extent to which the organization does a good job of facilitating coworker receptivity to accommodations requests by employees with disabilities, and the effectiveness of the organization's disability practices in general provides a comparison of perspectives to inform case study findings. Our prior work (Disability Case Studies Research Consortium 2009), as well as the focus groups we conducted for these case studies, have taught us that coworker reactions to accommodation requests on the part of employees with disabilities have important ramifications for the work experiences of people with disabilities.

It is also beneficial to conduct separate focus groups with managers to ask them about how well they think the organization is doing in recruiting, developing, engaging, and retaining people with disabilities, and whether there are disability policies and practices that they think are not as effective as they could be or that make their role as managers difficult, and why. Doing so supplements the perspective supplied by employees and provides valuable input regarding the disability practices that should be the focus of survey questions.

## Surveys

An important purpose of the previously described forms of information collection is to inform the design and content of a survey that will follow. Although researchers may embark on the research effort with specific hypotheses in mind, using information gathered from these interviews and focus groups prior to formulating a survey helps to (a) refine the specific set of disability practices and policies about which questions are included in the survey, (b) identify specific cultural issues or barriers that should be addressed, and (c) develop a clear understanding of how best to conceptualize work units and reporting relationships throughout the different parts of the organization.

This last point is critical for the design of surveys for multilevel research. Specifically, it is important to identify the work-unit level that is psychologically meaningful for employees. It is common practice in research conducted by organizational psychologists to think of meaningful work units as the units within which employees interact and are interdependent in some way, and within which coworkers engage in collective sense-making processes. Often, the specification of organizational units is based on expedience and likely to reflect the formal units about which the organization is accustomed to producing reports. Organizational representatives may initially suggest that the appropriate unit level of analysis to consider is their divisions or departments (Kozlowski and Klein 2000). However, these are usually too large to be psychologically meaningful for respondents. If within an identified unit there are many employees with whom an employee is unlikely to interact, then it is inappropriate to assume that those employees experience and understand that organizational unit similarly. Instead, their experiences are likely to be shared with employees in their more proximal or local subunit. If this is the case, then those subunits should be the focus of analysis (Klein, Dansereau, and Hall 1994; Kozlowski and Klein 2000).

Imagine, for example, when survey respondents answer questions about the inclusiveness of the work unit: if, within the identified work-unit level, respondents report to different managers who hold different beliefs about diversity and inclusion and have different leadership styles, and respondents also interact with a different subset of employees, then constructs aggregated to that particular work-unit level of analysis will be less reliable estimates of unit-level phenomena (Kozlowski and Klein 2000). Similarly, if respondents have different managers in mind when they respond to questions about their manager's treatment of disability issues or leadership style, then it makes little sense to aggregate their responses to represent the group's perception of the manager. As a rule, researchers should think about the theoretical level of a construct, then align the measurement level of the construct to it by carefully identifying which employees can meaningfully respond about the aspect of the work environment that is of interest (for more details, see Kozlowski and Klein 2000).

Once the appropriate unit level is identified, survey respondents should be directed to identify which unit they belong to (ideally using predetermined drop-down lists from which they can choose rather than allowing open-ended responses) and to think about that specific level of analysis when responding to any survey questions that refer to their work unit. Doing so helps to eliminate unwanted "noise" in survey responses. Subsequently, when survey data are analyzed using multilevel models, employees' responses can easily be aggregated using the unit identification variables included in the survey (Kozlowski and Klein 2000). For some types of jobs (assembly line or hospitality workers, for instance) it may be necessary also to include a survey question about respondents' work-shift membership so that the different shifts of employees doing the same work in the same department can be differentiated accurately within the data.

In cases when organizational administrative data and related metrics are available—for example, unit error, productivity, or sales data—and there is the possibility of linking it to survey data, another important consideration will be whether the unit level of analysis that has been identified as psychologically meaningful for employees aligns with the level at which the outcome data are reported. If there is a mismatch, then the researcher has to determine whether the smaller units identified in the survey (for example, customer-facing team and back-end employees of a restaurant or hotel) can be aggregated to match the larger units represented by the outcome data provided by the organization (for example, restaurant or hotel profits), and furthermore, whether there would then be a sufficient number of larger units in the data to provide the statistical power necessary to run desired analyses at the unit level of analysis. When using aggregated constructs in data analyses, the sample size is determined by the number of aggregated units rather than the number of individual responses that compose those aggregated constructs.

## Balancing Employer Needs

As stated earlier in this chapter, it is imperative that the research partnership be viewed as mutually beneficial. When developing the survey instrument and other parts of the case study research, researchers should pay careful attention to balancing research interests with the needs of the employer. This is important for a number of reasons. First, when stakeholders from the partner organization are afforded a voice in shaping the research agenda, they are much more likely to help market the survey and other data collection activities internally as being important for the organization. This in turn helps to boost response rates on surveys and cooperation in focus groups, interviews, and collection of organizational documents and existing metrics. Second, they can help to identify any survey items or case study activities that may trigger resistance within their organization (for example, from legal counsel) and disrupt the approval process. Third, it helps increase the chances that the results of the case study will be seen as relevant to addressing the organization's needs, thereby strengthening the possibility of having a significant impact on organizational behavior in the future and supporting the maintenance of a long-term research partnership with the organization (that is, for follow-up data collection efforts). Fourth, stakeholders can help ensure that the terms that are used in the research in general, and the survey in particular, are appropriate for their particular organizational context and are therefore more likely to be easily understood by respondents. Finally, even when the costs associated with the case study (for example, designing, programming, and administering the survey) are fully financed by the research team, the staff of the partner organization still needs to commit significant resources to make the partnership successful (for example, staff time, internal communication tools, internal social capital to garner and maintain support for the survey). The importance of these activities is nontrivial; successful and sustainable research partnerships rely on maintaining a healthy relationship between the employer and the research team.

## Important Considerations in Designing Case Studies

For all the value and unique insights offered by case studies, there are research and methodological cautions that need to be carefully considered and addressed. In this chapter we will mention ones we consider of highest importance: disability definition, anonymity versus confidentiality, common method bias, and self-identification.

*Definition of Disability*     Perhaps more so than is the case with other dimensions of diversity such as gender and race or ethnicity, the measurement of disability in the workplace is associated with numerous methodological challenges (Livermore and She 2007). As described in chapter 1, the two major conceptualizations of disability that dominate the field in the United States both recognize that "disability" results from interactions between a person and the physical and social environment (Weathers 2009, 29). These interactions may result in limitations to that person's capacity to function at work, in society, or in daily life. This "functional limitations" model can be contrasted with the "medical model," used by many government programs, which defines certain medical and health conditions as "disabilities." The existence of specified lists that define disability has contributed to the widespread use of the medical definition of disability in labor market research (Bernell 2003). It is also important to remember that most of the major definitions of disability ultimately rely on self-reporting by the person with a disability. Some people would not consider their condition to constitute an impairment and would thus not self-identify as a person with a disability (Colella and Bruyère 2011).

For public policy purposes, national surveys have often been used to assist in identifying the population with disabilities. Many disability researchers follow the lead of the U.S. Census Bureau's American Community Survey (ACS), which we discuss further later in this chapter (Livermore and She 2007). Using the same six ACS questions in survey research can allow for comparisons between the study population and national datasets (see chapter 3).

One of the issues inherent in deciding what type of disability definition or measure to use has to do with the level of specificity with which disability status is considered or respondents report about their disability. The advantage of including nuanced categories of disabilities is obviously that it provides the researcher with more information, and these categories can later be collapsed into larger groups of disabilities if necessary to create needed sample sizes for analyses; however, including nuanced categories increases respondent burden and perhaps also may raise greater concerns on the part of the respondent about privacy and identifiability. Because it is not uncommon for individuals to have multiple disabilities at the same time, terminology throughout the case study should allow for any number of disabilities as representing an employee's disability status.

Within the survey context, it is the case that when respondents disclose having multiple disabilities—especially disabilities that fall into different categories, such as physical and psychological disabilities—it is usually impossible to isolate the workplace outcomes associated with one of the disabilities independent of the effects of the other disabilities. For example, if such a respondent reports feeling mistreated by coworkers as a result of his or her disability status, there is no way to know whether coworkers are reacting to that individual's physical or psychological disability, or both.

*Anonymity and Confidentiality*     In addition to the disability-specific definitional issues of which researchers should be aware when conducting case studies, there are other issues germane to the research that are noteworthy. First is the issue of anonymity. In anonymous data collection, the participants' identities are not known to the researcher. In confidential data collection, identities of the participants may be known to the researcher, but individual responses (whether from surveys, interviews, or focus groups) are held confidential; that is, only aggregated results are shared with the organization that is being studied or with others (Ong and Weiss 2000). Given a choice, many organizations prefer to guarantee both confidentiality and anonymity to survey respondents, as these conditions tend to help respondents feel the most comfortable when providing answers to potentially sensitive questions, such as inquiries about their disability status or experiences with unfair treatment.

Every measure should be taken to guarantee the confidentiality of employees' interview, focus group, and survey responses. Examples include having online survey responses directed to a highly secure external server managed by the research team and not the organization, and reporting focus group results only in the aggregate. However, there are significant disadvantages associated with conducting anonymous research. Perhaps most important, when respondents remain anonymous and therefore cannot be identified in the data to be analyzed, it becomes impossible to link one data source to another. For example, responses cannot be linked to survey data collected at another point in time or to the partner organization's HR information systems that could be used in the analysis to include job type, function, demographics, tenure, absenteeism, individual performance ratings, pay, managerial level, history of job changes or promotions, and unit-level performance. In this situation, any and all information desired by the research team must be collected at one point in time using a single survey, thereby potentially increasing the length of the survey and associated respondent fatigue and limiting the richness and statistical robustness offered by multisource analysis. When this translates into the need to include a section asking respondents about their demographic and employment background, it can also increase respondent fears about being identified, despite assurances about the confidentiality of the data.

*Common Method Bias*    Another important consideration specific to the survey method of data collection in a case study is the reduction of "common method bias," which refers to when the correlations among measured variables are inflated as a function of a shared measurement method, as is the case in data from a single cross-sectional survey (Podsakoff, MacKenzie, Lee, and Podsakoff 2003). Common method bias is problematic to the extent that it presents a rival explanation for observed correlations among survey variables.

A number of techniques exist to reduce or even eliminate common method bias. Researchers should explicitly build these into their study design. One method is obtaining data for the independent and dependent variables from different sources, for example when employees provide data about one set of variables while their managers provide data about another, and the two sets of data are linked for analysis. Using manager data about employees is only appropriate when the manager can observe what is being assessed. Constructs that can be reliably assessed by either employees or managers are those that can be observed and reported relatively objectively, such as worker participation levels (Kozlowski and Klein 2000). Another common way of incorporating multisource data is to link survey data provided by employees or managers with data obtained from organizational records (for example, turnover). Keep in mind, however, that this requires that data not be anonymous. Another technique that can be used when examining relationships among aggregated (unit-level) constructs is the split-sample approach. In this approach, all units are split into two random halves, and the predictor variable is represented by data from split half A, while the criterion variable is represented by data from split half B (or vice versa). A final technique to consider is to separate the measurement of predictor and criterion variables by collecting survey data at two points in time or using different response formats to interrupt auto-responding. The former is not always desirable or possible, however, since it increases survey administration costs and can reduce the total sample size available for analyses, owing to respondent attrition over the two time periods.

*Self-Identification*    Perhaps one of the biggest challenges associated with conducting case study research on employment outcomes of employees with disabilities is that most organizations lack up-to-date and complete records about which employees have disabilities, and participant employees may not feel comfortable or willing to self-disclose their disability status within the research project. In most cases, organizations are aware of only a small subset of the actual number of employees with disabilities. This is because many disabilities are not visible; thus employees have a choice as to whether they want others to know about their disability. Given that people with disabilities continue to face stigmas (see, for example, Hebl and Skorinko 2005; Ragins, Singh, and Cornwell 2007; Wang, Barron, and Hebl 2010), many choose not to disclose their disability to their organization (Colella and Stone 2005). Thus, it is difficult or perhaps even impossible for organizations to accurately analyze their employee survey or HR administrative data based on disability status. It has been shown that individuals tend to feel more comfortable disclosing their disability in a survey administered and analyzed by an external third party. In fact, in our own case study work, company surveys have suggested that the actual proportion of employees with disabilities in an organization may be five to ten times larger than the proportion known to the organization prior to the survey conducted by the external researcher(s). This is encouraging for third-party researchers conducting a case study. However, as with research using other methodologies, partial reporting or misreporting of disability status must not be dismissed in evaluating case study conclusions.

## Questions That Can Be Addressed by Case Study Research

There are numerous subjective perceptions, attitudes, and experiences that researchers can learn about only by asking employees themselves. Asking a single organizational representative (an HR officer, for instance) to provide assessments about the subjective experiences of employees within the organization presents inherent challenges, of course. By their very nature, subjective experiences—including employee attitudes about their jobs, fairness perceptions, utility of available resources, quality of interactions with other individuals, and experiences of inclusion—differ across individuals. Thus, any one individual's account of how things are in an organization is unlikely to be representative of the range of attitudes, perspectives, and experiences actually present across employees. Organizations comprise socially complex, hierarchically nested systems. The strength of case study research is that it explicitly recognizes this, with the goal of understanding variance *within* an organization. Rather than being treated as error variance, as is necessary in organizational-level research, the within-organization variance in work attitudes and experiences becomes treated as true variance, as the focal point of the research (cf. Nishii and Wright 2008; Wright and Nishii 2013).

More and more, researchers are adopting a multilevel approach to their research to examine how phenomena at one level of analysis are associated with phenomena at other levels of analysis, either in top-down or bottom-up processes (Kozlowski and Klein 2000). Top-down processes refer to when aspects of the work context, such as managerial behaviors or group norms, affect individual-level phenomena, either directly or by moderating the relationship between individual-level constructs. Bottom-up, or emergent, processes refer to phenomena that have their theoretical origin in the cognition, affect, motivation, behavior, or other characteristics of individuals, which, when considered in the aggregate, emerge as unit-level phenomena (Bliese 2000; Chan 1998; Klein and Kozlowski 2000). Many relevant examples of emergent phenomena are available, including the proportion of individuals in a unit who have disclosed their disability, collective employee perceptions about the inclusiveness of work-group climate, and the pattern of relationships between particular managers and their employees.

In our current case study work, by surveying employees with disabilities about their experiences and matching their data with data collected from their managers about their perceptions of disability practices, as well as other data collected from coworkers, we were able to see how these organizational actors interact in shaping the experiences of employees with disabilities. Some additional interesting questions that we were able to explore through these case studies are briefly described in the remainder of this chapter.

Individual-Level Employee Experiences

One example of a research question that can be pursued at the individual level of analysis is whether individuals with disabilities report work attitudes and experiences significantly different from those of their peers without disabilities. The data that we collected as part of these case studies confirm a disparity in employment experiences when comparing employees with and without disabilities. These results were all significant at the 99 percent level. In particular, with regard to perceptions of the work-group context, we found that employees with disabilities report significantly less favorable perceptions of the fairness with which employment practices are implemented ($t = 34.58$; $p < .01$), were less likely to report that the work-group climate is open to and values differences among employees ($t = 31.40$; $p < .01$), that diverse employees are included in the group's decision-making processes ($t = 46.41$; $p < .01$), and that the group leader engages in authentic ($t = 7.68$; $p < .01$) and inclusive ($t = 5.94$; $p < .01$) leadership. Related to individual work attitudes, we found that individuals with disabilities report significantly less-favorable experiences regarding the receipt of adequate socialization once on the job ($t = 4.50$; $p < .01$), perceived organizational support ($t = 5.21$; $p < .01$), the quality of their relationship with the immediate manager ($t = 5.92$; $p < .01$), and the fit between one's skills and abilities and the demands of the job ($t = 9.92$; $p < .01$).

Our use of in-depth surveys also enabled an exploration of rates of disability disclosure, as well as some of the predictors and outcomes associated with it. In the federal agency, 58.6 percent of survey respondents with disabilities disclosed their disabilities to their supervisor, and 63.7 percent disclosed to their coworkers, but disclosure rates to more official entities was much lower: only 12.2 percent disclosed to HR, 15.5 percent using a self-identification form, and 7.5 percent to the EO office. Although disclosure rates were highest involving supervisors and coworkers, there appear to be greater psychological barriers to disclosure for individuals with mental and emotional disabilities, among whom only 38.5 percent disclosed to supervisors and 53.8 percent to coworkers. Given the interest that organizations have in being able to compile accurate statistics about the percentage of employees who have disabilities, disclosure to these official entities is of paramount importance, and therefore we further explored whether disclosure depends on disability visibility. We found that while 28.6 percent of individuals with very visible disabilities have disclosed to HR, 33.3 percent through the organization's self-identification form, and 25 percent to the EO office, only 9.1 percent of individuals with invisible disabilities reported disclosing to HR, 15.3 percent through the self-identification system, and 4.7 percent to the EO office.

Results from this case study research also provide a picture of the types of accommodations requested and why; and for those individuals with disabilities who have not requested an accommodation, we have data to understand the reasons why not. In our federal sample, accommodations were most frequently requested by individuals with physical impairments (59 percent of individuals with physical disabilities requested an accommodation) or vision impairments (59 percent), followed by individuals with chronic health (48 percent), mental/emotional (48 percent), cognitive (33 percent), and hearing (29 percent) disabilities. The most commonly requested type of accommodation included changes to work tasks, job structure, or job schedule (40 percent), followed by physical changes to the workplace (22 percent), requests for new or modified equipment (20 percent), policy changes (5 percent), and changes in communication practices (5 percent). In this sample, only a small percentage of employees with disabilities indicated that they had not requested an accommodation that they needed. Among that group, the most commonly cited reasons for not doing so involved concern about the negative impact on future opportunities and/or being seen differently by one's supervisor.

## Multilevel Relationships

Of primary interest in the research that we conducted as a part of the transdisciplinary team's efforts is understanding the factors that mitigate some of the negative work experiences that employees with disabilities report having. As indicated above, results of our case studies to date reveal that employees with disabilities tend to report significantly less favorable work attitudes and experiences on almost every work-attitude construct measured by these organizational surveys. A logical follow-up question is whether employees with disabilities who work in inclusive climates report more favorable experiences. Indeed, our survey results show that individuals with disabilities who work in inclusive climates report experiencing greater disability-related inclusion ($\beta$ = 0.14; p < .01), organizational commitment ($\beta$ = 0.26; p < .01), job satisfaction ($\beta$ = 0.29; p < .01), perceived fit between their skills and the demands of their job ($\beta$ = 0.25; p < .01), and perceived organizational support ($\beta$ = 0.27; p < .01).

In related research we conducted previously on disability inclusion, we found that the majority of managers surveyed reported being unaware of the various disability policies and practices in place within their organization (Nishii and Bruyère 2009). Thus in the current case studies, one of our goals was to see whether this finding would be replicated across different organizational contexts, and another was to explore the impact of managerial awareness on the experiences of employees with disabilities. To pursue this inquiry, we created a simple index (sum) across the eleven disability policies and practices we asked managers if they were aware of, and then averaged scores across the managers in a department. Results confirmed that the more managers overall were aware of disability policies and practices, the more favorable were employees' perceptions about the inclusiveness of the work environment ($\beta$ = 0.20; p < .01).

Moreover, we found that when managers believed that their organization had adopted disability policies for strategic reasons, they were more likely to cultivate work-group climates that were experienced by employees as inclusive ($\beta$ = 0.09; p < .01). However, when managers perceived that disability practices had been adopted merely to avoid looking bad to external stakeholders, employees working for these managers reported less favorable climate perceptions ($\beta$ = –0.04; p < .01). In turn, collective perceptions of the inclusiveness of work-group climate predicted to what extent employees with disabilities felt fairly treated by their coworkers ($\beta$ = 0.43; p < .01).

The multilevel analyses that we conducted using the data collected in the current case study research also revealed the critical role that managers' perceptions of disability initiatives had on the experiences of individuals with disabilities. For example, in our survey data, we found that the stronger the managers' perceptions were about the existence of barriers to the effective implementation of disability practices (for example, insufficient leadership support for and communication about disability, lack of training and reinforcement of training), the more employees with disabilities who report to them experienced disability-related exclusion from their coworkers ($r$ = 0.35–0.62; p < .01), depending on the particular perceived barrier.

Similarly, the more that managers perceived disability practices (such as centralized accommodation funds, disability awareness training, and accessibility reviews) to be effective within their organization, the less disability-related exclusion their employees with disabilities experienced ($r = -0.17$ — $-0.28$ depending on the disability practice; p < .01), and the more they perceived HR practices to be implemented in a fair way within their units ($r = 0.15$–$0.21$; p < .01). Managers play a more direct role in influencing whether individuals with disabilities experience disability-related exclusion as well, in that employees who enjoy high-quality relationships with their managers are elevated to in-group status within their work groups, thereby benefiting from "safe passages" (cf. Nishii and Mayer 2009), as evident in the relationship between the quality of employees' relationships with their direct supervisor and experiences of disability-related harassment ($\beta = -0.31$; p < .01).

Multilevel models have also enabled us to examine the influence that coworkers have on the experiences of individuals with disabilities. For example, in related prior research, we found that the prevalence of accommodation requests among coworkers (regardless of whether the requests are made for a disability) influences whether individuals with disabilities feel comfortable asking for an accommodation for their disability (Schur et al. 2014). We reasoned that when an organization fosters a culture of flexibility and accommodation as a means of enhancing employee engagement and productivity, employees with disabilities benefit because their requests for accommodations are much less unusual. In the current research, we also examined the impact that coworker awareness of, and reactions to, one's accommodation requests have on the experiences of individuals with disabilities. Our survey data revealed that when the coworkers of individuals with disabilities who had requested accommodations were aware of the accommodation request, the individuals with disabilities felt that coworkers were more likely to see them for who they are ($r = 0.21$; p < .05), and when coworker reactions to their accommodation request were positive, they reported significantly higher levels of organizational commitment ($r = 0.24$; p < .01). In contrast, when individuals with disabilities perceived that their coworkers reacted negatively to their accommodation, they felt less embedded within their jobs ($r = -0.12$; p < .05) and the organization more generally ($r = -0.17$; p < .05), reported lower perceptions of being supported by their organization ($r = -0.17$; p < .05), and also reported experiencing greater social isolation as a result of their disability ($r = 0.31$; $p < .01$). Furthermore, we found that when coworkers were able to appreciate the positive outcomes associated with the provision of an accommodation to an individual with a disability (for example, perceptions that the accommodation improved the individual's productivity, work-group safety, and the employee's interaction with coworkers), individuals with disabilities reported higher levels of embeddedness within their job ($r = 0.19–0.22$; $p < .01$) and organizational commitment ($r = 0.20–0.27$; $p < .01$).

An important next step in research about the role of managers in shaping the work experiences of individuals with disabilities is to examine the characteristics of managers that may influence the inclusion of people with disabilities. For example, we expect that managers who have a learning-goal orientation (VandeWalle 1997), or tend to approach situations with the goal of developing new understandings even if it means making mistakes, will be more adept at shaping work climates that are inclusive of individuals with disabilities. Given research that suggests that managers with learning-goal orientations can, through role modeling, establish group-level norms about engaging others openly and with the intent to learn across differences (Dragoni 2005), we expect that employees are likely to experience more positive interactions with their coworkers after disclosing their disability.

## Considerations for Future Research

Given the paucity of research on the within-organization factors that impact the employment experiences and attitudes of individuals with disabilities, there is a virtually endless list of research questions still requiring the attention of researchers. For example, research is needed that employs longitudinal designs to enable researchers to examine (a) how disclosure to different targets impacts long-term employment outcomes; (b) whether members of disability employee resource groups develop relational ties with a broader network of individuals with influence, thereby facilitating employment outcomes; (c) how experience working with an individual with a disability broadens the awareness and openness of managers and coworkers over time; (d) the content and design of disability training programs that are the most effective in changing employee and manager behaviors; and (e) the impact of having leaders in visible senior positions who disclose their disability on the inclusion experiences of lower-level employees with disabilities. Longitudinal research does not come without its share of challenges, however. Data collection involves significant administrative costs, particularly because the attrition of research subjects over time requires that researchers begin with samples that include substantially more participants with disabilities than are ultimately required to yield the statistical power needed to analyze the research models of interest.

In addition to these types of questions that are well suited for longitudinal research, we borrow from important trends in the broader diversity research to suggest three additional avenues for research. First, research has shown that developmental experiences that are challenging are critical for advancement into senior positions (DeRue and Wellman 2009; Dragoni et al. 2009; Dragoni et al. 2011), and the fact that women and people of color are less likely to be selected for stretch assignments may in part explain why they tend to be underrepresented in senior management positions (Eagly and Carli 2007; Eagly and Karau 2002; Ragins and Sundstrom 1989). There is good reason to believe that there are compounded benefits associated with having the opportunity to develop and be noticed early in one's career. When people have a chance to demonstrate their competence in visible assignments, they trigger a snowball effect wherein their experiences make them eligible for more such experiences, which quickly differentiate them from the rest. Research that examines the differential access that individuals with disabilities have to the range of developmentally challenging experiences that have been identified as critical for advancement would be highly valuable. Do individuals with certain types of disabilities (for example, psychological or cognitive versus physical) experience greater inequities in access to these job opportunities based on the stigmas or stereotypes associated with their disabilities (Cuddy, Fiske, and Glick 2007)? If individuals develop their disability after having had the opportunity to learn and advance from a key developmental assignment, are they able to overcome the biases that they might otherwise have experienced had they entered the organization with a preexisting disability?

Second, although it is reassuring to witness more and more organizations include disability as a focus of their broader diversity initiatives, it is important for research to help organizations to understand how the experiences of individuals with disabilities are similar to, but also different from, those of members of other marginalized groups. Perhaps the two most obvious ways in which disability as a diversity dimension differs from other dimensions of diversity such as race and gender are visibility and permeability. For many, their disability status may not be visible to others, and therefore they are faced with the decision of whether to disclose their stigmatized identity. This is an important aspect of disability identity that differs from gender and race, and one with nontrivial implications. Individuals with invisible disabilities have a choice between "passing" as someone without a disability versus "revealing" their disability (Clair, Beatty, and MacLean 2005). Although individuals who opt to hide their disability status or engage in "passing" may be able to avoid being discriminated against because of their disability, passing can be associated with higher levels of psychological strain, social isolation, strained relationships, and more limited social networks (Clair, Beatty, and MacLean 2005).

The challenge for organizations is to be aware of these potential side effects, and moreover, to shape the factors that signal to employees that it is safe to disclose their stigmatized identity. These factors include the inclusiveness of the climate, policies implemented that exceed minimal compliance standards, visible presence of other employees (ideally including leaders) who have disclosed their disability, and transparency of organizational decisions (Clair, Beatty, and MacLean 2005). While each of these factors is also important for promoting fairness and inclusion for members of other marginalized groups, research that helps to identify nuanced differences to which organizations should attend involving individuals with invisible disabilities would be valuable.

The second characteristic that sets disability apart from other dimensions of disability is the permeability of the boundaries of this identity group. Any individual can acquire a disability at any point in life, and disability intersects with other demographic identities that are fixed, serve as the basis of status differences, and categorize individuals into in-groups and out-groups (Ellemers, van Knippenberg, and Wilke 1990). As such, disability as a social identity has the unique potential to bring together people who would otherwise consider themselves separated across an "us versus them" boundary. Research on how disability status intersects with other social group memberships to influence identity-conflict versus identity-integration (Settles and Buchanan 2014) in diverse organizational contexts would thus be valuable. Also of interest would be research that examines whether priming people to understand the permeability of disability identity facilitates perspective taking and more earnest attempts at interpersonal learning, both of which are key ingredients for dismantling simplistic stereotypes and prejudice (Brewer and Miller 1984, 1988; Ensari and Miller 2006; Fiol, Pratt, and O'Connor 2009).

Finally, diversity research and practice more generally, as well as in relation to disability more specifically, have focused primarily on promoting fairness and eliminating discrimination (Dwertmann, Nishii, and van Knippenberg, forthcoming)—that is, on eliminating the obstacles to organizational entry, career advancement, and the social integration of members of historically marginalized groups. The primary emphasis is on eliminating negative outcomes or disparities. Despite the intuitive appeal of arguments about the business case for increasing diversity, there is very little empirical research on what might be called the "synergy" perspective of diversity according to which diversity is seen as a source of valuable information and perspectives that can, when carefully leveraged, benefit performance and innovation (Ely and Thomas 2001; van Knippenberg and Schippers 2007). Given that individuals with disabilities often require accommodations or changes to how they do their work, they have the potential to provide enormous informational benefits related to how work processes, systems, products, and services can be better designed. The idea here is not only that employees with disabilities have unique insights to offer, but that when work groups containing individuals with disabilities have the motivations, norms, and accountability structures necessary to encourage group members to challenge and debate each other's perspectives, the performance of the collective should also be enhanced (Mitchell, Nicholas, and Boyle 2009). Research that carefully examines the group conditions and processes involved in driving performance-benefits from disability diversity in work groups and organizations would represent a contribution not just to disability research but also to diversity research more generally.

# 7

## Translating Knowledge to Practice, and the Way Forward

Susanne M. Bruyère, Ellice Switzer, Sara VanLooy,
Sarah von Schrader, and Linda Barrington

By summarizing the experiences and findings of a transdisciplinary team of researchers from Cornell University working over a five-year period, this volume attempts to achieve three objectives: (1) to provide a variety of ways to identify how employers can improve the recruitment, hiring, retention, advancement, and full inclusion of individuals with disabilities; (2) to illustrate how researchers can work collaboratively with employers on workplace research; and (3) to present an example of the benefits and challenges of transdisciplinary research. Our focus has been on employer policies and practices. In this process, we have had as partners many employer associations and individual employer collaborators in both the private and federal sectors. We hope to reflect their insights and voices throughout our current and continuing work. Without their initial interest and commitment to this mission and their ongoing willingness to join us in this conversation and inquiry, this project would have been neither conceptually nor practically possible. We have ventured throughout these efforts to approximate the principles of true transdisciplinary research by deeply engaging our stakeholders and working with them to identify meaningful venues and methods to make this work both as rigorous and as useful as possible.

## Intersection of Transdisciplinary Research and Knowledge Translation

As a research team, we integrated the perspectives of our multiple disciplines to address in novel ways critical questions around the issues relating to employment disparities for people with disabilities. Through this approach, we committed ourselves to tackling questions of interest to the wide variety of knowledge users, including especially employers themselves and policy makers, key agents who can effect change around employment disparities. Following the principles of knowledge translation (KT) (Jacobson, Butterill, and Goering 2003), a focus on desired knowledge users must occur during all stages of the research process. The Cornell team engaged relevant stakeholders early and often throughout the research process, not only when sharing results at the conclusion of a research effort. The end goal of knowledge translation was part of the formulation of our research questions, hypothesis generation, and methods selection processes, and it also remained in view as we analyzed and summarized findings.

A critical element of these efforts has been end-user involvement. The Conference Board (TCB) and the Center for Advanced Human Resource Studies (CAHRS) at Cornell University's ILR School are employer organizations that are each uniquely connected to the priorities of the business community. As described more specifically in chapter 2, our Cornell team partnered with these organizations to convene several research working groups including their corporate and federal employer members. The goal of these groups was to further our understanding of existing employer practices in relation to disability, as well as to uncover the barriers to the implementation of promising practices identified in related prior Cornell research (Barrington, Bruyère, and Waelder 2014). Implicit in this process is the recognition that practitioner-experts have much to contribute to our understanding of what is working, what is not, and what types of resources for employers would be most influential. Gaps in existing knowledge related to the efficacy of specific practices (such as those that might lead to greater disclosure of non-visible disabilities) were useful in formulating a framework for research, including the in-depth federal and private sector case studies described in chapter 6.

We designed the dissemination activities of this effort to help employers answer some of the outstanding questions and concerns identified by the CAHRS and TCB groups, as well as to guide employers seeking on-demand technical assistance. We have been attuned to the distinct nature of each internal workplace environment and organizational climate and have customized our KT efforts (specifically consultation and training) to reflect varying levels of organizational readiness. At the same time, our KT activities must acknowledge the external environment of private and federal sector workforces, such as changing regulations and the composition of the local and regional labor markets, as much as internal processes and procedures. By doing so, we are able to directly connect new research, promising practices, and behavior change to business priorities, such as regulatory compliance.

## Policy Context—a Critical Time for Interventions

We are currently poised for new opportunities under recent revisions to the regulations that support employment rights and affirmative action on behalf of individuals with disabilities. In the decade after the Americans with Disabilities Act was implemented in 1990, the workforce participation rate of noninstitutionalized people with disabilities actually declined (Stapleton, Burkhauser, and Houtenville 2004). Although civil rights statutes established protections under the law for applicants and employees, earlier legislative efforts did not provide an incentive to employers to recruit and retain people with disabilities, and courts consistently interpreted disability discrimination law narrowly. However, the ADA Amendments Act of 2008 broadened the pool of people protected by the law, and new federal contractor regulations enacted in 2013 provide numerical goals for employers to increase the numbers of people with disabilities in their workforce. Direct interaction between employers and the Cornell team in the form of demands for technical assistance suggests that these efforts are beginning to have an impact.

Data collection on employer technical assistance requests to staff and faculty at the Employment and Disability Institute reflects trends in information needs. Between 2010 and 2014, 71.6 percent of employer technical assistance requests answered by Cornell University were related to the issue of recruiting people with disabilities. Over that time, we saw a sharp increase in requests related to new regulatory requirements regarding the employment of individuals with disabilities as a percentage of all requests for information. During the first half of 2014, large proportions of employers requested information on voluntary disclosure and self-identification (39 percent of all employer requests), and legal compliance requirements (34 percent) (von Schrader 2014, unpublished internal data). These trends are likely attributable to changes in the regulatory environment created by new rules promulgated under Section 503 of the Rehabilitation Act, and the Vietnam Era Veterans Readjustment Assistance Act.

The new rules of Section 503 are enforced by the Office of Federal Contract Compliance Programs (OFCCP) in the U.S. Department of Labor. They require companies with federal contracts of $10,000 or more to develop active outreach and recruitment efforts to increase the numbers of individuals with disabilities within the federal contractor workforce. Although the numerical goal has been defined as "aspirational," the aim is to achieve a 7 percent "utilization goal," that is, 7 percent of the workforce within each job category being individuals with disabilities (or 7 percent enterprise-wide for those with fewer than one hundred employees) (U.S. Department of Labor 2014b). Meeting this goal may require a strategic shift in contractors' approach to disability and employment, especially in regard to the creation of disability-inclusive workplace cultures. As employers focus now on bringing more people with disabilities into the workplace, they need to be prepared to retain these workers. Correspondingly, outreach efforts must support employers around the on-boarding, performance management, retention, and advancement processes to a greater degree.

There are also new and ongoing initiatives occurring within the federal sector to ensure that federal agencies become model employers of individuals with disabilities. Executive Order 13548 (2010) established a goal of adding one hundred thousand workers with disabilities to the federal workforce. Management Directive 715 from the U.S. Office of Personnel Management (MD 715) requires federal agencies to develop formalized plans to hire and retain people with disabilities, while creating greater transparency and accountability measures. It also requires agencies to set a specific numerical goal for hiring people with "targeted disabilities" each fiscal year.[1] In May 2014, the EEOC issued a notice of proposed rulemaking (NPRM) to amend the regulations under Section 501 of the Rehabilitation Act, which outlines disability nondiscrimination obligations of federal employers. Although, to date, the final rules have not been issued, the possibility exists that new rules under Section 501 will align with aspects of the new federal contractor rules under Section 503. Among the questions being assessed in the NPRM process is this: "Would requiring federal agencies to adopt employment goals for individuals with disabilities help them to become model employers of individuals with disabilities?" (Federal Sector's Obligation to Be a Model Employer 2014).

The end-user of the knowledge created through this Cornell research initiative is broadly defined as "employers." Put in the context of the regulatory environment described above, the most probable users, however, are those who are required (either by OFCCP or by MD 715) to create comprehensive affirmative action plans for the purpose of increasing the number of people with disabilities in their workforce, and are then required to measure their progress. Such is the case for federal agencies, as well as federal contractors and subcontractors. This segment of the end-user audience is composed mostly of large organizations, many of which operate internationally as well. From this perspective, our employer engagement through the CAHRS and TCB groups, as well as the case studies, has appropriately overrepresented this category of employer. Although ideally all employers—regardless of their sector, size, or industry—would proactively seek to include employees with disabilities in a strategic way, the likely reality is that the majority of information seekers would be larger organizations, federal sector employers, and/or government contractors.

In fact, international operations of many of the private sector companies studied by the Cornell team are in countries that have disability quota systems, driving concerns about recruitment, hiring, and other disability-inclusive policies and practices in international locations. Through our collaboration with employers, we heard a need for further development of resources to assist multinational companies to navigate complex disability issues across cultures, international statutes, and the global policy environment.

Translating Knowledge to Effect Change

As each research project within our initiative was completed, we began the process of disseminating our findings, keeping in mind our goal of influencing and improving employer practices. Effective knowledge translation consists of more than just the publication of results. Effective dissemination should help to effect changes in organizations to reflect the good practices identified through the research. Dissemination should reach the organizations for which the results are most relevant and demonstrate to them why they should adopt or reject specific policies or behaviors. Significant consideration was given to our approach in sharing information to reach and entice interested parties to learn more. We used a broad range of outreach approaches, both passive and active, targeting academic audiences as well as employers and policy makers. Passive strategies include efforts aimed at broad groups, whereas some dissemination efforts have included active involvement with individual organizations, in an effort to embed new knowledge within specific practices and policies.

*Business Publications and Presentations*    Traditionally, the first method of disseminating the results of academic research is the publication of scholarly articles in peer-reviewed journals. As is addressed in the rigor-relevance literature (see chapter 2), these kinds of articles add credibility to the research, but they do not have a large influence outside academia, and the time until publication can be lengthy. To share our work with the audiences we believe will ultimately assist in making the greatest definitive change in the employment of people with disabilities—employers and policy makers—we have employed several other approaches while working through the peer-reviewed journal process. Authoring business- and policy-focused briefs and reports helps put our findings into print more quickly. Presenting our findings through webcasts and at business and policy conferences such as those sponsored by the National Industry Liaison Group, the Society for Human Resource Management, the Conference Board, the American Association for Access, Equity, and Diversity, and others, enables us to reach a variety of employers. These briefs and reports refer readers to the scholarly working papers and subsequent publications once they are available. This substantiates our observations and recommendations with research-rooted metrics and helps the work maintain scientific legitimacy and gain acceptance across fields.

*Online Tools*     One of our more ambitious efforts at reaching audiences beyond the readers of traditional academic journals has been to offer direct access to information that might inform further research, policy formulation, and workplace practice. We designed online tools that could address the information needs of particular target audiences. For example, the result of our examination of employer characteristics associated with ADA charges was published in a peer-reviewed policy journal. However, we felt that policy makers, lawyers, employers, and disability advocates would value easier access to information on charges, so we developed an online tool to access state-level descriptive statistics about ADA charges (http://www.disabilitystatistics.org/eeoc/). These data can be enlightening. For example, the tool highlights the rapid rise in retaliation charges over time, suggesting that employers should ensure that they are creating a workplace climate that is inclusive and not retaliatory.

*Reaching Audiences in Their Own Media*     Practitioner magazines and media in general are effective channels to reach decision makers in the workplace. In addition to the reports just mentioned, our partner organizations such as SHRM and TCB each issued news releases and magazine articles about our findings. One team member conducted press interviews and published two different columns related to our findings in the monthly magazine of WorldatWork, the professional association of compensation practitioners (Hallock 2013a, 2013b). Our business association partners also release reports under their own brand and through their distribution networks. Having business associations publish results increases the visibility and credibility of the research to those audiences.

*State-of-the-Science National Conference*     One of our most effective approaches to reaching national policy makers was holding a State-of-the-Science (SOS) conference in Washington, D.C. We invited key policy makers to participate as speakers and panelists, shared key points of our research with them, and heard their reactions. During the conference we interviewed many participants to get their feedback and ideas on the next steps for research on employer practices. We recorded these interviews and used them, together with other material from the conference, to develop an interactive website that allows those who were unable to attend the conference to understand what was covered and learned.

*Multimedia Representations*    In addition to traditional articles and news stories, we captured video responses to our research from notable stakeholders within the employment, advocacy, and policy arenas and created multimedia presentations. We also overcame the challenge of quickly conveying the essence of our research by featuring a carefully selected statistic from our research on each project to be represented as a visually arresting, large-scale infographic. These posters were designed to present thought-provoking pieces of information requiring little time or effort to absorb, and to provide prompts for further discussions of the importance of disability issues in the employment environment.

*Social Media*    Social media is an increasingly popular way to reach people, and employers and policy makers are both active in this sphere. Webcasts and video presentations produced by the ILR School, including some related to this work, are archived in an open format on YouTube for future access. We continue to build our media networks and have been able to leverage the social media reach of the Cornell University ILR School with cross-promotional opportunities to share relevant information and events among the multiple projects. Such networking and collaboration efforts create feedback effects and have netted valuable attention in the mainstream media as well.

## A Novel Approach to Knowledge Translation

We realized early in the research process that employers were in need of practical strategies and user-friendly tools to guide them in their efforts to improve decision-making regarding applicants and employees with disabilities. We made it our goal to provide such resources.

Ultimately, we combined our research findings with our experience building online tools for data dissemination into an interactive website. This tool, BenchmarkABILITY, is designed to offer employers feedback about good employer practices around disability, with examples of both strategic and transactional human resource practices. The website presents both proactive forward-thinking principles and ideas contributing to the bigger picture and strategic direction of the organization (for example, regarding human capital development), and routine HR practices that are ongoing to support HR strategy. The examples will help employers become aware of the total employment life cycle in relation to disability, from application, to hire, to separation. If research is to have a real-world impact, the process of creating and sharing knowledge must be reciprocal. If we fail to consider our employer audience as we develop dissemination methods, the uptake and implementation of that information are likely to be poor. For this reason, employer feedback was incorporated in every stage of formulating BenchmarkABILITY, and employers will continue to be engaged as the tool matures in use, and as changes are made based on its efficacy and utility to the end user.

This online tool that offers employers usable (and in many cases measurable) strategies for recruitment, retention and advancement, accommodation, and inclusion of people with disabilities is a way to close the communications gap between researchers and employers. The BenchmarkABILITY platform recognizes that there are large numbers of individuals responsible for strategic human resource functions within organizations, for whom knowledge translation must occur in smaller, more easily digested, chunks. The following description of the approach taken to this product's design elements and its functionality offers an interesting example of carrying the transdisciplinary approach through the research stage and into dissemination.

## Use of Mental Modeling Technique

There are a variety of approaches to collecting user data to inform the design of websites and interfaces and make them more useful and intuitive. In the development of other employer-focused tools and websites, we have used a specific approach called "mental modeling" as a foundation (Young 2008; Malzer and von Schrader 2014). The mental modeling research process is generative rather than evaluative and uses nondirected, in-depth interviews to collect data on well-defined user groups. In our work, we have developed models of employers and their intersection with disability in the workplace. Task-based audience segmentation is a key component of mental model research, rather than a focus on demographics or characteristics (for example, employer size, industry). This technique defines a target audience by the tasks its members perform, including how they innately approach an objective, how they think about it, and how they ultimately accomplish it. This approach offers a way to think about designing products that does not rely on our assumptions about what would be intuitive, but instead relies on actual behavior and allows the design of products that use employers' own language.

## Knowledge of the HR Process

Our design of BenchmarkABILITY was informed by our employer-focused mental model and our team's extensive knowledge of the HR process from prior HR research and practice experience and teaching. For example, the categories under which promising practices are organized were informed by a conceptualization of the "work life-cycle" and the way in which disability-related transactions may occur within human resources, productivity management, and strategic processes throughout that cycle. Our team's deep understanding of organizations was invaluable to engaging an informed and active group of stakeholders in the development of research objectives, knowledge translation efforts, and ultimately BenchmarkABILITY.

## Selection of Topics for Inclusion

We were able to organize a series of over 90 action items against which an employer can self-assess organizational progress toward hiring and inclusion goals. Items are organized into checklists by category, following the concept of the employment life-cycle mentioned earlier. Within each category, individual items identified for inclusion range from what we perceive to be more transactional activities, such as providing notice to job applicants that accommodations are available, to strategic activities such as seeking out disability-owned businesses for procurement. One of the checklists consists of associated metrics to measure progress across key parts of the employment and accommodation experience. In addition, we included key evidence from across our discrete research studies that substantiates the case for considering each issue. For example, we highlighted that our SHRM member survey revealed that practices such as participating in internship programs for individuals with disabilities and having explicit organizational goals are associated with much higher rates (almost six times) of hiring people with disabilities (Erickson et al. 2014).

## Key Features

We know that HR professionals are busy and want to get real-time feedback. Each of the checklists consists of short, survey-like assessments that can be completed in relatively little time, and upon their completion a report can be generated to share results. The site itself is designed with the knowledge needs, time limitations, and the diverse organizational climates of segmented employer audiences in mind. The tool gives the employer the flexibility to address the issues of highest priority first (for example, an employer with solid recruiting practices may be more interested in assessing practices to improve retention). The real-time feedback and access to more information and the availability of on-demand technical assistance enhance functionality and provide added value for the user. The final step in the development process was to reengage employer stakeholders for feedback and user testing to assist the design team to better understand whether the product design and content were meeting the needs of its intended audience.

Over time the collection of user data will enable Cornell University to benchmark organizations against one another, examining differences between organizations by industry or organizational size. The manner in which the tool is used will also provide insight into employer behavior, which ultimately can generate new research questions, completing and restarting the knowledge-to-action cycle by returning the results of research activities to the researchers to inform new initiatives.

## Lessons Learned for an Effective Transdisciplinary Approach

This book highlights the data sources, methodologies, and disciplines that can contribute to an improved understanding of the employment status and experiences of people with disabilities. It has called for the engagement of employers in the identification and assessment of employer policies and practices that enhance employment outcomes for this group. People with expertise in a variety of fields collaborated to complete the comprehensive research conducted here and to bridge the areas where knowledge gaps remain in the various techniques employed. We have designed this book to convey the interrelatedness of these efforts, and we want to highlight the fact that stimulating synergies can occur when multiple fields work together with a common purpose and focus on a common theme. As ideas from unique perspectives intersect, they enhance the process of discovery. We have learned much in this process as researchers and individuals.

Building an outstanding transdisciplinary team that collectively reaches the desired goal takes a concerted effort over many months. The steps in our own research journey included the following:

- identifying the relevant disciplinary expertise needed
- becoming familiar with a body of literature that is diverse in both theoretical and methodological approaches
- identifying possible individual and organizational candidates for collaborative partnering
- cultivating mutual advantage in our approach
- taking time for clarifying and moving toward a more unified problem definition
- integrating initially independently formulated research assumptions and hypotheses into a cohesive perspective
- becoming mindful of team power relationships across varying disciplines, positions, and roles
- developing needed friendships and collegiality to build mutual trust and respect that ultimately can transcend the inherent disciplinary perspectives and biases

Transdisciplinary ventures are not without their challenges. It is worth identifying a few for those whom we may have inspired to pursue this path. Among the challenges of working across disciplines may be the need for more time to carry out projects, because it is inherently a group process; the need for more serious intellectual effort to understand the disciplinary perspectives of others; and the difficulty of evaluating the effectiveness and validity of particular outcomes when tools and methodologies vary between disciplines. Additionally, in academic scholarship, transdisciplinary research is still not necessarily understood or as highly valued in the processes of tenure and promotion as is discipline-specific research. We can transcend these potential barriers by sharing goals and identifying a common problem, building common "meaning" (beyond language) with a common conceptual framework, agreeing on the problem in question, and working toward true integration of group resources in the final research products and outcomes to be shared with the intended target audiences.

Individual researchers can experience personal challenges as well. This type of approach necessitates a conceptual representation across sometimes quite different social structures and research traditions, each with its own expected professional norms, methods of inquiry, and vernacular. This requires a willingness to move beyond the ideas of disciplinary superiority that many of us are taught to embrace. Each professional who desires to move toward a truly transdisciplinary approach to all facets of research must be personally mindful about cultivating an ability to listen openly and check perceptions. This gives all group members equal access to information, data, meetings, and project leaders, and guards against marginalization of any group discipline or member.

We have learned a great deal empirically about which employer policies and practices have significant positive effects on employment outcomes for people with disabilities, and we have been able to methodically catalog many of the data sources and research methods that best inform this kind of inquiry. We have made a meaningful effort to learn the best ways to share our findings with the key targets who we believe are the needed agents of change for improving employment outcomes for individuals with disabilities.

But we would be remiss if we did not talk about how much we have each learned about what it truly means to be a transdisciplinary team in the best sense of that concept. Each of us has needed to stretch our individual disciplinary and professional perspectives to open our minds to sometimes quite different ways of conceptualizing and approaching what we have all come to adopt as our common problem of focus. Many of our researchers, prior to this work, had only passing exposure to disability issues. But every research team member proactively applied their distinct expertise and energy with a high degree of rigor, sought meaningful relevance for the problem at hand from their own unique knowledge base, and over many months consistently engaged in a respectful and open dialogue to tap other members' distinct and different expertise and viewpoints. All of us would say that it has been a privilege to be a part of these efforts and of this collective team.

## Going Forward

Although we are proud of what these efforts have accomplished, much remains to be done to fully understand which employer policy and practice levers can be pulled in what manner to have the greatest positive impact on the labor market outcomes of individuals with disabilities. Throughout our initiative and as our current research efforts have come to fruition, we have identified promising next steps to heighten the possibility of further and richer findings, stronger employer engagement, and broader adoption of inclusive practices that can improve employment results for people with disabilities. We embrace the belief that transdisciplinary teams are best positioned to address these issues in a manner that puts the evolution of employer practices front and center. We encourage others to join us on this journey.

### Using National Survey Datasets

We designed informational outreach products and online tools as a part of our knowledge translation strategy with the idea that these would be resources available to our stakeholders in an ongoing and growing way. Therefore, maintaining and expanding the Disability and Compensation Variables Catalog (chapter 3) remains a top priority. The DCV Catalog will be most beneficial to researchers when it encompasses an even larger set of data files that provide unique information. Future endeavors on this front may include incorporating employer-level data, targeting key supplements from national surveys that collect disability information, and introducing national surveys linked to administrative datasets. The enhanced catalog can then be used to guide the choice of source data for research in a variety of new and continuing areas of concern, such as the impact of employer health benefits or employer accommodations on retention.

Expanding data access could encourage investigation of the impacts of the Affordable Care Act on employment patterns and job tenure among people with disabilities, as well as identify any inherent disincentives to work that are created by the current system of means-tested benefits allocation. Compensation is another area where further mining of existing national datasets could offer new insights. Far more is known, for example, about the factors that explain the pay gap for women than for people with disabilities. Questions also remain as to why different datasets produce such divergent point estimates of the pay gap between individuals with disabilities and those without. Further quantitative analysis is needed on this puzzle, and on how multiple characteristics (for example, gender and disability status, or type of disability status) interact in relation to compensation outcomes. We are hopeful that by extending the research using national datasets, we may also be able to establish methods to more accurately evaluate employer practices and related employment outcomes of people with disabilities across and within particular industry sectors.

## Administrative Data

Providing access to administrative data on employer practices continues to be a goal. We have begun developing public-use data aggregates of the EEOC charge data, and these have been used by researchers, employers, and others to better understand where in the employment process employers are experiencing charges. Beyond providing easier access to source data, there is much to be learned from additional research on administrative data, particularly through examination of organizational HR data and metrics, a relatively untapped data source. As more data related to disability are collected on employees in the private sector as a result of Section 503, the set of questions that can be addressed grows sizably. Currently, the federal government data on employment outcomes for people with disabilities are some of the best available, and the federal government has been leading the way for the private sector in implementing disability-related practices. There is much to learn in this sector.

One particular area where we see great value in expanding the coverage of federal administrative reports is the Equal Employment Opportunity Commission. The EEOC currently collects data from many employers on the composition of their workforce in terms of gender and race/ethnicity. As employers with federal contracts begin collecting data on disability, it would be highly informative to have this information reported in aggregate and available to researchers, allowing the replication of important work that has been done with other protected groups; but the first step is requiring employers to report this information. The EEOC is moving toward collecting compensation data within the EEO-1 framework, by the existing gender and race/ethnicity categories. Our research on pay gaps using national datasets suggests that expanding administrative data to include compensation of individuals with disabilities could further illuminate this continuing challenge.

Another future direction would be to use administrative data to understand the alignment of supply-side rehabilitation and training initiatives with demand-side needs and priorities. Within a given organization, we could explore how state initiatives, especially those that focus on skills training in technology, have made a difference in the hiring of people with disabilities. We could uncover which characteristics of such programs lead to greatest success inside the walls of a given workplace, and whether factors for success differ in relation to the management, employee culture, or organization.

## Surveying Employers and Individuals with Disabilities

While data sources already in existence can be used to study a plethora of ideas, much value is contributed by surveys developed with a specific research agenda in mind. Generating innovative surveys with the ability to track the career development and promotions of employees with a more nuanced understanding of outcomes will enable researchers to study the impacts of differing career development practices and policies for different disability populations. Partnerships with national employer associations and those representing the interests of an aging workforce can facilitate further study of the impact of proactive employer interventions to sustain employment with appropriate workplace accommodations, when illness or injury occurs in the aging process. Collaborations with disability advocacy networks and associations assure that individuals with disabilities and their family members have a voice in the research process. Working with federal agency representatives interested in the employment of individuals with disabilities would facilitate the development of federal sector surveys that could be used to test which practices are empirically associated with higher rates of employment among people with disabilities. The questions that can be addressed with employer surveys are many, and the current interest among the employer community around disability employment may mean greater engagement and response to a survey on this topic. Working with key stakeholders in the policy, employer, and disability communities can help guide the development of research questions and surveys that will make the results have maximum impact.

## Case Studies

Data are immensely powerful in testing theories, but to truly understand the reasons underlying observed outcomes or patterns of behavior it is necessary to get inside organizations and speak directly with employers and employees. By using case studies to gain insights about what actually transpires in the workplace, we can explore the effects of disclosing a disability to different targets on longer-term employment outcomes. Related to this is whether members of disability employee resource groups who network with a broader group of individuals with influence improve their employment outcomes. It would be enlightening to hear from managers and colleagues who work alongside an individual with a disability regarding whether they have had a shift in awareness and openness over time as a result. These same employees and managers may have ideas about the content and design of disability training programs that have been or could be the most effective in changing their own behaviors. Finally, to understand more about the inclusion experiences of lower-level employees with disabilities, research can be done on the impact of having those in top leadership positions who disclose their own disabilities. Carefully examining the group conditions and processes involved in driving performance benefits from disability diversity in work groups and organizations would represent a contribution not just to disability research but also to diversity research more generally.

## Knowledge Translation

The focus on conveying future research findings to the individuals and organizations that can use this information is key to truly impacting the lives of people with disabilities. The world of communication channels is multifaceted and expanding rapidly. It will be ever more important to leverage technological advancements to create customizable training and benchmarking tools that operate in the online space of today's diverse workplaces, as well as work within employer networks to distribute lessons learned through tried-and-true mediums such as conferences and research briefs. Future initiatives may uncover ways to articulate more clearly for employers the measurable benefits of hiring individuals with disabilities and may reveal creative ways to provide more inclusive and productive workplace climates.

Cultivating new behavioral insights that will compel further progress via informed and effective external *and internal* workplace policies takes a transdisciplinary approach. We hope our insights, findings, and these suggestions for going forward will capture the attention, imagination, and enthusiasm of an even broader array of employers, professionals, researchers, and disciplinary expertise in the months and years to come. Along this journey, knowledge translation needs to remain in lockstep if the intended destination of increased employment opportunities for people with disabilities is to be finally reached.

## A Final Word for Employers

Equitable employment participation and workplace inclusion for individuals with disabilities are issues that truly touch each of us, regardless of country and place in the world, moving beyond the boundaries of gender, race and ethnicity, religion, birth origin, and other differences that divide us. The workplace is the front line in this struggle. Complicated market forces and financial pressures create complex and ever-changing challenges for businesses of every size—challenges that ultimately lead to survival or demise. Despite or perhaps because of the intensity of the business environment today, bringing all available talent to the organizational table using the fullest array of human capital possible is a national imperative.

Perhaps, in finding a common cause in the pursuit of equity for people with disabilities, we can transcend the differences that can limit individuals, businesses, and economies from achieving their fullest potential. Equitable access to socioeconomic and employment opportunities, without barriers of discrimination, should be the rightful heritage for all humankind, and one that both underpins and fuels, not diminishes, competition and economic advancement. This is a goal well worth pursuing.

# NOTES

### 1. Disability and Employment: Framing the Problem, and Our Approach

1. USDE-NIDRR Grant No. H133B100017. For further information see the related Cornell University website at http://www.employerpracticesrrtc.org/.

2. For examples see Bagenstos 2004a, 2004b; Colker 1999; O'Brien 2001; Stein 2003, 2007.

3. Burkhauser, Butler, and Weathers 1999; Burkhauser and Daly 2002; Cook and Burke 2002; Haveman and Wolfe 2000; Schalock 2004; Scotch 2001; Silverstein 2000; Stapleton and Burkhauser 2003; Stapleton et al. 2006; Wittenburg, Mann, and Thompkins 2013; Yelin 1997.

4. Chan, Rosenthal, and Pruett 2008; Fabian, Leucking, and Tilson 1995; Gilbride, Stensrud, and Connolly 1992; Gilbride et al. 2000; Gilbride et al. 2003; Gold et al. 2012; Innis-Johnson 2012; Smart and Smart 2006; Stensrud 2007; Stoddard and Premo 2004.

5. Colella 1996, 2001; Colella, DeNisi, and Varma 1997, 1998; Colella, Paetzold, and Belliveau 2004; Colella and Stone 2005; Colella and Varma 1999; Hunt and Hunt 2004; Hyland and Rutigliano 2013; Ren, Paetzold, and Colella 2008; Schur et al. 2009; Stone and Colella 1996; Vornholt, Uitdewilligen, and Nijhuis 2013.

6. Geisen and Harder 2011; Habeck et al. 2010; McLellan, Pransky, and Shaw 2001; Rosenthal et al. 2007; Scotton 2009; Shrey and Hursh 1999.

### 2. Engaging Employers as Stakeholders

1. See http://www.hhs.gov/ohrp/index.html.

2. More about The Conference Board can be found at https://www.conference-board.org/about/.

3. More can be found about CAHRS at http://cahrs.ilr.cornell.edu/About/.

### 3. Exploring National Survey Data

1. Nazarov, Erickson, and Bruyère (2014) offer more examples of how national surveys can be used.

2. Additional detail can be seen in Barrington, Hallock, and Xin (2014) and Hallock, Xin, and Barrington (2014).

3. The link for the Disability and Compensation Variables Catalog is http://www.disability statistics.org/eprrtc/codebook.cfm.

### 4. Using Administrative Data

1. Of course, the entity gathering the administrative data bears a collection cost; however, the fact that the data are collected for the entity's own use means there is no cost to the researcher for the initial collection. That is not to say that access to preexisting administrative, or even survey, data is free, which is discussed later in this chapter.

2. The researcher can account for observed patterns before and after a policy change in addition to unobserved, individual characteristics that are time invariant.

3. It is important to note that while administrative data provide information on every recipient of the program, they fail to describe the overall participation rate. This failure is due to the fact that nonrecipients are not included in the data.

4. More information can be found at http://www.affirmativeactionlawadvisor.com/files/2014/10/Scheduling-Letter-final-09-12-2014.pdf.

### 5. Surveying Employers and Individuals with Disabilities

1. For example, http://www.qualtrics.com/university/researchsuite/advanced-building/advanced-options-drop-down/check-survey-accessibility/ and https://www.surveymonkey.com/mp/508-website-accessibility/.

2. DMI is a comprehensive, publicly available database that provides information on over 10 million U.S. business establishment locations in the United States, including public, private, and government organizations.

### 6. Conducting Case Studies

1. Chapters 3, 4, and 5 further address these topics.

### 7. Translating Knowledge to Practice, and the Way Forward

1. "Targeted disabilities" are disabilities that the federal government, as a matter of policy, has identified for special emphasis. The targeted disabilities are deafness, blindness, missing extremities, partial paralysis, complete paralysis, convulsive disorders, mental retardation, mental illness, and distortion of limb and/or spine.

# REFERENCES

Able Trust. 2003. "Dispelling Myths of an Untapped Workforce: A Study of Employer Attitudes toward Hiring Individuals with Disabilities." Tallahassee, FL: Able Trust. http://www.abletrust.org/news/Able_Trust_Employer_Attitudes_Study.pdf.

Abt Associates. 2005. *Cost and Benefits of HCAHPS: Final Report*. Cambridge, MA: Abt Associates Inc. http://www.cms.gov/Medicare/Quality-Initiatives-Patient-Assessment-Instruments/HospitalQualityInits/downloads/HCAHPSCostsBenefits200512.pdf.

American Anthropological Association. 2010. "Ethics Task Force—Draft Principle: Do No Harm." http://blog.aaanet.org/ethics-task-force/ethics-task-force-first-principle/.

Anderson, James C., James A. Narus, and Wouter van Rossum. 2006. "Customer Value Propositions in Business Markets." *Harvard Business Review* 84 (3). http://hbr.org/2006/03/customer-value-propositions-in-business-markets/ar/1.

Atkinson, Michael P., Adam Guetz, and Lawrence M. Wein. 2009. *A Dynamic Model for Post-Traumatic Stress Disorder among U.S. Troops in Operation Iraqi Freedom*. Stanford, CA: Institute for Computational and Mathematical Engineering.

Autor, David H. 2011. *The Unsustainable Rise of the Disability Rolls in the United States*. NBER Working Paper No. 17697. Vol. 2010. Cambridge, MA: National Bureau of Economic Research. doi:10.3386/w17697.

Bagenstos, Samuel R. 2004a. "The Future of Disability Law." *Yale Law Journal* 114 (1): 1–82.

————. 2004b. "Has the Americans with Disabilities Act Reduced Employment for People with Disabilities?" *Berkeley Journal of Employment and Labor Law* 25: 527–63.

Barrington, Linda, and Susanne M. Bruyère. 2012. "Introduction, Background, and History." In *Employment and Work*, edited by Susanne M. Bruyère and Linda Barrington, 1–58. Thousand Oaks, CA: Sage Publications.

Barrington, Linda, Susanne M. Bruyère, Peter Linkow, Sarah Potter, Nora Vele, and Stephen King. 2013. "Challenges on the Minds of Employers: Learnings from Employer-Participant Working Groups." In *Innovative Research on Employer Practices: Improving Employment for People with Disabilities; State of the Science Conference*. Ithaca, NY: Cornell University. http://www.epstateofthescience.org/.

Barrington, Linda, Susanne M. Bruyère, and Margaret Waelder. 2014. "Employer Practices in Improving Employment Outcomes for People with Disabilities: A Transdisciplinary and Employer-Inclusive Research Approach." *Rehabilitation Research, Policy, and Education* 28 (4): 208–24. doi:10.1891/2168–6653.28.4.208.

Barrington, Linda, and Kevin F. Hallock. 2013. "Can Compensation Design Issues Be Resolved Better by Having Organizations and Academics Combine Forces?" *World@Work Journal* 22 (2).

Barrington, Linda, Kevin F. Hallock, and Xin Jin. 2014. *The Pay Gap and the Total Compensation Gap*. Ithaca, NY: Cornell University Press.

Baruch, Yehuda. 1999. "Response Rate in Academic Studies—a Comparative Analysis." *Human Relations* 52 (4): 421–38.

Baruch, Yehuda, and B. C. Holtom. 2008. "Survey Response Rate Levels and Trends in Organizational Research." *Human Relations* 61 (8): 1139–60. doi:10.1177/0018726708094863.

Bernell, Stephanie L. 2003. "Theoretical and Applied Issues in Defining Disability in Labor Marker Research." *Journal of Disability Policy Studies* 14 (1): 36–45.

Bjelland, Melissa J., Susanne M. Bruyère, Sarah von Schrader, Andrew J. Houtenville, Antonio Ruiz-Quintanilla, and Douglas A. Webber. 2010. "Age and Disability Employment Discrimination: Occupational Rehabilitation Implications." *Journal of Occupational Rehabilitation* 20 (4): 456–71. doi:10.1007/s10926–009–9194-z.

Bjelland, Melissa J., Richard V. Burkhauser, Sarah von Schrader, and Andrew J. Houtenville. 2011. *2010 Progress Report on the Economic Well-Being of Working-Age People with Disabilities*. Ithaca, NY: Rehabilitation Research and Training Center for Economic Research on Employment Policy for Persons with Disabilities.

Blanck, Peter, and Helen A. Schartz. 2005. "Special Issue: Corporate Culture and Disability." *Behavioral Sciences & the Law* 23:1 2.

Bliese, P. D. 2000. "Within-Group Agreement, Non-Independence, and Reliability: Implications for Data Aggregation and Analysis." In *Multilevel Theory, Research, and Methods in Organizations: Foundations, Extensions, and New Directions*, edited by K. J. Klein and Steve W. J. Kozlowski, 349–81. San Francisco: Jossey-Bass.

Bowen, D. E., and C. Ostroff. 2004. "Understanding HRM-Firm Performance Linkages: The Role of the 'Strength' of the HRM System." *Academy of Management Review* 29 (2): 203–21.

Bowling, Ann. 2005. "Mode of Questionnaire Administration Can Have Serious Effects on Data Quality." *Journal of Public Health* 27 (3): 281–91. doi:10.1093/pubmed/fdi031.

Brannick, Alison, and Susanne M. Bruyère. 1999. *The ADA at Work: Implementation of the Employment Provisions of the Americans with Disabilities Act*. Alexandria, VA: Society for Human Resource Management.

Brewer, M. B., and Norman Miller. 1984. "Beyond the Contact Hypothesis: Theoretical Perspectives on Desegregation." In *Group in Contact: The Psychology of Desegregation*, edited by N. Miller and M. B. Brewer, 281–302. Orlando, FL: Academic Press.

———. 1988. "Contact and Cooperation: When Do They Work?" In *Eliminating Racism: Means and Controversies*, edited by P. Katz and D. Taylor, 315–26. New York: Plenum Press.

Broussard, Thomas G., Jr. 2006. "Who Is Accommodating Whom? Small Business Practices and Attitudes regarding Hiring People with Disabilities: An Exploratory Study." Dissertation, Brandeis University, Heller School for Social Policy and Management. UMI No. 3229896.

Bruyère, Susanne M. 1993. "Participatory Action Research: Its Implications for Family Members of Persons with Disabilities." *Journal of Vocational Rehabilitation* 3 (2): 62–68.

———. 2000. *Disability Employment Policies and Practices in Private and Federal Sector Organizations*. Ithaca, NY: Cornell University, Program on Employment and Disability. http://digitalcommons.ilr.cornell.edu/edicollect/63.

———. 2002. "Employer Perspectives on Disability Nondiscrimination Practices." In *Careers across America, 2002: Best Practices and Ideas in Career Development*, 33–42. Chicago: ERIC/CASS.

Bruyère, Susanne M., William A. Erickson, and Joshua Ferrentino. 2003. "Identity and Disability in the Workplace." *William and Mary Law Review* 44 (3): 1173–96.

Bruyère, Susanne M., William A. Erickson, and Richard Horne. 2002a. *Disability Employment Policies and Practices in U.S. Federal Government Agencies: EEO/HR and Supervisor Perspectives; Report by the Presidential Task Force on Employment of Adults with Disabilities*. Ithaca, NY: Cornell University, Program on Employment and Disability. http://digitalcommons.ilr.cornell.edu/edicollect/66.

———. 2002b. *Survey of the Federal Government on Supervisor Practices in Employment*. Ithaca, NY: Program on Employment and Disability. http://digitalcommons. ilr.cornell.edu/edicollect/65/.

Bruyère, Susanne M., William A. Erickson, and Sara A. VanLooy. 2000. "HR's Role in Managing Disability in the Workplace." *Employment Relations Today*, Autumn, 47–66. http://digitalcommons.ilr.cornell.edu/edicollect/119/.

———. 2005. "Information Technology and the Workplace: Implications for Persons with Disabilities." *Disability Studies Quarterly* 25 (2).

———. 2006. "The Impact of Business Size on Employer ADA Response." *Rehabilitation Counseling Bulletin* 49 (4): 194–206.

Bruyère, Susanne M., Thomas Golden, and Sara VanLooy. 2011. "Legislation and Rehabilitation Professionals." In *Medical Aspects of Disability*, edited by Steven Flanagan, Herb Zaretsky, and Alex Moroz, 4th ed., 669–86. New York, NY: Springer Publishing Company.

Bruyère, Susanne M., and Richard Horne. 1999. *Disability Employment Policies and Practices in U.S. Federal Government Agencies: Report by the Presidential Task Force on Employment of Adults with Disabilities.* Ithaca, NY: Program on Employment and Disability. http://digitalcommons.ilr.cornell.edu/edicollect/62/.

Burke, Jana, Jill Bezyak, Robert T. Fraser, Joseph Pete, Nicole Ditchman, and Fong Chan. 2013. "Employers' Attitudes towards Hiring and Retaining People with Disabilities: A Review of the Literature." *Australian Journal of Rehabilitation Counselling* 19 (01): 21–38. doi:10.1017/jrc.2013.2.

Burkhauser, Richard V., J. S. Butler, and Yang-Woo Kim. 1995. "The Importance of Employer Accommodation on the Job Duration of Workers with Disabilities: A Hazard Model Approach." *Labour Economics* 2 (2): 109–130. doi:http://dx.doi.org/10.1016/0927–5371(95)80049–4.

Burkhauser, Richard V., J. S. Butler, Yang-Woo Kim, and Robert R. Weathers II. 1999. "The Importance of Accommodation on the Timing of Disability Insurance Applications." *Journal of Human Resources* 34 (3): 589–611.

Burkhauser, Richard V., J. S. Butler, and Robert R. Weathers II. 1999. "How Policy Variables Influence the Timing of Social Security Disability Insurance Applications." *Social Security Bulletin* 64 (1): 52–83.

Burkhauser, Richard V., and Mary C. Daly. 2002. "Policy Watch: U.S. Disability Policy in a Changing Environment." *Journal of Economic Perspectives* 16 (1): 213–24.

CAHRS. 2011. *CAHRS Working Group—Attraction, Retention and Reward for Employees with Disabilities.* October 14. Ithaca, NY: Center for Advanced Human Resource Studies. https://est05.esalestrack.com/eSalesTrack/Content/Content.ashx?file=54a9007c-6246–4fbc-9c55-a269da23904f.pdf.

———. 2012. *CAHRS Working Group—Organizational Culture and Employer Practices with Respect to Persons with Disabilities.* Ithaca, NY: Center for Advanced Human Resource Studies. https://est05.esalestrack.com/eSalesTrack/Content/Content.ashx?file=4de0f9be-9dea-4500–9e71-c620531b3e3e.pdf.

Card, David, Raj Chetty, Martin Feldstein, and Emmanuel Saez. 2010. "Expanding Access to Administrative Data for Research in the United States." Berkeley: University of California. http://eml.berkeley.edu/~saez/card-chetty-feldstein-saezNSF10dataaccess.pdf.

Cartwright, B., P. R. Edwards, and Q. Wang. 2011. "Job and Industry Gender Segregation: NAICS Categories and EEO-1 Job Groups." *Monthly Labor Review* 134 (11): 37–50.

Chan, David. 1998. "Functional Relations among Constructs in the Same Content Domain at Different Levels of Analysis: A Typology of Composition Models." *Journal of Applied Psychology* 83 (2): 234–46. doi:10.1037/0021–9010.83.2.234.

Chan, Fong, David A. Rosenthal, and Steven R. Pruett. 2008. "Evidence-Based Practice in the Provision of Rehabilitation Services." *Journal of Rehabilitation* 74 (2): 3.

Chan, Fong, David Strauser, Robert Gervey, and Eun-Jeong Lee. 2010. "Introduction to Demand-Side Factors Related to Employment of People with Disabilities." *Journal of Occupational Rehabilitation* 20 (4): 407–11. doi:10.1007/s10926–010–9243–7.

Charles, Kerwin Kofi. 2004. "The Extent and Effect of Employer Compliance with the Accommodations Mandates of the Americans with Disabilities Act." *Journal of Disability Policy Studies* 15 (2): 86–96.

Chetty, Raj. 2012. "Time Trends in the Use of Administrative Data for Empirical Research." Cambridge, MA: Harvard University. http://obs.rc.fas.harvard.edu/chetty/admin_data_trends.pdf.

Clair, Judith A., Joy E. Beatty, and Tammy L. MacLean. 2005. "Out of Sight but Not out of Mind: Managing Invisible Social Identities in the Workplace." *Academy of Management Review* 30 (1): 78–95. 10.5465/AMR.2005.15281431.

Colella, Adrienne. 1996. "Organizational Socialization of Newcomers with Disabilities: A Framework for Future Research." *Research in Personnel and Human Resources Management* 14: 351–417.

———. 2001. "Coworker Distributive Fairness Judgments of the Workplace Accommodation of Employees with Disabilities." *Academy of Management Review* 26: 100–116.

Colella, Adrienne, and Susanne M. Bruyère. 2011. "Disability and Employment: New Directions for Industrial/Organizational Psychology." In *American Psychological Association Handbook on Industrial Organizational Psychology*, vol. 1, 473–503q. Washington, DC: American Psychological Association.

Colella, Adrienne, Angelo S. DeNisi, and Arup Varma. 1997. "Appraising the Performance of Employees with Disabilities: A Review and Model." *Human Resource Management Review* 7 (1): 27–53. doi:http://dx.doi.org/10.1016/S1053–4822(97)90004–8.

———. 1998. "The Impact of Ratee's Disability on Performance Judgments and Choice of Partner: The Role of Disability-Job Fit Stereotypes and Interdependence of Rewards." *Journal of Applied Psychology* 83: 102–11.

Colella, Adrienne, Ramona L. Paetzold, and Maura A. Belliveau. 2004. "Factors Affecting Coworkers' Procedural Justice Inferences of the Workplace Accommodations of Employees with Disabilities." *Personnel Psychology* 57 (1): 1–23.

Colella, Adrienne, and Dianna L. Stone. 2005. "Workplace Discrimination toward Persons with Disabilities: A Call for Some New Research Directions." In *Discrimination at Work: The Psychological and Organizational Bases*, edited by R. L. Dipboye and A. Colella, 407–43. Mahwah, NJ: Lawrence Erlbaum Associates.

Colella, Adrienne, and Arup Varma. 1999. "Disability-Job Fit Stereotypes and the Evaluation of Persons with Disabilities at Work." *Journal of Occupational Rehabilitation* 9 (2): 79–95.

Colker, Ruth. 1999. "The Americans with Disabilities Act: A Windfall for Defendants." *Harvard Civil Rights Civil Liberties Law Review* 34: 99–162.

Conyers, Liza, K. B. Boomer, and Brian T. McMahon. 2005. "Workplace Discrimination and HIV/AIDS: The National EEOC ADA Research Project." *Work* 25 (1): 37–48.

Cook, Judith A., and Jane Burke. 2002. "Public Policy and Employment of People with Disabilities: Exploring New Paradigms." *Behavioral Sciences & the Law* 20: 541–57.

Cornell University. 2015. "Quick Facts about Cornell University." http://irp.dpb.cornell.edu/university-factbook/quick-facts.

Cuddy, Amy J.C., Susan T. Fiske, and Peter Glick. 2007. "The BIAS Map: Behaviors from Intergroup Affect and Stereotypes." *Journal of Personality and Social Psychology* 92 (4): 631–48. doi:10.1037/0022–3514.92.4.631.

Cycyota, Cynthia S., and David A. Harrison. 2006. "What (Not) to Expect When Surveying Executives: A Meta-Analysis of Top Manager Response Rates and Techniques over Time." *Organizational Research Methods* 9 (2): 133–60.

Daly, Mary C., and John Bound. 1996. "Worker Adaptation and Employer Accommodation following the Onset of a Health Impairment." *Journals of Gerontology Series B: Psychological Sciences and Social Sciences* 51B (2): S53–60. doi:10.1093/geronb/51B.2.S53.

DeLeire, Thomas. 2000. "The Wage and Employment Effects of the Americans with Disabilities Act." *Journal of Human Resources* 35 (4): 693–715.

Denning, Stephen. 2006. "Effective Storytelling: Strategic Business Narrative Techniques." *Strategy & Leadership* 34 (1): 42–48.

DeRue, D. Scott, and Ned Wellman. 2009. "Developing Leaders via Experience: The Role of Developmental Challenge, Learning Orientation, and Feedback Availability." *Journal of Applied Psychology* 94 (4): 859–75. doi:10.1037/a0015317.

Deutskens, Elisabeth, Ko De Ruyter, Martin Wetzels, and Paul Oosterveld. 2004. "Response Rate and Response Quality of Internet-Based Surveys: An Experimental Study." *Marketing Letters* 15 (1): 21–36.

Dillman, Don. 2000. *Mail and Internet Surveys: The Tailored Design Method*. New York: Wiley.

Disability Case Study Research Consortium. 2008. *Conducting and Benchmarking Inclusive Employment Policies, Practices, and Culture*. Washington, DC: U.S. Department of Labor, Office of Disability Employment Policy.

Dixon, K. A., Doug Kruse, and Carl E. Van Horn. 2003. *Restricted Access: A Survey of Employers about People with Disabilities and Lowering Barriers to Work*. New Brunswick, NJ: Rutgers University Heldrich Center for Workforce Development.

Domzal, C., Andrew J. Houtenville, and R. Sharma. 2008. *Survey of Employer Perspectives on the Employment of People with Disabilities: Technical Report*. Prepared under contract to the Office of Disability and Employment Policy, U.S. Department of Labor. McLean, VA: CESSI.

Dragoni, Lisa. 2005. "Understanding the Emergence of State Goal Orientation in Organizational Work Groups: The Role of Leadership and Multilevel Climate Perceptions." *Journal of Applied Psychology* 90 (6): 1084–95. doi:10.1037/0021–9010.90. 6.1084.

Dragoni, Lisa, In-Sue Oh, Paul VanKatwyk, and Paul E. Tesluk. 2011. "Developing Executive Leaders: The Relative Contribution of Cognitive Ability, Personality, and the Accumulation of Work Experience in Predicting Strategic Thinking Competency." *Personnel Psychology* 64 (4): 829–64. doi:10.1111/j.1744–6570.2011.01229.x.

Dragoni, Lisa, Paul E. Tesluk, Joyce E. A. Russell, and In-Sue Oh. 2009. "Understanding Managerial Development: Integrating Developmental Assignments, Learning Orientation, and Access to Developmental Opportunities in Predicting Managerial Competencies." *Academy of Management Journal* 52 (4): 731.

Dwertman, David, Lisa H. Nishii, and Daan van Knippenberg. Forthcoming. "Disentangling the Fairness/Discrimination from Synergy Perspective of Diversity Climate: Time to Move the Field Forward." *Journal of Management*.

Eagly, Alice H., and Linda L. Carli. 2007. "Women and the Labyrinth of Leadership." *Harvard Business Review* 85 (9): 63–71.

Eagly, Alice H., and Steven J. Karau. 2002. "Role Congruity Theory of Prejudice toward Female Leaders." *Psychological Review* 109 (3): 573–98. doi:10.103 7/0033–295X.109.3.573.

Ellemers, Naomi, Ad van Knippenberg, and Henk Wilke. 1990. "The Influence of Permeability of Group Boundaries and Stability of Group Status on Strategies of Individual Mobility and Social Change." *British Journal of Social Psychology* 29 (3): 233–46. doi:10.1111/j.2044–8309.1990.tb00902.x.

Ely, Robin J., and David A. Thomas. 2001. "Cultural Diversity at Work: The Effects of Diversity Perspectives on Work Group Processes and Outcomes." *Administrative Science Quarterly* 46 (2): 229–73.

Ensari, Nurcan Karamolla, and Norman Miller. 2006. "The Application of the Personalization Model in Diversity Management." *Group Processes & Intergroup Relations* 9 (4): 589–607. doi:10.1177/1368430206067679.

Erickson, William A., Camille Lee, and Sarah von Schrader. 2014. *2013 Disability Status Report: United States*. Ithaca, NY: Cornell University, ILR School, Employment and Disability Institute. http://www.disabilitystatistics.org/.

Erickson, William A., Sarah von Schrader, Susanne M. Bruyère, and Linda Barrington. 2012. "Annotated Data, Statistics, Tables and Graphs." In *Employment and Work*, edited by Susanne M. Bruyère and Linda Barrington, 263–308. Thousand Oaks, CA: Sage Publications.

Erickson, William A., Sarah von Schrader, Susanne M. Bruyère, and Sara A. VanLooy. 2013. "The Employment Environment: Employer Perspectives, Policies, and Practices regarding the Employment of Persons with Disabilities." *Rehabilitation Counseling Bulletin* 57 (4): 195–208. doi:10.1177/0034355213509841.

Erickson, William A., Sarah von Schrader, Susanne M. Bruyère, Sara A. VanLooy, and David S. Matteson. 2014. "Disability-Inclusive Employer Practices and Hiring of Individuals with Disabilities." *Rehabilitation Research, Policy, and Education* 28 (4): 309–27.

Executive Order No. 13548. 2010. 75 FR 45309. July 30.

Fabian, Ellen S., R. Luecking, and G. Tilson. 1995. "Employer and Rehabilitation Personnel Perspectives on Hiring People with Disabilities: Implications for Job Development." *Journal of Rehabilitation* 61 (1): 42–49.

Federal Sector's Obligation to Be a Model Employer of Individuals with Disabilities. 2014. 79 FR 27824 (to be codified at 29 CFR 1614. 2014). https://federalregister. gov/a/2014–11233.

Fink, Arlene. 2009. *How to Conduct Surveys: A Step-by-Step Guide*. Los Angeles: Sage Publications.

Fiol, C. Marlene, Michael G. Pratt, and Edward J. O'Connor. 2009. "Managing Intractable Identity Conflicts." *Academy of Management Review* 34 (1): 32–55. doi:10.5465/ AMR.2009.35713276.

Flickinger, Miriam, Anja Tuschke, Tina Gruber-Muecke, and Marina Fiedler. 2014. "In Search of Rigor, Relevance, and Legitimacy: What Drives the Impact of Publications?" *Journal of Business Economics* 84 (1): 99–128. doi:10.1007/ s11573–013–0692–2.

Florey, Anna T., and David A. Harrison. 2000. "Responses to Informal Accommodation Requests from Employees with Disabilities: Multistudy Evidence on Willingness to

Comply." *Academy of Management Journal* 43 (2): 224–33. http://search.epnet.com/login.aspx?direct=true&db=buh&an=3034544.

Fowler, Floyd J. 2009. "Methods of Data Collection." In *Survey Research Methods*, 4th ed., 68–86. Thousand Oaks, CA: Sage Publications. doi:/dx.doi.org/10.4135/9781452230184.n5.

Francis, C. M., and N. Maxwell. 2013. *Public Use Data File Documentation for the Study "Using Administrative Data to Address Federal Contractor Violations of Equal Employment Opportunity Laws."* Ref No. 06971.300. Oakland, CA.

Freeman, R. Edward. 1984. *Strategic Management : A Stakeholder Approach*. Boston: Pitman.

Geisen, Thomas, and Henry George Harder. 2011. *Disability Management and Workplace Integration: International Research Findings*. Burlington, VT: Gower.

Gerstner, C. R., and D. V. Day. 1997. "Meta-Analytic Review of Leader-Member Exchange Theory: Correlates and Construct Issues." *Journal of Applied Psychology* 82: 827–44.

Gibbons, M., C. Limoges, H. Nowotny, S. P. Schwartz, and M. Trow. 1994. *The New Production of Knowledge: The Dynamics of Science and Research in Contemporary Societies*. London: Sage Publications.

Gilbride, Dennis, Robert Stensrud, and Morgan Connolly. 1992. "Employers' Concerns about the ADA: Implications and Opportunities for Rehabilitation Counselors." *Journal of Applied Rehabilitation Counseling* 23 (3): 45–46.

Gilbride, Dennis, Robert Stensrud, Connie Ehlers, Eric Evans, and Craig Peterson. 2000. "Employers' Attitudes toward Hiring Persons with Disabilities and Vocational Rehabilitation Services." *Journal of Rehabilitation* 66 (4): 17–23.

Gilbride, Dennis, Robert Stensrud, David Vandergoot, and Kristie Golden. 2003. "Identification of the Characteristics of Work Environments and Employers Open to Hiring and Accommodating People with Disabilities." *Rehabilitation Counseling Bulletin* 46 (3): 130–37. doi:10.1177/00343552030460030101.

Gofton, Ken. 1999. "Data Firms React to Survey Fatigue." *Marketing* (London: Haymarket Business Publications), April, pp. 29–30.

Gold, Paul B., Spalatin N. Oire, Ellen S. Fabian, and Nancy J. Wewiorski. 2012. "Negotiating Reasonable Workplace Accommodations: Perspectives of Employers, Employees with Disabilities, and Rehabilitation Service Providers." *Journal of Vocational Rehabilitation* 37 (1): 25–37.

Graham, I. D., J. Logan, M. B. Harrison, S. E. Straus, J. Tetroe, and W. Caswel. 2006. "Lost in Knowledge Translation: Time for a Map." *Journal of Continuing Education in the Health Professions* 26 (1): 13–24.

Grosse, S. D., S. L. Boulet, D. D. Amendah, and S. O. Oyeku. 2010. "Administrative Data Sets and Health Research on Hemoglobinopathies: A Review of the Literature." *American Journal of Preventative Medicine* 4 Suppl: 557–67.

Groves, Robert M., Stanley Presser, and Sarah Dipko. 2004. "The Role of Topic Interest in Survey Participation Decisions." *Public Opinion Quarterly* 68 (1): 2–31. doi:10.1093/poq/nfh002.

Habeck, Rochelle, Allan Hunt, Colleen Head Rachel, John Kregel, and Fong Chan. 2010. "Employee Retention and Integrated Disability Management Practices as Demand Side Factors." *Journal of Occupational Rehabilitation* 20 (4): 443–55. doi:10.1007/s10926–009–9225–9.

Hallock, Kevin F. 2012. *Pay: Why People Earn What They Earn and What You Can Do to Make More.* Cambridge: Cambridge University Press.

———. 2013a. "Compensation Data and Individuals with Disabilities." *Workspan: The Magazine of World@Work*, October, pp. 12–13.

———. 2013b. "The Wage Gap vs. the Total Compensation Gap." *Workspan: The Magazine of World@Work*, December, pp. 12–13.

Hallock, Kevin F., Xin Jin, and Linda Barrington. 2014. *Disabilities, Occupations, and Returns to Skills and Tasks.* Working Paper. Ithaca, NY: Cornell University.

Handel, Benjamin, and Jonathan Kolstad. 2015. *Health Insurance for Humans: Information Frictions, Plan Choice, and Consumer Welfare.* Cambridge, MA: National Bureau of Economic Research. http://economics.yale.edu/sites/default/files/handel-130502.pdf.

Haveman, Robert, and Barbara Wolfe. 2000. "The Economics of Disability and Disability Policy." In *Handbook of Health Economics*, edited by Anthony Culyer and Joseph Newhouse, 1: 995–1051. Amsterdam: Elsevier B.V. doi:10.1016/S1574–0064(00)80031–1.

Hebl, Michelle R., and Jeanine L. Skorinko. 2005. "Acknowledging One's Physical Disability in the Interview: Does 'When' Make a Difference?" *Journal of Applied Social Psychology* 35 (12): 2477–92. doi:10.1111/j.1559–1816.2005.tb02111.x.

Hernandez, Brigida, Christopher Keys, and Fabricio Balcazar. 2004. "Disability Rights: Attitudes of Private and Public Sector Representatives." *Journal of Rehabilitation* 70 (1): 28–37.

Hirsh, C. Elizabeth, and Sabino Kornrich. 2008. "The Context of Discrimination: Workplace Conditions, Institutional Environments, and Sex and Race Discrimination Charges." *American Journal of Sociology* 113 (5): 1394–1432.

Hotchkiss, Julie L. 2004. "Growing Part-Time Employment among Workers with Disabilities: Marginalization or Opportunity?" *Economic Review—Federal Reserve Bank of Atlanta* 89 (3): 25–40.

Hunt, Courtney Shelton, and Brandon Hunt. 2004. "Changing Attitudes toward People with Disabilities: Experimenting with an Educational Intervention." *Journal of Managerial Issues* 16 (2): 266–80.

Hurley, Jessica E. 2010. "Merit Determinants of ADA Title I Allegations Involving Discharge: Implications for Human Resources Management and Development." *Advances in Developing Human Resources* 12 (4): 466–83. doi:10.1177/1523422310379213.

Huynh, Minh, Kalman Rupp, and James Sears. 2002. *The Assessment of Survey of Income and Program Participation (SIPP) Benefit Data Using Longitudinal Administrative Records.* Working Paper No. 238. Social Security Administration. Washington, DC: U.S. Census Bureau.

Hyland, Patrick K., and Peter J. Rutigliano. 2013. "Eradicating Discrimination: Identifying and Removing Workplace Barriers for Employees with Disabilities." *Industrial and Organizational Psychology* 6 (4): 471–75. doi:10.1111/iops.12087.

Inniss-Johnson, Joy. 2012. "The Relationship of Rehabilitation Counselors' Knowledge of the Americans with Disabilities Act 1990, Attitudes toward Reasonable

Accommodation, and Job Development Efficacy." Wayne State University. UMI Number: 3503914.

Ipsen, Catherine. 2006. "Health, Secondary Conditions, and Employment Outcomes for Adults with Disabilities." *Journal of Disability Policy Studies* 17 (2): 77–87.

Jacobson, Nora, Dale Butterill, and Paula Goering. 2003. "Development of a Framework for Knowledge Translation: Understanding User Context." *Journal of Health Services Research & Policy* 8 (2): 94–99. doi:10.1258/135581903321466067.

Jette, Alan M. 2006. "Toward a Common Language for Function, Disability, and Health." *Physical Therapy* 86: 726–34.

Jobber, David, and John Saunders. 1993. "A Note on the Applicability of the Bruvold-Comer Model of Mail Survey Response Rates to Commercial Populations." *Journal of Business Research* 26 (3): 223–36. doi:/10.1016/0148-2963(93)90033-L.

Johns, Gary. 2001. "In Praise of Context." *Journal of Organizational Behavior* 22 (1): 31–42.

Kalev, Alexandra, Frank Dobbin, and Erin Kelly. 2006. "Best Practices or Best Guesses? Assessing the Efficacy of Corporate Affirmative Action and Diversity Policies." *American Sociological Review* 71 (4): 589–617. doi:10.1177/000312240607100404.

Karpur, Arun, Melissa J. Bjelland, and Zafar E. Nazarov. 2013. *Job Mobility for People with Disabilities: Impact of Employer-Paid Health Insurance.* Research brief. Ithaca, NY: Cornell University, ILR School, Employment and Disability Institute. http://digitalcommons.ilr.cornell.edu/cgi/viewcontent.cgi?article=1356&context=edicollect.

Karpur, Arun, and Susanne M. Bruyère. 2012. "Health Care Expenditure among People with Disabilities: Potential Role of Workplace Health Promotion and Implications for Rehabilitation Counseling." *Rehabilitation Counseling Bulletin* 56 (1): 7–22. doi:10.1177/0034355212439756.

Karpur, Arun, Sara A. VanLooy, and Susanne M. Bruyère. 2014. "Employer Practices for Employment of People with Disabilities: A Literature Scoping Review." *Rehabilitation Research, Policy, and Education* 28 (4): 225–41. doi:10.1891/2168-6653.28.4.225.

Kaye, H. Stephen. 2009. "Stuck at the Bottom Rung: Occupational Characteristics of Workers with Disabilities." *Journal of Occupational Rehabilitation* 19 (2): 115–28. doi:http://dx.doi.org/10.1007/s10926-009-9175-2.

———. 2010. "The Impact of the 2007–09 Recession on Workers with Disabilities." *Monthly Labor Review*, October 2010: 19–30.

Kessel, Frank, and Patricia L. Rosenfield. 2008. "Toward Transdisciplinary Research: Historical and Contemporary Perspectives." *American Journal of Preventive Medicine* 35 (2 Suppl): S225–34. doi:10.1016/j.amepre.2008.05.005.

Kessler Foundation. 2014. *nTIDE Jobs Report: Despite Economic Milestones, Employment Gap Remains for People with Disabilities.* West Orange, NJ: Kessler Foundation. http://kesslerfoundation.org/media/displaypressrelease.php?id=567.

Kessler/NOD. 2010a. *The ADA, 20 Years Later.* New York: Kessler Foundation, National Organization on Disability. http://www.2010disabilitysurveys.org/pdfs/survey results.pdf.

———. 2010b. *Survey of Employment of Americans with Disabilities.* New York: Kessler Foundation, National Organization on Disability. http://www.2010disabilitysurveys.org/octsurvey/pdfs/surveyresults.pdf.

Kieser, Alfred, and Lars Leiner. 2009. "Why the Rigour—Relevance Gap in Management Research Is Unbridgeable." *Journal of Management Studies* 46 (3): 516–33.

Klein, Katherine J., Fred Dansereau, and Rosalie J. Hall. 1994. "Levels Issues in Theory Development, Data Collection, and Analysis." *Academy of Management Review* 19 (2): 195–229.

Klein, Katherine J., and Steve W. J. Kozlowski. 2000. *Multilevel Theory, Research, and Methods in Organizations*. San Francisco: Jossey-Bass.

Kmec, Julie A. 2003. "Collecting and Using Employer-Worker Matched Data." *Sociological Focus* 36 (1): 81.

Kozlowski, Steve W. J., and Katherine J. Klein. 2000. "A Multilevel Approach to Theory and Research in Organizations: Contextual, Temporal, and Emergent Processes." In *Multilevel Theory, Research and Methods in Organizations: Foundations, Extensions, and New Directions*, edited by K. J. Klein and Steve W. J. Kozlowski, 3–90. San Francisco: Jossey-Bass.

Kwak, Nojin, and Barry Radler. 2002. "A Comparison between Mail and Web Surveys: Response Pattern, Respondent Profile, and Data Quality." *Journal of Official Statistics* 18 (2): 257–73.

Laplume, André O., Karan Sonpar, and Reginald A. Litz. 2008. "Stakeholder Theory: Reviewing a Theory That Moves Us." *Journal of Management* 34 (6): 1152–89. doi:10.1177/0149206308324322.

Lazear, Edward P. 2000. "Performance Pay and Productivity." *American Economic Review* 90 (5): 1346–61.

Lengnick-Hall, Mark L., Philip M. Gaunt, and Mukta Kulkarni. 2008. "Overlooked and Underutilized: People with Disabilities Are an Untapped Human Resource." *Human Resource Management* 47 (2): 255–73. doi:10.1002/hrm.20211.

Link, Michael W., Michael P. Battaglia, Martin R. Frankel, Larry Osborn, and Ali H. Mokdad. 2008. "Practicability of Including Cell Phone Numbers in Random Digit Dialed Surveys: Pilot Study Results from the Behavioral Risk Factor Surveillance System." https://fcsm.sites.usa.gov/files/2014/05/2007FCSM_Link-II-C.pdf.

Linkow, Peter, Linda Barrington, Susanne M. Bruyère, Ivelys Figueroa, and Mary Wright. 2013. *Leveling the Playing Field: Attracting, Engaging, and Advancing People with Disabilities*. R-1510–12-RR. Research Report. New York: The Conference Board. http://digitalcommons.ilr.cornell.edu/edicollect/1292/.

Linkow, Peter, and Ivelys Figueroa. 2013. *Leveling the Playing Field: Executive Summary*. New York: The Conference Board. http://digitalcommons.ilr.cornell.edu/edicollect/1321/.

Livermore, Gina A., and Peiyun She. 2007. *Limitations of the National Disability Data System*. Ithaca, NY: Cornell University, ILR School, Employment and Disability Institute. http://digitalcommons.ilr.cornell.edu/edicollect/1245/.

Malzer, Valerie B., and Sarah von Schrader. 2014. *Mental Modeling: A Qualitative Method for Mapping Audience Behaviors and Designing Social Marketing Initiatives*. Ithaca, NY: Cornell University, ILR School, Employment and Disability Institute. http://digitalcommons.ilr.cornell.edu/edicollect/1354/.

Mashaw, Jerry L., and Virginia P. Reno. 1996. *Balancing Security and Opportunity: The Challenge of Disability Income Policy*. Washington, DC: National Academy of Social Insurance.

McKee, R., and Bronwyn Fryer. 2003. "Storytelling That Moves People." *Harvard Business Review* 81 (6): 51–55.

McLellan, Robert, Glenn Pransky, and William S. Shaw. 2001. "Disability Management Training for Supervisors: A Pilot Intervention Program." *Journal of Occupational Rehabilitation* 11 (1): 33–41. doi:10.1023/A:1016652124410.

McMahon, Brian, Ron Edwards, Phillip Rumrill, and Norman Hursh. 2005. "An Overview of the National EEOC ADA Research Project." *Work* 25:1–7.

McMahon, Brian T., L. Shaw, and D. Jaet. 1995. "An Empirical Analysis: Employment and Disability from an ADA Litigation Perspective." *NARPPS Journal* 10 (1): 3–14.

McNabb, Jennifer, David Timmons, Jae Song, and Carolyn Puckett. 2009. "Uses of Administrative Data at the Social Security Administration." *Social Security Bulletin* 69 (1): 75–84. http://www.ssa.gov/policy/docs/ssb/v69n1/v69n1p75.html.

Meyer, B., and W. Mok. 2006. *Disability, Earnings, Income and Consumption*. Harris School of Public Policy Studies, Working Paper Series No. 610. Chicago: University of Chicago, Harris School of Public Policy Studies. http://econpapers.repec.org/paper/harwpaper/0610.htm.

Mindruta, Denisa. 2013. "Value Creation in University-Firm Research Collaborations: A Matching Approach." *Strategic Management Journal* 665 (December 2012): 644–65. doi:10.1002/smj.

Mitchell, Rebecca, Stephen Nicholas, and Brendan Boyle. 2009. "The Role of Openness to Cognitive Diversity and Group Processes in Knowledge Creation." *Small Group Research* 40 (5): 535–54. doi:10.1177/1046496409338302.

Mitchell, Susan, Anne Ciemnecki, Karen Cybulski, and Jason Markesich. 2006. *Removing Barriers to Survey Participation for Persons with Disabilities*. Ithaca, NY: Cornell University, ILR School, Employment and Disability Institute.

Moore, Mark E., Alison M. Konrad, and Judith Hunt. 2010. "Creating a Vision Boosts the Impact of Top Management Support on the Employment of Managers with Disabilities: The Case of Sport Organizations in the USA." *Equality, Diversity and Inclusion: An International Journal* 29 (6): 609–26. http://www.emeraldinsight.com/journals.htm?articleid=1881504.

Morgan, Sandra, and Robert F. Dennehy. 1997. "The Power of Organizational Storytelling: A Management Development Perspective." *Journal of Management Development* 16 (7): 494–501. http://search.proquest.com/docview/216355906?accountid=10267.

Moss, Kathryn, Jeffrey Swanson, Michael Ullman, and Scott Burris. 2002. "Mediation of Employment Discrimination Disputes Involving Persons with Psychiatric Disabilities." *Psychiatric Services* 53 (8): 988–94.

Moss, Kathryn, Michael Ullman, Matthew C. Johnsen, Barbara E. Starrett, and Scott Burris. 1999. "Different Paths to Justice: The ADA, Employment, and Administrative Enforcement by the EEOC." *Behavioral Sciences & the Law* 17: 29–46.

Moss, Kathryn, Michael Ullman, Barbara E. Starrett, Scott Burris, and Matthew C. Johnsen. 1999. "Outcomes of Employment Discrimination Charges Filed under the Americans with Disabilities Act." *Psychiatric Services* 50 (8): 1028–35.

Nazarov, Zafar E., William A. Erickson, and Susanne M. Bruyère. 2014. "Rehabilitation-Related Research on Disability and Employer Practices Using

Individual-Based National and Administrative Data Sets." *Rehabilitation Research, Policy, and Education* 28 (4): 1–23.

Nazarov, Zafar E., and Sarah von Schrader. 2014. "Comparison of Employer Factors in Disability." *Rehabilitation Research, Policy, and Education* 28 (4): 1–19.

Nelson, C. 2006. *What Do We Know about the Differences between CPS and ACS Income and Poverty Estimates?* Washington, DC: U.S. Census Bureau. http://www.census.gov/hhes/www/poverty/about/datasources/nelson_082906.pdf.

Nicolai, Alexander T., Ann-Christine Schulz, and Markus Gobel. 2011. "Between Sweet Harmony and a Clash of Cultures: Does a Joint Academic-Practitioner Review Reconcile Rigor and Relevance?" *Journal of Applied Behavioral Science* 47 (1): 53–75. doi:10.1177/0021886310390866.

Nishii, Lisa H. 2010. "Managers' Diversity Practice Attributions: Why We Should Care." Paper presented at the 16th Annual Wharton Organizational Behavior Conference, Philadelphia.

———. 2014. "Leveraging OB Theories and Multilevel Methods to Expand HRM Research." Paper presented at the Spanish Academy of Management Conference, Tarragona, Spain.

Nishii, Lisa H., and Susanne M. Bruyère. 2009. "Protecting Employees with Disabilities from Discrimination on the Job: The Role of Unit Managers from Workplace Policies and Practices Minimizing Disability Discrimination; Implications for Psychology." In *117th Annual Convention of the American Psychological Association*. Toronto.

Nishii, Lisa H., David P. Lepak, and Benjamin Schneider. 2008. "Employee Attributions of the 'Why' of HR Practices: Their Effects on Employee Attitudes and Behaviors, and Customer Satisfaction." *Personnel Psychology* 61 (3): 503–45. http://search.proquest.com/docview/220135538?accountid=10267.

Nishii, Lisa H., and David M. Mayer. 2009. "Do Inclusive Leaders Help the Performance of Diverse Groups? The Moderating Role of Leader-Member Exchange in the Diversity to Group Performance." *Journal of Applied Psychology* 94 (6): 1412–26. doi:10.1037/a0017190.

Nishii, Lisa H., and P. M. Wright. 2008. "Variability at Multiple Levels of Analysis: Implications for Strategic Human Resource Management." In *The People Make the Place: Dynamic Linkages between Individuals and Organizations*, edited by D. B. Smith, 225–48. Mahwah, NJ: Lawrence Erlbaum Associates.

Nissani, M. 1997. "Ten Cheers for Interdisciplinarity." *Social Science Journal* 34 (2): 201–14.

O'Brien, Ruth. 2001. *Crippled Justice: The History of Modern Disability Policy in the Workplace*. Chicago: University of Chicago Press.

OECD. 2012. "Good Practices in Survey Design Step-by-Step." In *Measuring Regulatory Performance: A Practitioner's Guide to Perception Surveys*. Paris: OECD Publishing. doi:http://dx.doi.org/10.1787/9789264167179-en.

O'Hara, Brian James. 2000. "Discrimination against Persons with Disabilities: Issues in Employment Transitions." Dissertation, University of Notre Dame. UMI No. 9967306.

Ong, Anthony, and David Weiss. 2000. "The Impact of Anonymity on Responses to Sensitive Questions." *Journal of Applied Social Psychology* 30 (8): 1691–1708.

Pfeffer, J. 1981. "Management as Symbolic Action: The Creation and Maintenance of Organizational Paradigms." *Research in Organizational Behavior* 3: 1–52.

Pitt-Catsouphes, Marcie, Ellen Ernst Kossek, and Stephen Sweet. 2006. "Charting New Territory: Advancing Multi-Disciplinary Perspectives, Methods, and Approaches in the Study of Work and Family." In *The Work and Family Handbook: Multi-Disciplinary Perspectives, Methods, and Approaches*, edited by Marcie Pitt-Catsouphes and Ellen Ernst Kossek, 1–16. Mahwah, NJ: Lawrence Erlbaum Associates.

Podsakoff, Philip M., Scott B. MacKenzie, Jeong-Yeon Lee, and Nathan P. Podsakoff. 2003. "Common Method Biases in Behavioral Research: A Critical Review of the Literature and Recommended Remedies." *Journal of Applied Psychology* 88 (5): 879.

Pohl, Christian. 2011. "What Is Progress in Transdisciplinary Research?" *Futures* 43 (6): 618–26. doi:10.1016/j.futures.2011.03.001.

Porter, Stephen R., Michael E. Whitcomb, and William H. Weitzer. 2004. "Multiple Surveys of Students and Survey Fatigue." *New Directions for Institutional Research* 2004 (121): 63–73. doi:10.1002/ir.101.

Powers, Elizabeth, and David Neumark. 2005. "The Supplemental Security Income Program and Incentives to Take Up Social Security Early Retirement: Empirical Evidence from the SIPP and Social Security Administrative Data." *National Tax Journal* 58 (1): 5–26. http://econpapers.repec.org/RePEc:ntj:journl:v:58:y:2005:i:1:p:5–26.

Qin, Jian, F. W. Lancaster, and Bryce Allen. 1997. "Types and Levels of Collaboration in Interdisciplinary Research in the Sciences." *Journal of the American Society for Information Science* 48 (10): 893–916.

Ragins, Belle, Romila Singh, and John M. Cornwell. 2007. "Making the Invisible Visible: Fear and Disclosure of Sexual Orientation at Work." *Journal of Applied Psychology* 92 (4): 1103–18.

Ragins, Belle, and Eric Sundstrom. 1989. "Gender and Power in Organizations: A Longitudinal Perspective." *Psychological Bulletin* 105 (1): 51–88. 10.1037/0033–2909.105.1.51.

RAND Corporation. 2008. *Invisible Wounds of War: Psychological and Cognitive Injuries, Their Consequences, and Services to Assist Recovery*. Santa Monica, CA: RAND Center for Military Health Policy Research.

Randolph, Diane Smith. 2004. "Predicting the Effect of Disability on Employment Status and Income." *Work* 23 (3): 257–66.

Rea, Louis M., and Richard Parker. 2005. *Designing and Conducting Survey Research : A Comprehensive Guide*. 4th ed. San Francisco: Jossey-Bass.

Reason, P., and H. Bradbury. 2008. Introduction to *The Sage Handbook of Action Research: Participative Inquiry and Practice*, 5–10. Thousand Oaks, CA: Sage Publications.

Ren, Lily Run, Ramona L. Paetzold, and Adrienne Colella. 2008. "A Meta-Analysis of Experimental Studies on the Effects of Disability on Human Resource Judgments." *Human Resource Management Review* 18 (3): 191–203. doi:http://dx.doi.org/10.1016/j.hrmr.2008.07.001.

Rimmer, J. H. 2005. "The Conspicuous Absence of People with Disabilities in Public Fitness and Recreation Facilities: Lack of Interest or Lack of Access?" *American Journal of Health Promotion* 19: 327–29.

Rivera, L. 2012. "Diversity within Reach: Recruitment versus Hiring in Elite Firms." *Annals of the American Academy of Political and Social Science* 639 (1): 71–90. doi:10.1177/0002716211421112.

Rosenfield, Patricia L. 1992. "The Potential of Transdisciplinary Research for Sustaining and Extending Linkages between the Health and Social Sciences." *Social Science & Medicine* 35 (11): 1343–57. http://www.ncbi.nlm.nih.gov/pubmed/1462174.

Rosenthal, David A., Norman Hursh, John Lui, Rodney Isom, and Joy Sasson. 2007. "A Survey of Current Disability Management Practice: Emerging Trends and Implications for Certification." *Rehabilitation Counseling Bulletin* 50 (2): 76.

Roy, Abhijit, and Paul Berger. 2005. "E-Mail and Mixed Mode Database Surveys Revisited: Exploratory Analyses of Factors Affecting Response Rates." *Journal of Database Marketing & Customer Strategy Management* 12 (2): 153–71. doi:10.1057/palgrave.dbm.3240252.

Rudstam, Hannah, Wendy Strobel Gower, and LaWanda Cook. 2012. "Beyond Yellow Ribbons: Are Employers Prepared to Hire, Accommodate and Retain Returning Veterans with Disabilities?" *Journal of Vocational Rehabilitation* 36 (2): 87–95.

Rudstam, Hannah, Margo Hittleman, Sukyeong Pi, and Wendy Strobel Gower. 2013. "Bridging the Knowing-Doing Gap: Researching a New Approach to Disability and Employment Programming." *Journal of Vocational Rehabilitation* 39 (1): 43–60. doi:10.3233/JVR-130641.

Rumrill, Philip D., Jr., James L. Bellini, and James M. Webb. 1999. "Perspectives on Scientific Inquiry: Survey Research in Rehabilitation." *Journal of Vocational Rehabilitation* 13 (3): 195–98.

Rutigliano, Pete, and Meg O'Connell. 2013. "Employees with Disabilities: The Forgotten Diversity Segment; Tracking Trends." Findings from a joint SIROTA / National Organization on Disability Survey. http://www.nod.org/assets/downloads/Disabilities_2013_Sirota-NOD_20130227_FINAL.pdf.

Schalock, R. L. 2004. "The Emerging Disability Paradigm and Its Implications for Policy and Practice." *Journal of Disability Policy Studies* 14 (4): 204–15. doi:10.1177/1044 2073040140040201.

Scheuren, Fritz. 2004. *What Is a Survey?* Chicago: NORC. https://www.whatisasurvey.info/overview.htm.

Schiele, Holger, and Stefan Krummaker. 2011. "Consortium Benchmarking: Collaborative Academic–Practitioner Case Study Research." *Journal of Business Research* 64 (10): 1137–45. doi:http://dx.doi.org/10.1016/j.jbusres.2010.11.007.

Schur, Lisa A. 2002. "Dead End Jobs or a Path to Economic Well Being? The Consequences of Non-standard Work among People with Disabilities." *Behavioral Sciences & the Law* 20 (2): 601–20. doi:10.1002/bsl.512.

———. 2003. "Barriers or Opportunities? The Causes of Contingent and Part-Time Work among People with Disabilities." *Industrial Relations* 42 (4): 589–622. doi:10.1111/1468–232X.00308.

Schur, Lisa A., and Douglas Kruse. 2002. *Non-standard Work Arrangements and Disability Income*. Urbana: University of Illinois, Urbana-Champaign.

Schur, Lisa, Douglas Kruse, and Peter Blanck. 2013. *Sidelined or Mainstreamed? Political Participation and Attitudes of People with Disabilities in the United States*. Cambridge: Cambridge University Press.

Schur, Lisa, Douglas Kruse, Joseph Blasi, and Peter Blanck. 2009. "Is Disability Disabling in All Workplaces? Workplace Disparities and Corporate Culture." *Industrial Relations* 48 (3): 381–410.

Schur, Lisa, Lisa Nishii, Meera Adya, Douglas Kruse, Susanne M. Bruyère, and Peter Blanck. 2014. "Accommodating Employees with and without Disabilities." *Human Resource Management* 53 (4): 593–621. doi: 10.1002/hrm.21607.

Scotch, Richard K. 2001. *Transforming Federal Disability Policy*. Philadelphia: Temple University Press.

Scott, L. 2008. "Save Money, Live Better, and the Full Potential of Walmart: Address to the Walmart Shareholders' Meeting 2008." http://news.walmart.com/executive-viewpoints/save-money-live-better-the-full-potential-of-walmart.

Scotton, L. 2009. "A New Approach to Disability Management." *Risk Management* 56 (9): 54.

Settles, Isis, and Nicole T. Buchanan. 2014. "Multiple Groups, Multiple Identities, and Intersectionality." In *The Oxford Handbook of Multicultural Identity*, edited by Veronica Benet-Martinez and Ying-yi Hong, 160–80. Oxford: Oxford University Press. doi:10.1093/oxfordhb/9780199796694.013.017.

Shrey, Donald E., and Norman C. Hursh. 1999. "Workplace Disability Management: International Trends and Perspectives." *Journal of Occupational Rehabilitation* 9 (1): 45.

Siebens, J. 2013. *Extended Measures of Well-Being: Living Conditions in the United States, 2011*. Household Economic Studies. Washington, DC: U.S. Department of Commerce, Economics and Statistics Administration. http://www.census.gov/prod/2013pubs/p70–136.pdf.

Silverstein, Robert. 2000. "Emerging Disability Policy Framework : A Guidepost for Analyzing Public Policy." *Iowa Law Review* 85:1691.

Siperstein, Gary N., Neil Romano, Amanda Mohler, and Robin Parker. 2006. "A National Survey of Consumer Attitudes towards Companies That Hire People with Disabilities." *Journal of Vocational Rehabilitation* 24 (1): 3–9.

Slud, Eric V., and Leroy Bailey. 2006. "Estimation of Attrition Biases in SIPP." In *ASA Section on Survey Research Methods*, 3713–20.

Smart, Julie F., and David W. Smart. 2006. "Models of Disability: Implications for the Counseling Profession." *Journal of Counseling & Development* 84 (1): 29–40. doi:10.1002/j.1556–6678.2006.tb00377.x.

Society for Human Resource Management. 2014. *SHRM Survey Findings: 2014 Strategic Benefits—Health Care*. Alexandria, VA. http://www.shrm.org/research/surveyfindings/articles/pages/2014-shrm-strategic-use-of-benefits-health-care.aspx.

Society for Industrial and Organizational Psychology. 2015. "What is I-O?" http://www.siop.org/.

Stainback, Kevin, and Donald Tomaskovic-Devey. 2012. *Documenting Desegregation: Racial and Gender Segregation in Private-Sector Employment since the Civil Rights Act*. New York: Russell Sage Foundation.

Stapleton, David C., and Richard V. Burkhauser. 2003. *The Decline in Employment of People with Disabilities: A Policy Puzzle*. Kalamazoo, MI: W. E. Upjohn Institute for Employment Research.

Stapleton, David C., Richard V. Burkhauser, and Andrew J. Houtenville. 2004. *Has the Employment Rate of People with Disabilities Declined?* Policy Brief. Ithaca, NY: Cornell University, ILR School, Employment and Disability Institute. http://digitalcommons.ilr.cornell.edu/edicollect/92/.

Stapleton, David C., and Gina Livermore. 2011. *Costs, Cuts, and Consequences: Charting a New Course*. Vol. 11. Washington, DC: Center for Studying Disability Policy. http://www.aapd.com/resources/publications/hunter-publications.pdf.

Stapleton, David C., Bonnie L. O'Day, Gina A. Livermore, and Andrew J. Imparato. 2006. "Dismantling the Poverty Trap: Disability Policy for the Twenty-First Century." *Milbank Quarterly* 84. doi:10.1111/j.1468–0009.2006.00465.x.

Stein, Michael Ashley. 2003. "The Law and Economics of Disability Accommodations." *Duke Law Journal* 53 (1): 79–191. http://www.jstor.org/stable/1373190.

———. 2007. "Disability Human Rights." *California Law Review* 95 (1): 75–121. http://www.jstor.org/stable/20439088.

Stensrud, Robert. 2007. "Developing Relationships with Employers Means Considering the Competitive Business Environment and the Risks It Produces." *Rehabilitation Counseling Bulletin* 50 (4): 226–37. http://rcb.sagepub.com/content/50/4/226.abstract.

Stiles, Paul G., and Roger A. Boothroyd. 2012. *Ethical Use of Administrative Data for Research Purposes*. St. Petersburg: Louis de la Parte Florida Mental Health Institute, University of South Florida. http://impact.sp2.upenn.edu/aisp_test/wp-content/uploads/2012/12/0033_12_SP2_Ethical_Admin_Data_001.pdf.

Stock, Paul, and Rob J. F. Burton. 2011. "Defining Terms for Integrated (Multi-Inter-Trans-Disciplinary) Sustainability Research." *Sustainability* 3 (12): 1090–1113. doi:10.3390/su3081090.

Stoddard, Susan, and Brenda Premo. 2004. "Expanding Employment Opportunities: Independent Living Center Employment Services and Collaboration with Vocational Rehabilitation." *Journal of Vocational Rehabilitation* 20 (1): 45–52.

Stone, Dianna L., and Adrienne Colella. 1996. "A Model of Factors Affecting the Treatment of Disabled Individuals in Organizations." *Academy of Management Review* 21 (2): 352–401.

Sudsawad, Pimjai. 2007. *Knowledge Translation: Introduction to Models, Strategies, and Measures*. Austin, TX: Southwest Educational Development Laboratory.

Sue, Valerie M., and Lois A. Ritter. 2014. *Conducting Online Surveys*. Thousand Oaks, CA: Sage Publications.

Thakker, Daksha, and Phyllis Solomon. 1999. "Factors Influencing Managers' Adherence to the Americans with Disabilities Act." *Administration and Policy in Mental Health* 26 (3): 213–19. doi:10.1023/a:1021366731025.

Toosi, Mitra. 2012. "Labor Force Projections to 2010: A More Slowly Growing Work-force." *Monthly Labor Review* 135 (1): 43–64.

Towers Watson. 2014. "U.S. Employers Expect Health Care Costs to Rise 4% in 2015." http://www.towerswatson.com/en-US/Press/2014/08/us-employers-expect-health-care-costs-to-rise-4-percent-in-2015.

Trochim, W. 2006. "Ethics in Research." *Web Center for Social Research Methods: Research Methods Knowledge Base*. http://www.socialresearchmethods.net/kb/ethics.php.

Turnbull, A. P., B. J. Friesen, and C. Ramirez. 1998. "Participatory Action Research as a Model for Conducting Family Research." *Research and Practice for Persons with Severe Disabilities* 3 (1): 178–88.

Ullman, Michael, Matthew C. Johnsen, Kathryn Moss, and Scott Burris. 2001. "The EEOC Charge Priority Policy and Claimants with Psychiatric Disabilities." *Psychiatric Services* 52 (5): 644–49. doi:10.1176/appi.ps.52.5.644.

*Ultimate Business Dictionary: Defining the World of Work.* 2003. s.v. "Value Proposition." Cambridge, MA: Perseus Publishing.

Unger, Darlene D. 2002. "Employers' Attitudes towards People with Disabilities in the Workforce: Myths or Realities?" *Focus on Autism and Other Developmental Disabilities* 17 (1), 2–10.

U.S. Bureau of Labor Statistics. 2014a. *Congressional Budget Justification*. Washington, DC. http://www.dol.gov/dol/budget/2014/pdf/cbj-2014-v3–01.pdf.

———. 2014b. "Employer Costs for Employee Compensation—September 2014." USDL-14–2208. News Release. Washington, DC: Bureau of Labor Statistics. http://data.bls.gov/cgi-bin/print.pl/news.release/ecec.nr0.htm.

———. 2014c. "Employment Situation of Veterans—2013." News Release. USDL-14–0434. Washington, DC: Bureau of Labor Statistics.

———. 2014d. "Persons with a Disability: Labor Force Characteristics 2013." News Release. USDL-14–1076. Washington, DC: Bureau of Labor Statistics. http://www.bls.gov/news.release/disabl.toc.htm.

U.S. Department of Education. 2010. Application Package for New Grants (CFDA No. 84.133B-3, FY2010).

U.S. Department of Health, Education, and Welfare. 1979. *Belmont Report: Ethical Principles and Guidelines for the Protection of Human Subjects of Research; Report of the National Commission for the Protection of Human Subjects of Biomedical and Behavioral Research*. Washington, DC: Department of Health, Education, and Welfare. http://www.hhs.gov/ohrp/humansubjects/guidance/belmont.html.

U.S. Department of Health and Human Services. 2014. *International Compilation of Human Research Standards*. Washington, DC: Department of Health and Human Services. http://www.hhs.gov/ohrp/international/.

U.S. Department of Labor. 2014a. "Notice of Proposed Rulemaking : Government Contractor Requirement to Submit Equal Pay Report." http://www.wageandhour.dol.gov/ofccp/EqualPay/EqualPayReport_NPRM_FactSheet_JRF_QA_508c.pdf.

———. 2014b. Office of Federal Contract Compliance Programs (OFCCP). "Frequently Asked Questions; New Section 503 Regulations." http://www.dol.gov/ofccp/regs/compliance/faqs/503_faq.htm.

U.S. Equal Employment Opportunity Commission. 2003. "Equal Employment Opportunity Management Directive 715." http://www.eeoc.gov/federal/directives/md715.cfm.

―――. 2011. *Annual Report on the Federal Work Force: Part II*. Washington, DC. http://www.eeoc.gov/federal/reports/fsp2011_2/upload/fsp2011_2.pdf.

U.S. Office of Personnel Management. 2012. *Agency Financial Report, FY 2012*. Washington, DC: Office of Personnel Management. http://www.opm.gov/about-us/budget-performance/performance/2012-agency-financial-report.pdf.

―――. 2014a. *Federal Employee Viewpoint Survey: Employees Influencing Change*. Washington, DC: Office of Personnel Management. http://www.fedview.opm.gov/2014/Reports/DisComp.asp?AGY=ALL.

―――. 2014b. *2013 Federal Employee Viewpoint Survey Results: Employees Influencing Change*. Washington, DC: Office of Personnel Management. http://www.fedview.opm.gov/2013/Reports/DisComp.asp?AGY=ALL.

U.S. Senate. 2013. *High Expectations: Transforming the American Workforce as the ADA Generation Comes of Age*. Washington, DC: United States Senate.

VandeWalle, D. 1997. "Development and Validation of a Work Domain Goal Orientation Instrument." *Educational and Psychological Measurement* 57 (6): 995–1015. doi: 10.1177/0013164497057006009.

van Knippenberg, Daan, and Michaéla C. Schippers. 2007. "Work Group Diversity." *Annual Review of Psychology* 58 (1): 515–41. doi:10.1146/annurev.psych.58.110405.085546.

Vannieuwenhuyze, Jorre T. A. 2014. "On the Relative Advantage of Mixed-Mode versus Single-Mode Surveys." *Survey Research Methods* 8 (1): 31–42.

Vargo, Thomas J., and George W. Grzanowicz. 2002. "Strategies for Effective Disability Management." *Employee Benefit Plan Review* 57 (6): 24–27.

Virnig, Beth, and Anjali Madeira. 2012. *Strengths and Limitations of CMS Administrative Data in Research* (ResDAC Article 156). ResDAC Knowledgebase. Washington, DC: Centers for Medicare and Medicaid Services. http://www.resdac.org/resconnect/articles/156.

von Schrader, Sarah, Susanne M. Bruyère, Valerie B. Malzer, and William A. Erickson. 2013. *Absence and Disability Management Practices for an Aging Workforce*. Ithaca, NY: Cornell University, ILR School, Employment and Disability Institute. http://digitalcommons.ilr.cornell.edu/edicollect/1320/.

von Schrader, Sarah, Valerie B. Malzer, and Susanne M. Bruyère. 2013. "Perspectives on Disability Disclosure: The Importance of Employer Practices and Workplace Climate." *Employee Responsibilities and Rights Journal* 26:237–55. doi:10.1007/s10672-013-9227-9.

von Schrader, Sarah, and Zafar E. Nazarov. 2014. "Employer Characteristics Associated with Discrimination Charges under the Americans with Disabilities Act." *Journal of Disability Policy Studies*, April. doi:10.1177/1044207314533385.

von Schrader, Sarah, Xu Xu, and Susanne M. Bruyère. 2014. "Accommodation Requests: Who Is Asking for What?" *Rehabilitation Research, Policy, and Education* 28 (4), 329–44.

Vornholt, Katharina, Sjir Uitdewilligen, and Frans J. N. Nijhuis. 2013. "Factors Affecting the Acceptance of People with Disabilities at Work: A Literature Review." *Journal of Occupational Rehabilitation* 23 (4): 463–75, 1–13. doi:10.1007/s10926–013–9426–0.

Wallgren, A., and B. Wallgren. 2007. *Register-Based Statistics: Administrative Data for Statistical Purposes*. Hoboken, NJ: John Wiley.

Walter, Alexander I., Sebastian Helgenberger, Arnim Wiek, and Roland W. Scholz. 2007. "Measuring Societal Effects of Transdisciplinary Research Projects: Design and Application of an Evaluation Method." *Evaluation and Program Planning* 30 (4): 325–38. doi:10.1016/j.evalprogplan.2007.08.002.

Wang, Katie, Laura G. Barron, and Michelle R. Hebl. 2010. "Making Those Who Cannot See Look Best: Effects of Visual Resume Formatting on Ratings of Job Applicants with Blindness." *Rehabilitation Psychology* 55 (1). doi:10.1037/a0018546.

Wasti, S. Arzu, and Christopher Robert. 2004. "Out of Touch? An Evaluation of the Correspondence between Academic and Practitioner Concerns in IHRM." In *Managing Multinationals in a Knowledge Economy: Economics, Culture*, 207–39. Oxford: Elsevier Ltd. doi:10.1016/S0747–7929(03)15010-X.

Weathers, Robert R., II 2009. "The Disability Data Landscape." In *Counting Working-Age People with Disabilities: What Current Data Tell Us and Options for Improvement*, edited by Andrew J. Houtenville, David C. Stapleton, Robert R. Weathers II, and Richard V. Burkhauser, 27–67. Kalamazoo, MI: Upjohn.

Whyte, W. F. 1991. *Participatory Action Research*. Thousand Oaks, CA: Sage Publications.

Wickson, F., A.L. Carew, and A.W. Russell. 2006. "Transdisciplinary Research: Characteristics, Quandaries and Quality." *Futures* 38 (9): 1046–59. doi:10.1016/j.futures.2006.02.011.

Wilson, Erin, Robert Campain, Megan Moore, Nick Hagiliassis, Jane McGillivray, Daniel Gottliebson, Michael Bink, Michelle Caldwell, Robert Cummins, and Joe Graffam. 2013. "An Accessible Survey Method: Increasing the Participation of People with a Disability in Large Sample Social Research." *Telecommunications Journal of Australia* 63 (2): 411. doi:10.7790/tja.v63i2.411.

Wittenburg, David, David R. Mann, and Allison Thompkins. 2013. "The Disability System and Programs to Promote Employment for People with Disabilities." *IZA Journal of Labor Policy* 2 (1): 4. doi:10.1186/2193–9004–2–4.

World Health Organization. 2001. *International Classification of Functioning, Disability, and Health*. Geneva, Switzerland: World Health Organization.

———. 2011. *World Report on Disability*. Geneva, Switzerland: World Health Organization.

Wright, P.M., and Lisa H. Nishii. 2013. "Strategic HRM and Organizational Behavior: Integrating Multiple Levels of Analysis." In *Innovations in HR*, edited by D. Guest, 97–110. Oxford: Blackwell Publishing.

Yang, Yang, and Alison M. Konrad. 2011. "Understanding Diversity Management Practices: Implications of Institutional Theory and Resource-Based Theory." *Group & Organization Management* 36 (1): 6–38. doi:10.1177/1059601110390997.

Yelin, Edward H. 1997. "The Employment of People with and without Disabilities in the Age of Insecurity." *Annals of the American Academy of Political and Social Science* 549: 117–28.

Yeo, Rebecca, and Karen Moore. 2003. "Including Disabled People in Poverty Reduction Work: 'Nothing about Us, without Us.'" *World Development* 31 (3): 571–90. doi:10.1016/S0305-750X(02)00218-8.

Yin, Michelle, Dahlia Shaewitz, and Mahlet Megra. 2014. *An Uneven Playing Field: The Lack of Equal Pay for People with Disabilities*. Washington, DC: American Institutes for Research. http://www.air.org/resource/uneven-playing-field-lack-equal-pay-people-disabilities.

Young, I. 2008. *Mental Models: Aligning Design Strategy with Human Behavior*. Brooklyn, NY: Rosenfeld Media.

Zikmund, William G. 2003. *Business Research Methods*. Mason, OH: Thomson/South-Western.

Zwerling, Craig, Paul S. Whitten, Nancy L. Sprince, Charles S. Davis, Robert B. Wallace, Peter Blanck, and Steven G. Heeringa. 2003. "Workplace Accommodations for People with Disabilities: National Health Interview Survey Disability Supplement, 1994–1995." *Journal of Occupational and Environmental Medicine* 45 (5): 517–25.

# CONTRIBUTORS

**Linda Barrington** is executive director of the Institute for Compensation Studies and Associate Dean for Outreach at the ILR School, Cornell University.

**Susanne B. Bruyère** is director of the K. Lisa Yang and Hock E. Tan Institute on Employment and Disability and professor of Disability Studies at the ILR School, Cornell University.

**Hassan Enayati** is a research associate at the K. Lisa Yang and Hock E. Tan Institute on Employment and Disability at the ILR School, Cornell University.

**William A. Erickson** is a research specialist at the K. Lisa Yang and Hock E. Tan Institute on Employment and Disability at the ILR School, Cornell University.

**Kevin F. Hallock** is the Kenneth F. Kahn '69 Dean and Joseph R. Rich '80 Professor at the ILR School, Cornell University.

**Arun Karpur** is an extension associate at the K. Lisa Yang and Hock E. Tan Institute on Employment and Disability at the ILR School, Cornell University.

**Lisa H. Nishii** is associate professor of Human Resource Studies at the ILR School, Cornell University.

**Ellice Switzer** is a technical assistance specialist at the K. Lisa Yang and Hock E. Tan Institute on Employment and Disability at the ILR School, Cornell University.

**Sara VanLooy** is a publications assistant at the K. Lisa Yang and Hock E. Tan Institute on Employment and Disability at the ILR School, Cornell University.

**Sarah von Schrader** is the assistant director of research at the K. Lisa Yang and Hock E. Tan Institute on Employment and Disability at the ILR School, Cornell University.

# INDEX

Page numbers in italics refer to figures and tables.